Carl Sandburg. (Photograph by Editta Sherman.)

CARL SANDBURG

LINCOLN
of Our
LITERATURE

Read the Space killer

a Biography by
NORTH CALLAHAN

1970

New York   NEW YORK UNIVERSITY PRESS

Copyright © 1970 by North Callahan
Library of Congress Catalog Card Number: 76–92521
SBN: 8147–0069–1 (cloth)
SBN: 8147–0070–5 (paper)
Manufactured in the United States of America

Acknowledgments

Excerpts from Carl Sandburg's *Chicago Poems*, copyright © 1916 by Holt, Rinehart and Winston, Inc.; copyright © 1944 by Carl Sandburg. Reprinted by permission of Holt, Rinehart and Winston, Inc.

Excerpt from Carl Sandburg's *Cornhuskers*, copyright © 1918 by Holt, Rinehart and Winston, Inc.; copyright © 1946 by Carl Sandburg. Reprinted by permission of Holt, Rinehart and Winston, Inc.

Permission to quote and to paraphrase excerpts from the following books by Carl Sandburg has been granted by Harcourt, Brace and World, Inc.: *The Chicago Race Riots; Smoke and Steel; Slabs of the Sunburnt West; Good Morning, America; The People, Yes; Abraham Lincoln: The War Years*, Vol. IV; *Home Front Memo; Remembrance Rock; A Lincoln Preface; Abraham Lincoln: The Prairie Years* and *The War Years*, one volume edition; *The Sandburg Range; The American Songbag*, copyright © 1928, 1939, 1941, 1947, 1948, 1950, 1953, 1954, 1956, 1957, 1964, 1967 by Carl Sandburg; copyright © 1919, 1920, 1922, 1936, 1948 by Harcourt, Brace and World, Inc.

Permission has been granted by Harcourt, Brace and World, Inc. to quote and to paraphrase excerpts from Harry Hansen's *Midwest Portraits* and *Modern American Poetry* edited by Louis Untermeyer, copyright © 1923, 1936, 1964 by Harcourt, Brace and World, Inc.; copyright © 1951 by Harry Hansen.

Excerpt from the review by Stephen Vincent Benet of Carl Sandburg's *Abraham Lincoln: The War Years, The Atlantic Monthly* (December 1939), copyright © 1939, 1967 by The Atlantic Monthly Company, Boston, Mass. Reprinted with permission.

Excerpt from Allan Nevins' "Carl Sandburg as Historian," *The Journal of the Illinois State Historical Society* (winter 1952), copyright © 1952 by *The Journal of the Illinois State Historical Society*. Reprinted with permission.

Excerpt from Charles A. Beard's "The Sandburg Lincoln," *Virginia Quarterly Review* (winter 1940), copyright © 1940 by William Beard and Miriam Vagts. Reprinted with permission.

Excerpts from Robert Sherwood's review of Carl Sandburg's *Abraham Lincoln, The New York Times*, December 5, 1939, copyright © 1939 by The New York Times Company. Reprinted by permission.

Excerpt from Newton Arvin's "Carl Sandburg," *The New Republic* (September 9, 1936), copyright © 1936 by *The New Republic*. Reprinted with permission.

Excerpts from Perry Miller's review of Carl Sandburg's *Remembrance Rock, The New York Times*, October 10, 1948, copyright © 1948 by The New York Times Company. Reprinted by permission.

Excerpts from Associated Press dispatches of May 28, 1952; June 1, 1958; March 4, 1961; December 25, 1964, copyright © 1952, 1958, 1961, 1964 by Associated Press. Reprinted with permission.

Excerpts from Bruce Weirick's "Political Circuit Rider," and Catherine McCarthy's "Carl Sandburg: the Lincoln Years," *The Lincoln Herald* (spring 1968), copyright © 1968 by *The Lincoln Herald*. Reprinted with permission.

Excerpts from *The Letters of Carl Sandburg*, copyright © 1968 by Lilian Steichen Sandburg, Trustee. Reprinted by permission of Harcourt, Brace and World, Inc.

Excerpt from Allan Nevins' "A Tribute to Carl Sandburg," *The Lincoln Herald* (spring 1968), copyright © 1968 by *The Lincoln Herald* and Allan Nevins. Reprinted with permission.

Excerpt from Carl Haverlin's "He Heard America Sing," *The Journal of the Illinois State Historical Society* (winter 1952), copyright © 1952 by *The Journal of the Illinois State Historical Society*. Reprinted with permission.

Excerpt from James G. Randall's "Carl," *The Journal of the Illinois State Historical Society* (winter 1952), copyright © 1952 by *The Journal of the Illinois State Historical Society*. Reprinted with permission.

Permission to quote and to paraphrase Adda George's "The Galesburg Birthplace of Carl Sandburg," *The Journal of the Illinois State Historical Society* (winter 1952), copyright © 1952 by *The Journal of Illinois State Historical Society*.

Excerpts from Carl Sandburg's "The American Songbag," *The Journal of the Illinois State Historical Society* (winter 1952), copyright © 1952 by *The Journal of the Illinois State Historical Society*. Reprinted with permission.

A biography, sirs, should begin—with the breath of a man when his eyes first meet the light of day—then working on through to the death when the light of day is gone.

—Honey and Salt

Foreword

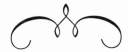

DURING THE WHOLE of a quiet and balmy Saturday afternoon in eastern Texas, I was seated at my typewriter in a newspaper office —pecking away at an equally unexciting feature story for the Sunday edition. Suddenly, from nowhere it seemed, a man bounded into the view, a white mane of hair hanging down over one eye. He flung himself into the chair beside my desk, stuck out a huge hand, and boomed:

"Sandburg's my name!"

So Carl Sandburg came into my life, just as he did into countless others. To say my world was different after meeting him, might be an exaggeration but certainly, anyone who met him even once was conscious of him afterwards.

The next time I saw him was some fifteen years later in the majestic Smoky Mountains in western North Carolina. Here he lived at "Connemara," a National Historic Site but at that time just a serene and secluded estate, so fitted to the evening of his fruitful life. My home, at one time in the Smokies, now was New York City and the members of the Civil War Round Table there had just elected me president. One of my goals was to get Carl Sandburg, who had finished his great biography of Lincoln, to speak to our organization. I had been told this was impossible; that he had stopped appearing before such groups, had slowed down and was confining himself to his woodland farm and finishing some writing he had long intended to do.

But I did not accept this as fact and was determined to seek him out and somehow persuade him to come and speak. It would have been useless to write or telephone. The answer would surely have been "No" and he probably would not even have given that answer personally. So, along with my cousin Milton Callahan of Chattanooga, I drove to Connemara, slowly easing the car up the last bit of the winding, wooded road to his huge white house for fear that we would be sighted and shooed away.

In front of the mansion we paused. I was on the point of getting out of the car when a huge, muscular, black dog appeared beside it and sobered this thought to a dim wish. The dark animal came closer and looked at us with questioning eyes. My heart sank. But not for long; if it required being mangled to get to the Sandburg doorway it might as well be now, I muttered to Milton as I slowly opened the car door and ventured out. The dog stood his ground. Somehow I found the courage to reach out a trembling hand and pat him on the head, half expecting part of the hand to disappear. The dog turned up his mouth—I was near paralysis—but then a warm red tongue emerged and licked my hand. My relief verged on collapse as I made my way to the front porch.

After I had rung the doorbell three times, a trim lady with gray hair and sharp but kindly eyes came to the door and asked what I wished. Quickly I spoke the names of mutual friends of

Mr. Sandburg's and mine—Allan Nevins, Carl Haverlin, and John Pemberton—and was pleased to note she recognized them. I was just passing by, I added, and simply wished to shake the hand of the poet-historian and to present him with a book of mine which he might find appropriate because it was titled "Smoky Mountain Country." Mrs. Sandburg nodded very slowly, asked me to wait a moment, and then faded back into the recesses of the house.

By this time Milton had joined me on the porch, and we both stood and waited hopefully in silence. After what seemed a long time, although actually it wasn't, I saw a white-haired figure, staring blinkingly from under an old blue eyeshade, make his way to the front door. As he opened the door, I repeated my introductory words; we shook hands and I reminded him we had once met at the newspaper office in Texas. He nodded and seemed to remember, and I handed him the copy of my book for which he thanked me.

"Mr. Sandburg," I said, "the next time you are in New York, would you please come to our Civil War Round Table and receive an award?"

"An award for *what?*" he roared.

It was a pretext to which I had given little thought, but I managed to reply that it would be set forth on the plaque. He mumbled a kind of assent and, before he could say more, I added that of course we hoped he would say a few words on the occasion.

Months later, Carl Sandburg did appear before our Round Table in New York. I spent half a day with him before the meeting, having been warned that if one did not keep an eye on him, he might well forget an occasion and not show up. After he had been interviewed by a young reporter from the *New York Times*—during which he admonished him, "Young man, now don't you put words in my mouth"—Sandburg and I stood for twenty minutes in the rain at Madison Avenue and 54th Street, trying to get a taxicab. Finally, the historian himself nabbed one and we rode down to the New York University Faculty Club at Washington Square where the meeting was to be held.

As we moved slowly along through the rain, I asked, "Mr. Sandburg, why, of all those people on national television last night dedicating the Overseas Press Club, did you alone read your remarks?'"

He paused for a moment and replied, "Well, Lincoln read his Gettysburg Address!"

At the Round Table meeting, Sandburg spoke to a capacity crowd about Lincoln and the Civil War. When he was presented with the plaque, he looked at it and exploded:

"Now that's a fine piece of calligraphy! If I were a dentist, I could hang that on my wall and it would do me some good."

Among those at the head table that night was Oscar Cargill, professor and author and a former teacher of mine. He had promised me he would attend the Round Table at some time when we had "somebody like Carl Sandburg." And he kept his promise. The idea of my writing a biography of Sandburg did not occur to either of us on that interesting evening which now seems so long ago. Yet when Dr. Cargill recently asked me to do just this, that Round Table, so memorable for those present, came vividly to mind.

There have been a number of articles and books on the life of Carl Sandburg and there will of course be more. But most of those that have already appeared were done during his lifetime. Now that he has gone (July 23, 1967), we can have a little better perspective on his full life, but it will be many years before the definitive assessment of his place in our history and literature can be made. It is hoped that this volume will be a beginning.

A biography of Sandburg is plainly no easy task. He was such a many-faceted man—poet, musician, biographer, historian, and novelist—that it is difficult to know how his achievements should be depicted and evaluated. Certainly it is impossible here to pass positive judgment upon the degree to which his contributions will endure. It is better to set forth the story of his uniquely colorful personality, to recall the manner in which he strode so flaringly across our land, and to examine his songs and writings and their effect upon his wide audience. Time will determine their place in the hierarchy of human greatness.

Sandburg, despite his often unconventional activities, was primarily a family man and his devoted wife and three daughters probably played as vital a part in his career as any family ever did in the life of a famous man. Accordingly, it was especially desirable to obtain the cooperation of the Sandburg family in the writing of this book, and I am exceedingly grateful to Mrs. Sandburg and her daughters, Margaret, Janet, and Helga, for helping in every way they were asked. Visits to lovely Connemara have been valuable and rewarding, although of course there is a quiet emptiness about the place since Sandburg's passing.

Margaret Sandburg, the eldest daughter, has been particularly helpful, spending long hours reminiscing about her beloved father and patiently going through huge files of letters, aiding me in extracting those appropriate for this work. She has a critical eye for accuracy and it is hoped that such will be consistently present in the forthcoming pages.

Appreciation is expressed to Vincent Starrett, Jonathan Warner, Hilda Lindley, Robert Land, Edward MacConomy, Robert Blake, Bernard Hoffman, Donald Leavitt, Mayme Wortelboer, M. L. Rein, Sam Ragan, Mr. and Mrs. Henry Belk, Norman Corwin, Harry Hansen, Einer Tangen, Mary C. Hogan, Joseph Schiffman, Fingel Rosenquist, Steven Lee Carson, Warren Titus, John N. Tangen, David M. Delo, Sophocles Papas, Robert V. Breen and Hallmark Cards, Inc., Mrs. Fred Hearn, Charles A. Pearce, Joe M. White, Martin Litvin, Don Shoemaker, Glenn Tucker, John Frost, Charles F. Gosnell, Edward Whitman, Grace Mayer, Rita Vaughan, Susan Cosalaro, and Marguerite Reese.

North Callahan

New York University
New York City

Contents

To Milton

The Young Idea
Takes Shape

THE CONTRAST OF the seasons in which Carl Sandburg entered upon this earth and took his departure from it was no sharper than that of the circumstances. He was born on a cold morning, January 6, 1878 at Galesburg in northwestern Illinois, the son of an illiterate blacksmith, and died, world-famous, eighty-nine years later in July at his North Carolina mansion home.

In those years covering nearly a century, Sandburg led at least three lives, and if one counts carefully, several more. He made his slow, struggling way along the main roads, but loved to go off at unexpected times into intriguing byways. Until his last years he was always on the move, either in external travels or striving for literary achievement inside his home or office. And even when age and weariness forced him to slow down, he relived in his warm memory the travels made by his active body and ebullient mind.

The story began just after midnight in the Sandburg home on Third Street in Galesburg, beside the Chicago, Burlington and Quincy Railroad for which his Swedish father worked. In the three-room frame home, the Sandburg's first baby, a girl named Mary, had been born three years earlier. Carl was the first son and therefore especially welcome, as he was to concede later.

The baby was put into a cradle his father had made which had been Mary's until Carl took over. It had three legs on each end. A year and a half later, Carl was in turn displaced by a new brother Mart. Carl Sandburg always loved to recall his boyhood days; in fact in many ways, he never outgrew them. One of the saddest things to him was that growing up was necessary in this life; yet to the end of his long span of years, he was to recount the charms of his golden days, and if now and then he threw in a sad note, he usually made it disappear with a great burst of laughter that sounded down the intervening years.

He was christened Carl August Sandburg but he himself decided in his first years in school to use the name Charles instead, believing that it sounded less Swedish. At about the same time, he and his brother and sister began to spell their last name "burg" instead of "berg." Among Carl's many early memories was that of carrying pails of water from a cistern in the family yard to fill washtubs, one having warm water and a washboard for soaping and rubbing, the other, with a wringer attached to it, holding cold rinsing water. He often turned the wringer handle and later carried the washing to a clothes line in the back yard. When the weather was cold—and in Galesburg it gets very cold in the winter—Carl would often have trouble when the clothes froze, bounced against his head in the wind, and became generally unwieldy. When bath time came, often at the urging of a discerning mother, the same washtubs were filled with warm water, soap was furnished and the boys took over the kitchen for scrubbing, while the girls waited and took turns shortly afterward.

Carl Sandburg was never a stickler for food yet always seemed to appreciate good edibles. Perhaps this was because his earliest meals consisted mainly of the Swedish dishes of boiled herring and boiled potatoes. Even in his last years, his menus at Connemara were simple ones, with boiled potatoes again forming a sturdy adjunct. Cabbage heads were heaped in the Sandburg cellar in October to be used during the winter. As to another source of sustenance, Carl himself has reminisced:

> In the triangle closet under the stairs from the first floor to the cellar, Papa used to keep a barrel of apples in winter months, when he could afford it. He put a lock on the door and hid the key. He had seen that when a barrel of apples stood where everyone could get at it, we would soon be at the barrel bottom. He would have put a board over the gap above the door had he known what Mart and I were doing. By hard wriggling, our boy bodies could squeeze through the gap and drop down to the apple barrel. We took two apples at a time and only every other day. What we stole wasn't noticed and we said, "When two of us steal two apples and divide them, that's only stealing one apple apiece and stealing one apple isn't really stealing, it's snooking." [1]

Life picked up somewhat for the family when the elder Sandburg bought a larger house on Berrien Street in Galesburg. But the payments seemed bigger than the house, especially when they came at the same time as those on the parcel of farm land the father also bought in this sudden splurge. For a while, the family dreamed of leaving Galesburg and moving onto the farm. There were visions of big crops of wheat and corn, apples and pears. Tradition pictured the farmer as independent, living off what he raised on his land; he was his own boss and could not be discharged. But then came the Panic of 1893 when the New York stock market collapsed and the price of gold fell off, followed by business failures, unemployment, strikes, and a depression. Corn went to ten cents a bushel in Kansas and land went down in price. As a sad consequence, August Sandburg sold his land. In 1894 Coxey's Army marched on Washington. Hard times harried Galesburg as they did other communities. Work on the railroad dropped from a ten-hour to a four-hour day and the Sandburg pay check, like others, was less than half what it had been formerly.

None bore the depression with more spirit, however, than the Sandburgs. They ate bread that had been spread with lard; sometimes even the lard ran out and molasses was substituted. Fortunately, the potato crop was good and this welcome staple helped them ride out the crisis. Occasionally neighbors banded together and killed hogs, dividing up the carcasses—succulent spare ribs, loins, chops, and all the other delectable parts—which added variety to the plain, drab diet they had become accustomed to.

Powdered coke was used for fuel instead of the better lumps. Young Carl learned to break big lumps of coke small enough to fit into the coal bucket and the stove. He found this to be hard work but consoled himself that many miners he had read about went through more hardships than he did. Only a small part of the house was heated in those cold winter nights in Galesburg, and Carl and his brother Mart, who slept in the third-floor garret, used to stand before the kitchen stove in their underwear, get real warm, then dash upstairs and into bed before the cold could close in on them. Later when the family had acquired a gasoline stove for cooking and a heating stove with an insinglass door and an ashpan at the bottom—which Carl emptied endless times on the outside ashpile—memories remained of the cherished old kitchen stove before which they had so delightfully warmed their haunches on icy winter nights before jumping into bed.

The Sandburgs must have spent much time in the kitchens of their earlier homes, for Carl recalled the scenes as long as he lived. There they were crowded into a kitchen twelve by fifteen feet, with cupboard, sink, stove, table, and chairs. It was not only a kitchen, he recalled, but a dining room, study-playroom, and workshop. There Carl's mother mixed bread and oven-baked the dough into savory brown loaves. There clothes were patched, the boys' hair was cut by their father, and their shoes were half-soled. Corn was popped, taffy made, and nuts were cracked on flatirons and eaten voraciously.

"Papa shaved at the kitchen sink," Carl remembered,

> before a small looking glass. A serious father with lather over cheeks, chin and neck looks less serious to his children. The sound of the scraping razor mowing down the three days' growth of whiskers had a comic wonder for us. He couldn't shave without making faces at himself. There were times when his face took on so fearful and threatening a look we were a little scared. We saw his razor travel over cheeks, chin, upper lip, below the jaws, everywhere except a limited area under his chin. There he left a small tuft of hair. At intervals over a few weeks, we would see him take scissors and trim this goatee.[2]

Though much of Carl's boyhood centered about play, work of various kinds made impressions more lasting than those of the indelible pencil his father used on special occasions to record something of importance. There was a pump in the back yard with a personality all its own, a demanding one when his father wanted fresh water and Carl had to go out and pump it. In summer the pump needed priming and he would have to go back into the house and fetch a pail of rain water to pour into the reluctant conveyor. On winter mornings, the pump handle often would not move, so Carl had to douse it with hot water until it was thawed. Its two-way stretch had a rhythm similar to some lines of the Sandburg poetry.

As time went on, the appearance of the houses in the neighborhood changed. For years, all the residences had been fenced in on the sides, back, and front. This apparently was because of numerous horses, cows, pigs, and chickens belonging to virtually all the families around; it was necessary to protect one's property as well as one's safety. But as the numbers of the livestock dwindled, the fences began to disappear, first the front ones, then the sides and back. The wealthier families got rid of them first and the less affluent followed suit until, finally, all the fences were gone.

At the age of six, Carl Sandburg saw his first political meeting. Down on Seminary Street a crowd of men had gathered under torchlights for a Republican rally. As they began to march, a brass band led the procession and to this sound was added those of extra horns blowing and drums beating. All his life, Carl seemed to hear the sound of drums of some kind, whether real or in fancy; it reminds one, in recounting his far-reaching life, that the poet and biographer, like Thoreau, must have heard "a different drummer."

One group at this rally yelled rhythmically, "Blaine, Blaine, James G. Blaine," while across from them with equal fervor, a competing crowd screamed, "Hurrah for Cleveland." In return, the opposition retorted that they thought Cleveland should be hanged, but instead, a few months later, Cleveland had been elected President of the United States, a great disappointment for the elder Sandburg who was a rabid Republican.

U. S. Grant, another Republican, died when Carl was only seven years old, and Galesburg held a sort of collateral funeral for him which made a strong impression on the youngster. Local stores closed for this July afternoon in 1885 and a parade began on Seminary Street, moved along Main Street, and ended in the public square. Crowds lined the sidewalks and Carl and his father had trouble seeing what was going on in the streets. Finally the boy was placed on his father's shoulders and he could see that a marshal on a sorrel horse headed the parade—resplendent with shiny bridle and saddle. Police marched two abreast and a fife and drum corps followed. Grant had been the most famous general in America if not the world, and members of his old ranks, the Grand Army of the Republic, marched as well, a few of them escorting a symbolic black box on a black cart pulled by eight black horses. Then came a procession of Negroes pacing to slow and sad music, for Grant had led the armies which set them free. This event lingered in the memory of Carl Sandburg, as did most military spectacles, and it fired his imagination as to what was the real significance of the death of a man who had fought for a cause that came to mean so much to so many. This early interest in history was widened by reading especially by the time Carl was in the fifth grade. With avid interest, he devoured John S. C. Abbott's *History of Napoleon Bonaparte*, both volumes. The boy learned not only that Napoleon was a great soldier but also that, despite his autocratic career, he accomplished some good things for his people and set a colorful example the world will never forget. Carl was so impressed with the emperor that he put a leather strap around his waist and a wooden sword inside it and strutted around the house like the "Little Corporal" himself. Other volumes he read thoroughly included J. T. Headley's *Napoleon and His Marshals* and *Washington and His Generals;* also *Boy Travellers* by Thomas W. Knox, and Hezekiah Butterworth's *Zigzag Journeys.*

But Carl recalled:

> Best of all was the American history series by Charles Carleton Coffin. *The Boys of '76* . . . made me feel I could have been a boy in the days of George Washington and watched him on a horse, a good rider sitting easy and straight, at the head of a line of ragged soldiers with shotguns. I could see Paul Revere on a horse riding wild and stopping at farmhouses to holler the British were coming. I could see old curly-headed Israel Putnam, the Connecticut farmer, as the book told it: "Let 'em have it!" shouted Old Put, and we sent a lot of redskins head over heels into the lake. . . . A few days later . . . the French and Indians ambushed us. We sprung behind trees and fought like tigers. Putnam shot four Indians. . . . One of the Frenchmen seized Rogers's gun, and the other was about to stab him, when Put up with his gun and split the fellow's head open.[3]

Other books by Coffin that Carl enjoyed were *Old Times in the Colonies* which related how the pioneers built cabins, cleared the timbers, and shoved crude plows into new ground while watching out for the Indians, and *The Story of Liberty* which revealed what attracted people to Europe and described tyrants who intrigued the curiosity of the young Sandburg. Strangely, Carl found *The Boys of '61* by Coffin not nearly so interesting as his volume on the Revolution, yet Coffin was supposed to have been a correspondent in the Civil War.

In studying Sandburg's career, one wonders how much he might have been influenced by Mark Twain, especially since Twain lived until Sandburg was thirty-two years old. They had some similar qualities, but Sandburg appears to have been little conscious of any influence of Twain. This may have been partly because the first of Twain's books that Sandburg read, *Huckleberry Finn* and *Tom Sawyer*, made little impression upon him for some reason. But there is definitely one quality the two had in common—wishing to make people happy and rejoicing in it when they did. While Twain made people laugh, Sandburg made them laugh and cry. Even the crying usually had a tinge of joy. And helping folks to feel better lay deep in the roots of Sandburg's boyhood.

The first biography Carl ever owned was an accidental but significant discovery. He found it lying on a sidewalk on his way to school and when he had picked it up and cleaned the dirt off, he discovered a very small book with a glossy paper cover and a color picture of Major General P. T. Beauregard of the Confederate Army. It had only thirteen pages of text but this was enough to enhance his curiosity about the Civil War and the men who figured in it. In the back of the book was a list of other such volumes which came in the packages with a certain brand of cigarettes. Carl persuaded two older friends of his to purchase some of these and eventually he became the owner of biographies not only of Beauregard but of Cornelius Vanderbilt, Sarah Bernhardt, George Peabody, Robert Ingersoll, and John Ericsson who invented many features of the Union ship, *Monitor*. Through these books Carl became entranced with history, especially the period of our Civil War. His mother was glad that he had the history books; but his father was skeptical and wondered out loud what good it would do. Such taunts hurt Carl, though he did not say so. They doubtless drove him to prove later on just how much good could come from them.

In 1891 when Carl Sandburg was thirteen and had finished the eighth grade, he dropped out of school, and temporarily stopped his studies. His education for almost a decade came from experience and occasional contacts with newspapers, magazines, and a few random volumes, but mostly, as always, from people. He was still a boy, however, and no one ever savored the keen delights of boyhood more than he, when he had the chance. He and his friends played the ageless game of mumble peg, trying to flip an open knife from the hand so as to stick the blade in a particular spot of ground. Or, on the wooden sidewalks of Berrien Street, they flung tops in gay abandon, the radish-shaped forms landing with a whining hum on their metal tips, sometimes upright and correct, sometimes at a dizzying angle that could not be sustained and ended in a flip-flop across the walk and a coming to rest as still as young death. There was the gratifying game of two-eyed cat in which two batters stood facing each other, a catcher-pitcher behind each one. When the ball was hit, the batters ran and changed sides until scores piled up and young muscles finally gave out. Sometimes a good batter would just stand up and knock mighty fly balls toward eager outstretched arms away out in the cow pasture. When the hit was wide, one of the boys running to catch it would at times slip and fall ignominiously in a fresh puddle of soft cow manure. This they called "third base."

When the players stayed so late that dusk fell as they journeyed home, they would pass the lamplighter at his work. He carried a small ladder which he would set against the lamppost and slowly he would climb up and open the door of the glass compartment which held the gas burner; he would reach in and turn the gas on, then with a lighted taper, he would put flame to the gas escaping from the tiny outlet in the center of the lamp. This aroused the poetic sense of young Carl who later described with such vividness the glories of the night world. Soon the gas lamps were replaced by the more mundane electric lights which brought into bright focus the raw ugliness of Galesburg.

The hometown team aspired to more than sandlot baseball. Galesburg played teams such as those of Peoria, Chillicothe, and Rock Island on the campus of Knox College. Knox was a non-sectarian, coeducational institution opened by Congregationalists and Presbyterians and chartered in 1837. It was to be combined with Lombard College in the years to come and both Knox and Lombard had a part in the life of Carl Sandburg. When the town baseball teams played on the campus, the kids from Berrien Street, who usually lacked the price of admission, watched through knotholes in the fence or climbed a tree not too far from the diamond and saw the game almost as well as those close by.

Baseball, with its heated activity and competition, most probably influenced young Sandburg, for in many ways the game remained with him to the end of his life. At one point he wanted to be a professional, and at times in the summers he played from eight in the morning until it was too dark to handle the ball, only chasing home at noon for a bite of lunch and racing back. His head was filled with baseball names and stars, and he knew the names of the teams of both the National and American Leagues, including those who led in batting and fielding and the pitchers who won the most games.

An abrupt end came to his baseball ambitions. Early one afternoon in October, 1894, Carl took his secondhand fielder's glove to a pasture to practice catching fly balls. A friend hit a high ball and Carl ran headlong for it. As he raced along, he later recalled, he had visions of making a great catch in the style of big-league baseball. This dream was interrupted when his right foot went into a hole and he found himself face down on the ground. His foot hurt and when he looked at it blood was oozing from his sock, and a broken beer bottle which had cut him lay nearby. He managed to make his way to the home of a nearby doctor and have the cut dressed and four stitches taken, before he limped home. His mother was sorry, his father disdainful, and the combination of all factors completely ended Carl's ambitions for big-time baseball. But he never lost his love for it and it colored his mature vocabulary.

Between nine and twelve years of age, Carl Sandburg experienced one of the pleasures boys fortunate enough to live in that day had: along with his friends he attended the county fair. That this required almost a five-hour walk each way to reach the fair grounds just outside of Knoxville, Illinois, was simply part of the pleasure to him. Usually the roads were dusty, for barefoot boys this provided a delightful powder to squish up between the toes and splash gently over the balls of the feet in soft rhythm as they plodded joyously along, the fair already in their nostrils, the thrill of the crowds already sounding in their young ears. They had shoes, not to waste on the dust of the road, but to carry in their hands until they reached the fair and there proudly put on to keep bare toes from being stepped on and skinned by the crowd.

Most things at the fair cost a nickel then. Carl and the Larson brothers, his friends, invested one each in the new Edison Talking Phonograph. They had to put on earphones to listen while other people stood around awaiting their turn to "take in" the great, new wonder which brought so near the sound of words and music from far-off places. In later years, Carl always seemed fascinated with sound reproduction. He was to make resonant sounds of his own, especially on records which, fortunately for posterity, hold his warm folk singing and his poetry recitation until this day. He never seemed happier than when he was in some big-city studio, singing or speaking into a microphone for radio, or recording for television or films. When work was over, he joshed with the studio personnel and often said things as priceless as those he produced for formal occasions. Some that have been recaptured will be found in this volume.

At the county fair, Carl saw slices of midwestern life which were always to be part of his own nature and expression—horses and cows, hogs and chickens, ducks and sheep. These were only part of the panorama of the prairie farms on display, their red and blue ribbons bright evidence of prizes won in sweating com-

petition between ardent but fair-minded farmers from the surrounding countryside. Not only did the farmers compete but they
learned from example how to make the land produce more each
year in crops and profits, until finally the system would develop
that gave a small percentage of people sway over a powerful
kingdom of mechanical giants, wresting from the soil its rich
fruitfulness. Carl saw the rawboned farmers in their crude but
clean clothing, muscles prominent underneath, sturdiness plain
in their earnest faces. Their women, who should have retained
their beauty, were all too much like the Grant Wood painting
that reveals femininity worn and wearied by toil and inexorable
demands of family life on the prairie.

On one visit to the fair, Carl hitched a ride back home in a
hayrack, a comfort and joy to his aching feet and exuberant
heart. The smell of the hay as the horses jogged along caught in
his nostrils and never left him when he came to write about his
Middle West and its people who turned to the great cities to
compete in a harsh industrial system that the young Swedish-
American never quite accepted. The luxuriant grass, as thick as
his own hair, was a symbol to him of the surface of the prairie.
Although he never gave the grass the prominence in his titles
that Whitman did, Sandburg whom Whitman influenced was
just as conscious of it and vastly more familiar with this hirsute
adornment of rural nature than his earlier Brooklyn counterpart.

Another strand in this youthful experience that bore so
strongly upon the sensitive mind of young Sandburg was the
Barnum and Bailey Circus. When it came to town he was up
early to watch the unloading of the animals down by the railroad
tracks, and hear the man who rode ahead of the elephants an-
nounce in exaggerated but beloved tones that the great beasts
were coming down the street—something he could hardly have
concealed had he tried. Once Carl even saw Mr. Bailey himself,
in a long black coat with tails, noisily supervising the setting up
of the circus in a large field outside Galesburg. Characteristically,
the boy wondered where Barnum was, not realizing that it was
unusual for even one of the owners to appear at such a compara-

tively small place on the circus itinerary. Carl got a job carrying water for the elephants, and this was not a small task for the pay involved a ticket for the day's performance. But he considered the show a rich reward, with its grand march of all the performers around the spacious interior of the great tent, the antics of the acrobats, the hilarious carrying-on of the clowns, and—the climax that forever remained with him—the hippodrome chariot race lavishly presented as it had been, at least in the words of the master of ceremonies, in the time of the Roman Emperor Nero. Other features that stuck in the fertile Sandburg mind were the spieler with the long mustache and stentorian voice, the inevitable wild man of Borneo, the world's smallest dwarf and tallest giant, a man-eating python, a dog-faced boy, an unbelievably fat woman, the tattooed man who had fish, birds, girls, and boats all over his skin. Carl felt sorry for the freaks because he sometimes felt like a freak himself and sympathized when they were stared at. Yet the time was to come when he would feel inadequate in public unless he himself was stared at. Indeed he cultivated a colorful appearance for the very purpose of bringing this about, particularly when it meant success on the stage or in front of the microphones.

Not long afterward—perhaps the influence of the circus was to blame—Carl went into Olson's store and made his first purchase on credit. It was a stick of licorice and it cost only a nickel but that was more than Carl possessed. He thought that this was a marvelous way to get something for nothing; but he did not reckon with his thrifty mother. When he arrived home with the dark and sticky candy showing on his face, she inquired how he came by it and he told her. Whereupon, she slapped him and admonished him never to abuse the family credit again on peril of a real licking.

Such episodes were exceptional, however, for Carl's recollections were mostly pleasant, especially the occasions of his first singing. The local cigar store was the scene of gatherings of his boy friends between work and play times. On balmy nights, and on Sundays when the little store was closed, he and his friends would gather on the sidewalk for a session of youthful harmony. Among the participants were tall and skinny John Hultgren, a Swedish boy who worked in a local broom factory, and stout, bright-cheeked John Kerrigan, a young Irishman who worked as an apprentice plumber, both of whom sang tenor. Willis Calkins and Carl Sandburg sang baritone and bass interchangeably, which they considered quite acceptable, but since there were no demanding critics, it made little difference. Examples of their musical offerings were "In the Evening By the Moonlight," "Carry Me Back to Old Virginny" in its original version, and the popular "Suwanee River."

Such sentiment fused into the religious when Carl watched the local cobbler do his work and philosophize at the same time. The latter would cut his leather for a half-sole and fill his mouth with wooden pegs for the job, meanwhile trying to talk. The boys watched with fascination as he proceeded, and remembered his mouth as much as his words. But they knew that he worked from early morning until early evening each day and that he liked his work, something which made a special impression on Carl as he huddled around the cozy little coal stove on chilly winter days. But memorable also were the cobbler's devout words. He made it clear that he had Jesus in his heart, that he prayed to him day and night, and that the boys would never go wrong if they followed Jesus, for He was the light of the world and if one believed in Him, one should never be afraid. The cobbler emphasized that this is a short life, and proved it by dying early from consumption. This experience made a sharp impression on the young Sandburg, although even now it is hard to estimate just how orthodoxly religious he ever became. But it is certain that in later years he often made reference to God, especially in some of his writings. One has the feeling that Carl Sandburg, like Jefferson and Lincoln, was religious in his own special but adequate way.

In his teens, Carl heard one of the foremost speakers of the day, William Jennings Bryan. The "Great Commoner" arrived in Galesburg by train, and from a platform on Mulberry Street next to the railroad tracks he made one of his eloquent speeches. The boy has not recorded what impression the famous orator made the first time he heard him, but evidently it had a definite impact, for not long afterward when Bryan was speaking in Monmouth, a town some sixteen miles from Galesburg, Carl and some of his friends rode the cowcatcher of a train on a cold October night to hear him again. Whatever the orator said this time must not have made much impression on Sandburg; nor did his principle of abstinence from the bottle make much of a dent, for one of the boys bought a pint of blackberry brandy which was sampled by the group and found to bring marked relief from the cool weather. In what appears from his own reminiscing, Carl was equally unimpressed with a speech by Robert Ingersoll who appeared that fall in a tent on the Knox College campus and delivered an excoriation of the Democrats and Free Silver, which the local boys listened to obligingly. Meanwhile the blackberry brandy had apparently not become habit-forming for the boys had apparently decided that they would leave booze alone thereafter. Instead, their main dissipation, for a time at least, consisted of walking the main street of the hometown and voraciously eating cream puffs.

Of more import was the first musical instrument that Carl Sandburg played. It was a willow whistle which he cut out for himself, putting a pencil between his teeth, he rapped out the tune against his teeth with his right thumb. Next came a comb with a paper over it on which he tried to vocalize but without much success. With a dime sweet-potato-like kazoo, Sandburg could imitate large musical instruments or the sounds of chickens. Then he tried a tin fife, a flageolet, and the octarina, but none to much effect. His first string instrument was a banjo which he made himself from a cigar box. He never learned to play any instrument very well, but from his success in singing folk songs and strumming a guitar or a banjo later on, it seems that few detected it.

Whether by performing musically, or by writing, or speaking, Carl Sandburg always had a knack of making money, even though he made so little at times that it seems a wonder that it was sufficient to sustain him. (His first regular paid job, following a series of odd assignments such as hunting for rags, bones, iron, and bottles to sell, was with the local real-estate firm of Callender and Rodine, located in the main part of town. His task was to open the office each morning before the owners arrived and sweep it from end to end. There was dust all over the wooden floor and in cracks and corners; Carl dealt with it by the simple method of sweeping it out into the hall and down the stairs into the street. Also part of the daily stint was cleaning the spittoons of both Mr. Callender and Mr. Rodine. Carl carried the heavy and smelly brass receptacles to a nearby faucet where he emptied them, then washed and rinsed them until they were brightly clean. Every few weeks, the lad polished the spittoons until they shone like a brass tuba. For this chore, that really required only a few minutes each morning, Carl received the sum of twenty-five cents a week.)

Inevitably for an American boy growing up in that era, Carl carried newspapers. This he did for the *Galesburg Republican-Register*. The papers came off a flatbed press and the carrier boys, who gathered right after school each day, took them to a table where they folded and counted them. Carl learned how to fold the papers so they could be thrown sharply against the front doors. With a bundle of them under his arm, he dashed downstairs to Main Street and turned north. Most of the houses were near enough to the sidewalk so that, without stepping off the walk, he could fire the papers smack against the door bottoms on the wooden porches. Now and then he would find a big house set back so far from the walk that he had to go inside the yard to make his pitch. Possibly here at this early age began Carl Sandburg's resentment of those who had what seemed to him too much as opposed to his own class which had too little. Especially, he became unpleasantly conscious of the local Republican Party boss of the county, a fat man who often waddled out to meet him and take the paper from his hand, so greedy, thought Carl, was the roly-poly one to read the news of the world, particularly that which fed his own likes and dislikes. The great three-story stone house, biggest in town, seemed to the boy to have a particularly forbidding appearance of wealth, with its towers and fancy curvatures. When he had finished his two-mile delivery rounds—greeting friends, shyly looking at girls now and then—he turned south again, with one copy of the newspaper left over for himself. In addition, the *Republican-Register* paid him one shiny and appreciated silver dollar a week.

This typical American midwest landscape which young Carl saw as he delivered his papers made a deep impression on him, leaving a kind of Gothic etching in his mind that later was to appear in the vivid images of both his poetry and prose. The trees stood out in bold relief, stark and bare against the winter sky, lush and green in spring and summer days. In autumn some of the apple trees were too beckoning for him not to pause and partake of their fruit; for surely no one was ever hungrier than a schoolboy carrying newspapers. Carl, in contrast, also got to know the sizes and shapes of the backhouses or privies; every yard, rich or poor, had one, only varying from elegant lattice-fronted structures, spacious and containing soft paper, to dinky and broken ones with apertures open to the elements and catalogs the mainstay of their equipment.

On these rounds came the inspiration which was to stay with Carl until the end of his long life and mark him in many primary ways, a journalist at heart and in much practice and association. He saw the reporter for the newspaper going along the street and getting personal items from the most prominent people who were either coming or going, expecting company or a baby, or perhaps had had a sickness or a death in the family. It was a leisurely process then and a pencil was used on the copy paper instead of a typewriter. The sight of this working journalist thrilled Carl and filled him with an admiration that spurred him to eventual emulation.

In fact, he got deeper into the newspaper field even then by carrying a morning route of Chicago papers. This required diligence and every morning he found himself on the railroad platform when the fast mail train from Chicago came in soon after seven. From the depths of the mail car as the train rolled to a stop, came hard, fat rolls of the city papers, the boys grabbing them and quickly sorting them out for their routes. The newspapers included the *Chicago Tribune, Chicago Times, Chicago Herald,* and *Chicago Chronicle.* On Sunday mornings, Carl would pull a small wagon filled with the Chicago newspapers and sell them for five cents a copy, making a penny for himself. All in all, he came to make about twelve dollars a month—to say nothing of the invaluable experience he received in his varied contact with all kinds of people, the feeling he acquired for the business, and his hearty absorption of the joys and sorrows he encountered.

Of equal interest and value were his days peddling milk from a wagon, although this episode in his life was a rather brief one. Carl was nearly fifteen years of age when a dairyman hired him to help deliver milk to the local residents. The milk barn was two miles away and instead of riding this distance, which cost a nickel, the young man walked. He had hardly begun work when he and his family came down with diphtheria, and Carl was kept from his job for some time. The dairyman held little attraction for Carl, so when he paid him for his work, the boy told him he wished to quit and this was mutually agreed upon.

After a short period of working for a drunken tinner, and another of washing bottles in a pop bottling plant where Carl drank so much free pop that he felt he had had enough to do him the rest of his life, he quit this for still another job, this time in a drugstore. He had the key for opening the store and at seven in the morning he appeared and diligently swept the floor, then took a chamois skin and wiped off the showcases. Carl quickly learned how to fill bottles with wine and whiskey, as well as those labeled sulphuric and muriatic acid, wood alcohol, turpentine, and other kinds of medicine. Mr. Hinman, the pharmacist, reminded Carl of Edgar Allan Poe, being slim, dark-skinned, and wearing a neat little mustache. He had a frequent smile and an ever-present sense of humor.

Perhaps no boy ever had such varied jobs as Carl Sandburg. For weeks he worked nights in what was called an ice harvest on a nearby lake when the thermometer was near zero. Carl walked from home for several blocks, then caught a street car which ran for over a mile out to the lake. The ice was thick, up to eighteen inches, and men worked over it at first with ice cutters. Large blocks from ten to fifteen feet in size were cut and moved to the ice house at the edge of the lake. The ice was then cut up into smaller cakes and these were stored in rows with sawdust sprinkled in between to keep them until the warm weather came when they were greatly cherished.

"I had overshoes and warm clothes and enjoyed the work," Carl reminisced in later years:

> The air was crisp and you could see a fine sky of stars any time you looked up, sometimes a shooting star and films of frost sparkles. I never had a night job that kept me til the sun came up. I got acquainted with a little of what goes on over the night sky, how the Big Dipper moves, how the spread of the stars early in the night keeps on with slow changes into something else all night long. I did my wondering about that spread of changing stars and how little any one of us is, standing and looking up at it.[4]

When soon afterward Carl was put in the ice house to work, he found that the chutes fed him so many cakes of ice that it was a cold, hard struggle to keep up with them. As he did in his life to come, however, he adjusted his efforts and his strength and handled the ice cakes well. Throwing iron tongs into these heavy blocks and maneuvering them into proper position proved to be heavy work, straining the muscles in his back and shoulders. Doubtless such labor added to the size of his huge hands which were always conspicuous whether he was typing out a newspaper story or plunking on his guitar. He found that like many beginners he went at the work too diligently and unskillfully. Now and then he would try to rest a few minutes, but evidently the foreman did not relish this, for he would walk over and tell the young man to get busy. At least he called him by his name and this helped. Carl was just about ready to quit, when the foreman kindly reminded him that in only a few more days the ice-gathering job would be over. This gave Carl a second wind and he tore into the task with new vigor. He worked harder, slept better, and best of all his taut muscles relaxed. He found that if he relaxed, he could work better and last longer. This was a lesson he never forgot.

All his life too he relished sports. A year after his experience with the ice, he worked for a time at the local racetrack, carrying water and helping to dry and sponge the tired horses after their runs. This was interesting, but best of all to him was being near some of the best race horses in the world. Here was competition at its keenest; he learned what it took to win. Yet some days were wet and then the horses and trainers and riders had to wait for the weather to change, something none could control but all complained about just the same. Over them all, however, there was a complacency which was a good example to the young man who was to express man's struggle in song, poetry, and prose and to show the lasting influence of such molding experiences.

At the Galesburg grammar school one night, Carl saw a diorama of the Battle of Gettysburg and even this simple portrayal sketched itself in his mind and never left it. Admission to the show was five cents. Succeeding curtains revealed the unfolding events of the great battle and a man with a long pointer explained the struggle. Although his voice was squeaky and monotonous, Carl absorbed the spirit of the presentation and remembered details which in later years he was to convey not only in writing but to interviewers who walked with him across the battlefield itself, as he reflected the image of Abraham Lincoln there.

Striking too was the impression made upon the boy at the same series of performances by the appearance of John Peter Altgeld who was then running for governor of Illinois. From what he had read in the Chicago newspapers, Carl half expected him to be some sort of monster breathing violence. Instead he saw a gentle man who stood in one spot during his whole speech and never gesticulated once. Altgeld talked quietly and Carl immediately felt empathy with him.

John L. Sullivan, the heavyweight boxer and symbol of the cleanness of the sport at that time, also came to Galesburg. He played in a skit that had little relation to athletics but did give the audience an opportunity to see and hear this strong man who had won the admiration of the boxing fans of the world. Sullivan whetted the appetite of the young Sandburg for sports, as did Gentleman Jim Corbett who appeared soon afterward with his punching bag on which he demonstrated his skill. But Carl got little thrill out of seeing Fridtjof Nansen, the adventure-story writer, or Henry M. Stanley, the African explorer, though the boy did sense something of importance in these figures with whose background he had little familiarity.

Some of Carl Sandburg's first stage experience came when he helped backstage with the play "The Count of Monte Cristo" when it came to town with James O'Neill as the star. In fact, the young man helped roll the canvas sea that O'Neill swam in when he made his escape. "Uncle Tom's Cabin" also played the town, and Carl remembered long afterward how disappointed all the local people were at not seeing two of each character in the play as had been advertised. Carl even had a small part in a Civil War play, *Shenandoah,* by Bronson Howard. A favorite was Al Field's minstrel show, for here was a rousing display of the art of banjo-playing by Field himself. Carl usually saw these shows from the balcony known as "Nigger Heaven," a cheaper and noisier part of the auditorium where the cracking of peanut shells mingled with sounds from the stage.

Despite the interest and variety of Carl's many jobs, he began to realize that he was not getting anywhere and decided that he wanted to learn a trade. But he found no opportunities among the plumbers, carpenters, painters, or machinists. Then he heard of an opening for a porter at the Union Hotel barbershop. By this time, he felt some desperation and rationalized that here was a real opportunity for work, travel to other towns, and possible openings into more promising fields of endeavor. So he went down and got the job. The barbershop was under a bank—in a basement with large windows through which he could see the feet of pedestrians on the sidewalk. These feet were of special interest to Carl because the shoes of many of them he was to shine and the result would be a few welcome tips to add to the slender coffer. Later when he was to write of the lowly, he knew the lowly.

In this barbershop Carl met the so-called upper crust of Galesburg and he was not overly impressed with them. Barbershops are not always busy and he found that at early noon he could go up a back stair to the main office of the hotel and, although he was too young to be admitted legally, into a swanky saloon. There he found a brass rail and a long mirror with fancy wood carving around it. At the end of the bar was the proverbial free lunch of those days, ham and cheese and pickles—and there Carl got his lunch without buying a drink—for which he was duly thankful. The most prominent people who passed through Galesburg usually appeared at the hotel and Carl learned who they were by reading the *Police Gazette* in the barbershop, so he could recognize many of them when he saw them. A high spot in Carl's barbershop era came when on the death of the local Congressman, he took to his shoeshine stand and there brightly shined the shoes of four Senators, eight Congressmen, and two majors, as well as two pairs of knee-high boots such as Lincoln wore. Their wearers had of course come for the funeral, and that day Carl made an unprecedented $1.40.

Saturday was a special day in the barbershop. It was bath day. Next to the shop was a bathroom with tubs which cost a quarter to use. Some of the customers would call Carl in to scrub their backs, for which he usually received a quarter. Often he talked with other barbershop porters and they would compare notes on what was the best polish for shoes and how to wheedle the biggest tip out of a customer. Sometimes some of the shine boys would go to the hotel on Sundays and order the best dinner, just so they could say they had associated with the bon ton of the town and did not have to be lackeys all the week long. The barbershop fascinated Carl, but by spring of 1893, he was ready to leave it. He felt he was not cut out to be a barber.

Serious thoughts were besetting him. He observed:

> Every morning for sixteen months or more I walked from
> home at half-past six, west on Berrien Street, crossing the
> Q. Switchboard tracks, on past Mike O'Connor's cheap
> livery stable, past the Boyer broom factory, then across the
> Knox College campus and past the front of the Old Main
> Building. Every morning I saw the east front of Old Main
> where they had put up the platform for Lincoln and
> Douglas to debate in October, 1858. At the north front of
> Old Main many times I read on a bronze plate words
> spoken by Lincoln and by Douglas. They stayed with me
> and sometimes I would stop to read these words only,
> what Lincoln said to twenty thousand people on a cold,
> windy October day: "He is blowing out the moral lights
> around us, when he contends that whoever wants
> slaves has a right to hold them." I read them in winter
> sunrise, in broad summer daylight, in falling snow or rain,
> in all the weathers of a year.[5]

It was probably at this point in the young **man**'s life that he began to ally himself with Lincoln as a force, an unknown quantity,
an enigma—having no notion that one day he, Carl Sandburg,
would be moved to write the world's most spectacular biography
of the Civil War president.

This was on Carl's second milk-route job. Also on this job he
found his first romantic love. Once he saw her face, it stayed
with him day and night. She lived in a home that required a
quart of milk each day, so he would pour it into the crock waiting
on the porch, knowing that usually, through the window above
him, she was looking. Sometimes when there was no message in
the crock, she would come out and smile at him and ask him personally to leave the milk. He left his heart also. But this did not
last long. One night he had the opportunity to walk home with
her from the Knox Street Congregational Church and found that
she had little to say and less to offer, so he shied away from her
from then on, a disillusioned but not too downcast boy.

But girls had a very small part in Carl's life. He did not understand them nor know what to say to them. Now he was nineteen years old and restless. His jobs had led nowhere and he sensed a frustration that often depressed him. He began to feel that, though his hometown had many shortcomings, he did too—and so he blamed himself for his uneasy state of mind. He realized, however, that it was up to him to do something about this restless state. So in June of 1897 he headed west, having heard from hoboes that anyone could wander about without money or job and get along all right, at least in their demi-world. His family had not favored the idea—his mother burst into tears and his father scowled. But Carl was determined and there was little they could do but let him go. He had no valise, just his clothes and a few toilet articles in his pockets, plus $3.25 and anticipation.

Into The Mainstream

CARL LEFT ON a bright afternoon when a Santa Fe Railroad freight train was standing near the station. He hopped into a box car and was soon a considerable distance from Galesburg, crossing the Mississippi River and jumping off at Fort Madison where he procured a nickel's worth of cheese and crackers and felt more uncertain about his mission than he had thought he would. At Keokuk he met a real tramp who told him how he filched food from gullible housewives and proved it by showing Carl several sandwiches he had so obtained. Using his own initiative, Carl found an old tin can, bought a cheap brush and some liquid asphalt, and went from house to house getting jobs blacking rusty stoves. He earned a little money this way, enjoyed some good meals, and learned that housewives were the same as in Galesburg—credulous when a young man told them he was working his way through college.

In Keokuk the young Sandburg landed a job as waiter in a tiny restaurant whose owner was evidently a drunk who came and went as the drinking notion struck him. But Carl did not leave this job until he had learned some of the art of waiting on hungry customers, and how to feed himself and fix a batch of hearty sandwiches for his use on the road. Then he boarded another freight car which took him into the center of Missouri. In a little place called Bean Lake, he worked for a few weeks on the railroad, tamping cross ties and cutting weeds. But he tired of the monotony, the rigidity of the boss, and the endless diet of pork, potatoes, and coffee, so he soon departed for Kansas City. There he worked again briefly in a restaurant, mostly washing dishes. This naturally grew tiresome so in keeping with the pattern he had already set, he quit and moved on. The freight train this time did not turn out to be such an easy ride. A brakeman spotted him and ordered him off the train, and when Carl did not readily comply, the former struck the young man in the mouth with his fist, but allowed him to remain on board.

A memory of these days which remained with Carl was getting off the train in Emporia, Kansas, and walking past the office of the *Emporia Gazette* but not having the courage to stop in and see the editor, William Allen White. What good it would have done for the youth to have seen him under the circumstances is not clear from the later reminiscences, but apparently even at that age, Carl realized who the "Sage of Emporia" was and how significant it was to be in his locality.

On to Hutchinson, Kansas, where Carl learned that by calling at houses which were not too near the railroad tracks, he stood a better chance of getting food handouts, although at times he had to work for them. By now he was getting used to the hand-to-mouth life but one day he was shocked to hear some Swedes on a farm where he was working refer to him as a "bum." He asked himself if this were true—and concluded that it was. Even so, he apparently derived a bizarre enjoyment from his contacts with the other hoboes and it is certain he learned from them some of the elementary facts of life he would never have absorbed anywhere else. He was meeting fellow travelers and though they were rough, they were Americans. Even if he was not climbing upward conventionally in the social scale, he was gaining some kind of respect for his own ability to make a go of things. His open road was even more raw and revealing than that of Walt Whitman.

By degrees Carl made his way across the Great Plains. He was stirred by the Rocky Mountains and saw Pikes Peak with pride. In Denver, he washed dishes at a hotel for two weeks. But time had brought some homesickness, so that, when he contemplated either going on to the West Coast or returning, it did not take him long to decide on the latter. He hopped a Pullman train, lay on the top of a car until he reached McCook, Nebraska, and there paused for a few days to eat and to wash his grimy clothes. He chopped wood and picked apples in return for some warm clothing, and when he was on his way eastward in the cool fall weather, asked to spend one night in a city calaboose so as to keep warm. Carl reached Galesburg in mid-October; as he was welcomed by his relieved family, he realized that he had at last grown up in many ways.

He was not to remain idle long. Work on a farm some three miles east of Galesburg appealed to him and he began a routine of arising at four-thirty in the morning and currying two horses, then milking eight cows while the owner milked fourteen. The milk was put into large cans and Carl drove into town with it, pouring out pints and quarts for the customers. He bought a Chicago newspaper regularly and on his way back to the farm read a series of lectures on history and government by University of Chicago professors. His intellect was beginning to be whetted. After leaving the farm work, Carl hired out to a Swedish painter

in order to learn the trade. But mostly, he scraped old paint off
buildings and sandpapered the surface in preparation for the
real painting by more experienced men.

In February of 1898, Carl heard of the sinking of the battleship *Maine* in Havana harbor and, like most other uniformed
Americans, believed the propaganda—that the Spaniards who
had killed thousands of Cubans who wanted a republic, had also
had a hand in the blowing up of the ship. Though Carl was as
aroused as most of his countrymen, he went on with his sand-
papering for a time. But he knew what he was going to do. On
April 26th, he enlisted for two years in the Sixth Infantry Regiment of the Illinois Volunteers. He was acquainted with most of
the men in his company for they were from Galesburg and its
vicinity and were proud of the fact that no regular army personnel were part of the organization. The Sandburg family took
the matter soberly. They did not try to keep Carl from going,
but did let him know that they fervently hoped he would return
alive; to which he answered that most soldiers did return.

The local company of troops was quartered in a big brick
building on the fair grounds at Springfield, Illinois. Carl Sandburg
could not have been unaware that here in this land of Lincoln,
he too was serving in a local military outfit as did the illustrious
late President in another war. The fact that the men were staying
in a building that ordinarily housed livestock did not diminish
their sense of historic importance. Carl was given a heavy blue
uniform and a Springfield rifle (named for the Massachusetts
city where they were manufactured). He learned that these were
the same uniforms worn by Grant's and Sherman's men some
thirty-five years earlier. Carl recorded that he felt honored to
wear the uniform, but for some reason had a mistrust of it.

During a few leisure hours, Carl and his companions had an
opportunity to walk around the capital grounds and past the
home of Abraham Lincoln. But soon they were in train coaches
headed southward, their food being mainly canned beans,
canned salmon, bread, and coffee. Canned goods were not yet
taken for granted; and it was well that these men did not know

that before this short enlistment was over, more men were to die from the effects of "embalmed beef" than from enemy bullets.

The train made its slow way to Washington, D. C., then on to Falls Church, Virginia, where the men bivouacked temporarily before continuing their journey. From May to June the company drilled and the recruits became familiar with Army equipment and its use in the field. About a fifth of the company had relatives in the Civil War, a fact that made itself felt not only among them but permeated to others in the ranks, including the young and impressionable Sandburg. He learned that men join the military for various reasons: love of country, often vaguely felt; desire for adventure, sometimes soon regretted; troublesome wives who doubtless live to be remorseful; and hope of pensions which usually is rewarded.

When he was on leave one day, Carl made a trip to Washington and for the first time saw the Capitol and Ford's Theater and the Peterson House across the street. Soon the regiment was on an Atlantic Coast Line train en route to action, making its way across Virginia and North Carolina to Charleston, South Carolina. There the men in Yankee blue were somewhat surprised at the friendly treatment accorded them by the local people. The cotton plantation life was still evident, but the Negroes took off their hats to these soldiers who to them still represented their emancipators.

The Illinois men boarded a captured Spanish freighter, were issued more canned rations, and in due time landed at Guantanamo Bay, Cuba. There the ship lay at anchor—because of confusion in the orders from Washington regarding it, and because there were several hundred cases of yellow fever ashore. Finally the ship got under way, wandered around, and put its soldiers ashore at Guanica, Puerto Rico.

Carl's dream of getting into action was frustrated by lack of action to get into, and by uncertainty as to the future. Mostly the fight was with mosquitoes. Although some shooting could be heard in nearby towns, it did not affect the Illinoisians and they continued to march, eat their canned rations, fight insects, and endure the heat which was caused to a great extent by the heavy underwear, wool pants, shirts, and socks which had been worn by the Army of the Potomac in 1865. The Puerto Ricans appeared glad to be taken over by the Americans after four hundred years of Spanish rule. They were gladder than the American soldiers who were each bearing, besides a heavy uniform, a cartridge belt, a rifle, bayonet, blanket roll, half of a canvas pup tent, haversack, and rations. Some of the men, including Private Sandburg, tore off part of their blankets and threw them away to lighten the weight and heat of the great load.

Camping above a town called Ponce, the Americans were sleeping one night when shrieks rang out in the darkness and hundreds of men dashed from their sleeping places down a slope, sure that the enemy was in hot pursuit. True, it was hot and there was pursuit by mosquitoes, but the dishevelled and bruised men soon learned that the commotion was all caused by the moving around of one of the bulls used for hauling carts. The animal had accidentally trampled on a sleeping soldier who let out a blood-curdling yell. The men called this their "First Battle of Bull Run."

Carl observed that, even though it was a small war, it was the first in which our country had sent troops to fight on foreign soil and acquire island possessions. Soon it was over and a transport took the Americans back to New York. Our "hero" bought on the docks a loaf of white bread and a quart of milk and thought he was dining on nectar and ambrosia. It was not long before he was welcomed back in Galesburg, this time with the feeling that though he had been away for only five months, he had gone "somewhere."

The homecoming was heartening to the young temporary soldier. In the late summer days of September, 1898, Carl marched with his company through the streets of Galesburg, to the cheers of the welcoming homefolks. He had an additional pride from the fact that he drew $122 in discharge pay from the army. He gave part of this to his father in repayment of a loan.

With some of the rest of the money, he bought books and clothes to use in his new activity—enrollment in Lombard College which had offered him free tuition for the first year "in recognition for his valorous service in the late war." The college was only a few blocks away from the Sandburg home. Although Carl had not been to high school, he was admitted to the college, making it a point to avoid taking mathematics. (He was awarded a diploma from Galesburg High in 1963 on his eighty-fifth birthday.) His subjects were history, English, public speaking and dramatics, Latin, and chemistry. Philip Green Wright was a professor at Lombard and his son Quincy recalled that Carl Sandburg was often at their home, talking with the professor about Walt Whitman and other subjects in the field of literature. Thus began the influence of Whitman upon Sandburg. They discussed also economic reform and socialism. The younger Wright remembered that Carl was at that time husky in appearance, with black hair which lent the impression of robustness.

In Professor Philip Green Wright, Sandburg found a kindred political spirit, an advocate of economic reform in the United States, for which the latter was to put forth vigorous journalistic efforts for years to come.

During these days, Carl read a book by Edward Eggleston entitled *How To Educate Yourself*. In this volume were posed the questions: What does a person do when he thinks? What is thinking? Can one be too careful about thinking? Can one's thinking fool a person? A sentence in the book set Carl to pondering: "An unreasoning skepticism is as bad as the unreasoning credulity, but the habit of holding the mind open to conviction and the habit of questioning everything for the sake of learning more about it, are certainly exceedingly valuable ones." Carl never quite understood just what this meant.

To help pay his expenses at Lombard, he rang the bell for classes to assemble and while he was in the tower where the huge bell was located, he read Universalist books, which seemed to him ironical because across the street was the traditional Lutheran church of his family. This study helped to locate for him a middle ground in his attitude toward religion and this remained with him.

At Lombard, Carl played basketball on a winning team and participated to some extent in other sports on the campus. He found time to read Kipling, Turgenev, and some of Mark Twain. His membership in the "Poor Writer's Club" brought him in contact with writers who had made some progress in their work. Evincing his flair for dramatics early, the young Sandburg appeared in a musical play entitled *The Cannibal Converts* which was written by Professor Wright and produced at the local opera house. The plot concerned an imaginary aerial trip to some Pacific islands by a group of Lombard students. Carl played a blackened character who talked in a strange tongue and was involved in successful efforts to prevent the students from being eaten by cannibals.

At this time, the second year of his attendance at Lombard, Carl was offered—to his surprise—an opportunity to apply for entrance to the United States Military Academy at West Point. He passed the physical examination without difficulty and was at the academy for a few weeks. But when it came to mathematics, he failed. Apparently this was not his only difficulty, because years later Sandburg said, "I always thought it was just arithmetic I failed. But not long ago I came on the West Point letter. It was arithmetic—and grammar." So ended ironically his military career.

During his first two years at Lombard, Carl worked as a part-time fireman to help pay expenses. For this easy duty he was paid $10 a month, although his associates felt that he was more adept at reading books on the job than fighting fires. In 1901, he became editor of the college yearbook which that year was appropriately called "The Cannibal." The incidental writing he did for the publication has been called his first published work, but his first major effort soon appeared in the form of a small book. It was produced by Professor Wright who had been a printer in his youth and who had in his basement a small Gordon press. On this the Sandburg book was printed in Caslon Old Face type. It consisted of fifty pages, was composed of poems, and was entitled *In Reckless Ecstasy*. The professor wrote a foreword and Carl showed his appreciation by writing one for the former's book of verses called *The Dial of the Heart*. Only fifty copies were printed of the Sandburg volume; they were bound in cardboard covers and held together by ribbon. The little volume is now a collectors' item. The foreword states that Sandburg was "just a rough-featured, healthy boy, possessed of indomitable energy and buoyancy of spirit."

In all, Carl Sandburg spent almost four years at Lombard College in Galesburg but he did not graduate. Just why is not clear. The extant accounts and the recollections of members of his family throw little light on the reasons why he chose to depart when he "felt the call elsewhere."

Margaret Sandburg, his daughter, when asked why her father did not graduate, replied, "It is difficult to explain. He didn't believe so much in degrees. He didn't think a degree would be of any use to him as he didn't intend to teach or anything like that. And to get the degree, I think he would have had to go into other subjects that would have taken up his time that he thought would be better spent writing or something else."

Carl attended Lombard from the fall of 1897 to the spring of 1902. According to the office of the president of Knox College,

> Lombard, which had been started as the "Illinois Liberal Institute" in 1851, was liberal with Sandburg. He took the courses he enjoyed and best understood, such as English and public speaking, and was not required to enroll for some of the mathematics and science essential for the bachelor's degree. So he did not graduate in 1902, but he received an exceptional education at Lombard College, especially in creative writing and appreciation of scholarship.[1]

In 1928, Lombard College bestowed upon Sandburg the honorary degree of Doctor of Literature. He hardly added to the dignity of the occasion when he entered the office of the president of the college on the June morning of the commencement exercises and asked of the amazed attendant, "Where do I get the Ku Klux Klan regalia?"

Knox College awarded him an honorary degree also in 1928, and in 1930 the two Galesburg colleges were united under the name of Knox College, named after Henry Knox, the noted American soldier and statesman.

As an undergraduate, Carl Sandburg played baseball, football, and basketball. He developed a keen interest in Abraham Lincoln and read everything on him he could get his hands on.

As a boy Sandburg had sometimes passed on the streets Newton Bateman, the president of Knox College who was known as "the fellow who used to know Abe Lincoln." He had a white beard and wore a tight-fitting, square-cornered, single-breasted black coat that came down to his knees. He would nod to Carl without speaking, so the young man did the same automatically. Much earlier, Bateman had been Superintendent of Public Instruction of the State of Illinois and had his office in the state house in Springfield next to the one Lincoln used when he was a candidate. It was said that Lincoln called him "Little Newt, the big schoolmaster of Illinois," and he was also said to have been the last man to shake hands and say goodbye to President-elect Abraham Lincoln before the train pulled out from Springfield bound for Washington and the inauguration.

Bateman was succeeded by John Huston Finley who was twenty-nine years of age and at that time the youngest college president in the United States. Carl thought him to be an educator, orator, politician, salesman, and a man who could make a speech about any subject on two minutes' notice. He made Knox College known over the country as the place where Lincoln and Douglas had debated, both having faced an audience of 20,000 people from a platform next to the main building of the institution on October 7, 1858. The Lincoln-Douglas-Knox connection was first heard of in a general way when President Finley con-

ducted an anniversary celebration on October 7, 1896. At this
time, Chauncy M. Depew, president of the New York Central
Railroad, spoke at Galesburg, and Carl Sandburg slipped out to
hear him because he was not only an important executive but was
known as the most popular after-dinner speaker in the United
States.

Robert Todd Lincoln, the son of Abraham Lincoln, also made
a short speech that afternoon. Looking at him with some awe,
Carl wondered what kind of talks he had had with his father in
the White House, what kind of Secretary of War he had been in
the cabinets of Presidents Garfield and Arthur, and in general,
how he reflected the character of his famous parent. In Carl's
memory was the information he had read that the younger Lincoln had been nominated at succeeding Republican national
conventions, getting only one vote each time. The young Sandburg seemed disappointed, even at this early date, that Robert
Todd Lincoln was an attorney for the Pullman Company and
had been in favor of the company's attitude in the violence-
ridden strike of 1894. His speech did not impress his Galesburg
hearers. . . .

Something got into Carl Sandburg in the year 1902, something
that made wanderlust stronger than desire for academic ad-
vancement, so he left the town of his birth and spent two years
seeking an answer to whatever it was that impelled him. He
sought and found jobs, tried to write some, and found that most
of his companions were bums—and that was what he was too.
Carl made his way east via the railroad freight cars and found
himself in New York which he soon left again. Across New Jersey
he went, selling stereopticon pictures door to door, then to Philadelphia en route westward. Through a relative, he had managed
to get a pass on some of the railroads. As he traveled, he was
writing and writing, anything that came to his mind, poems,
essays, and just sentences. He listened to the heartbeat of the
nation from an odd and elemental angle and tried amateurishly
to reproduce it. Once at McKee's Rocks, Pennsylvania, Carl was

pulled off a freight train with eight other hoboes and arrested. He spent ten days in the county jail in Pittsburgh, staying in a cell with two war veterans and another character he called a "genus homo bohunk."

Writing to his sister Mary about one meal he ate on the road, the wanderer mentioned: "Irish waitress this morning. Steak and eggs. Eggs. Fried? Yes. Both sides? No, only the outside. Biff, bang and a batter of wheat cakes!"

It was not easy for Carl Sandburg to leave Galesburg. He never really left it, for it was a microcosm of America, exemplifying for him especially its sturdy, earthy, and burgeoning Middle West. He was to express this in the meat and meter of his poems, in the nasal but pleasant timbre of his songs, and in the bigness of his biography. But there came a time in 1906 when being there physically seemed impossible for his dreamed-of purposes. He had returned briefly. Then he purchased another old guitar, put it under his arm, and departed from his home country, never to come back except in occasional visits during his eventful career.

In that year of the dynamic administration of Theodore Roosevelt, Carl had written a number of pieces for a little Chicago magazine fittingly called *Tomorrow* and the reaction of some who read them was that here was a probable major figure in American literature. Paul Jordan Smith recalled that "in those days, Sandburg's hair was as black as a crow's wing, but he was the same folksy, friendly fellow he has remained down the years. He seemed to me then as now, earthy, honest, loving, and lovable."

Carl sensed that people around the country would like to hear a fellow sing and might like to buy some pictures, so he took off for the hinterlands and proved his point. This scheme he followed until his late and most affluent years when he did not have to think about making a living except by his writings. As he moved about our land, he was all ears for the tunes it produced. He heard songs and copied their words; he memorized the melodies so that later he could include them in his own songbook. Although he never learned to play the guitar very well—and always wanted to—he did such a good job of pretending to play that this, with his dramatic and resonant voice, convinced his listeners that he was a performer par excellence.

Drifting into Chicago, Carl landed a job as associate editor of the *Lyceumite*. Here he read more of Walt Whitman and was impressed with the free style and robust message of this new American voice in poetry. Carl memorized a lecture on Whitman and delivered it with some success in Indiana, Pennsylvania, and Michigan. In Chicago he had met Winfield R. Gaylord, state organizer of the Social-Democratic Party in Wisconsin, and liked him. This party was the forerunner of the Socialist Party in the United States and Carl Sandburg subscribed heartily to its philosophy of a better life for the average man. He was offered a job with it so he left the magazine and went to work for the party in Milwaukee.

In 1908 there was great social ferment in Wisconsin. Milwaukee was the capital of liberal ideas and Carl Sandburg entered into the spirit of this with gusto. He planned meetings, made speeches, arranged for the distribution of party literature, and helped the organization obtain new members and friends. This was not too difficult since there was then, as now, much sympathy in Milwaukee for the underprivileged. Carl worked also as a reporter and editorial writer. He went from the *News* to the *Sentinel* to the *Journal* and then to the *Leader* somewhat in the haphazard manner of a water bug. The immigrant Germans of Milwaukee at that time were influenced by Carl Schurz who had fled to America after the Revolution of 1848 in Germany and who had become a friend and supporter of Abraham Lincoln. Theodore Roosevelt was now President, Robert M. La-Follete was United States Senator from Wisconsin, and a group of Socialist city officials were pushing and getting reforms in local government. Fresh in the minds of the people were the works of the muckrakers such as *The History of the Standard Oil Company* by Ida M. Tarbell, *The Shame of the Cities* by Lincoln Steffens, *The Jungle* by Upton Sinclair, and *The Pit* by Frank Norris. Carl Sandburg must have read and absorbed these works for he reflected their philosophy in his own endeavors. In his reading, speaking, and writing, Sandburg plunged ahead in the drive for clean government and the recognition of individual rights.

One day in the Social-Democratic headquarters, he chanced to meet a slender and winsome girl with pink cheeks and bright eyes named Lilian Steichen, another party worker and sister of Edward Steichen, a native of Luxembourg, who was to become a famous modern photographer.

Lilian had originally been named Mary Ann Elizabeth Magdalen Steichen, but her mother took care of this when she found a character in a book named Lilian and changed the name of her daughter accordingly. Later, Lilian was called Paula, a Luxembourg pet name. She attended Ursuline Academy in London, Ontario, where she was said to have read everything she could get her hands on. Later she entered the University of Illinois and next the University of Chicago because she was attracted to the work in this institution on social problems, especially on child labor.

Lilian now lived only sixteen miles away at Menominee Falls and was home on vacation from her job as a Latin teacher at the high school in Princeton, Illinois. She had eventually graduated from the University of Chicago where she had become a member of Phi Beta Kappa, one among the top academic three in her class. Carl often referred to this in later years, adding that he had to obtain his membership in the scholastic fraternity by the honorary route. Lilian Steichen had translated social classics from the French and German and was a liberal intellectual whose achievements impressed Sandburg.

After she returned to Princeton, they corresponded for about six months, seeing each other only twice during this period. But that was enough. They became engaged with the understanding that when they were married, if at any time during their lives together, either became tired of the marriage, they would simply dissolve it in mutual agreement. They never did. Carl sent Lilian some of his writings on labor and politics and a few of his poems. She liked his work but felt his characters should be of the laboring class. His letters to her were romantic and even lyrical and his poetry evidently did have a definite effect on her.

An example was his letter to her written on March 21, 1908, from Manitowoc, Wisconsin:

> Dear girl:—I will look for you on the 4:45 P.M. at the C. M. and St. Paul station on Friday the 27th. I expect to have everything cleared up and be ready for anything that can happen, gallows or throne, sky or sea-bottom! Yours Thoughtfully alias Paula will be dictator and mistress of ceremonies. You will announce the events and the gladiators will gladiate like blazes! The joy-bells on high will clang like joy. Motley will have vent and psalms will be sung and three or four paeans will go up to the stars out of pure gladiosity.—I believe you asked about my cussedness. This is some of it. I am cussedest when I am glad, and so are those around me. Admonish me gently to behave and I may or I may not. For whatever is in must come out. That is the snub and sumstance of expression and great is expression.[2]

Another example of Carl's letters to Lilian was that penned from Two Rivers, Wisconsin, on April 23, 1908:

> Back from a long hike again—sand and shore, night and stars and this restless inland sea—Plunging white horses in a forever recoiling Pickett's charge at Gettysburg—On the left a ridge of jaggedly outlined pines, their zigzag jutting up into a steel-grey sky—under me and ahead a long brown swath of sand—to the right the ever-repelled but incessantly charging white horses and beyond an expanse of dark—but over all, sweeping platoons of unguessable stars! Stars everywhere! Blinking, shy-hiding gleams —blazing, effulgent beacons—an infinite, travelling caravanserie—going somewhere! "Hail!" I called. "Hail!—do you know? do you know? You veering cotillions of worlds beyond this world—you marching imperturbable splen-

dors—you serene, everlasting spectators—where are we going? do you know?" And the answer came back, "No, we don't know and what's more, we don't care!" And I called, "You answer well. For you are time and space—you are tomb and cradle. . . ." There—it's out of me, Pal. It was a glorious hike. I shall sleep and sleep to-night. And you are near to-night—so near and so dear—a good-night kiss to you—great-heart—good lips—and good eyes—My Lilian—Carl . . . P.S.P.S.S.!—No, I will never get the letter written and finished. It will always need postscripts. I end one and six minutes after have to send more. All my life I must write at this letter—this letter of love to the great woman who came and knew and loved. All my life this must go on! The idea and the emotion are so vast it will be years and years in issuing. Ten thousand love-birds, sweet-throated and red-plumed, were in my soul, in the garden of my under-life. There on ten thousand branches they slept as in night-time. You came and they awoke. For a moment they fluttered distractedly in joy at stars and odors and breezes. And a dawn burst on them—a long night was ended." [2]

According to Margaret, she asked him once, "How do you manage to write so well in such different fields?" This was a question which was to challenge his critics during all of his later life.

Lilian invited him out to her family farm nearby and the couple walked and talked. They were close to the good earth and it helped to bring them together. They had addressed each with increasing affection and their happy sojourn together on the farm intensified their love. Carl and Lilian were married on June 15, 1908. It was the beginning of what the family described as a happy and lasting union.

They set up housekeeping in Appleton, Wisconsin, where Carl was working for the Social Democrats. The couple rented three rooms in a one-and-a-half-story house for which they paid four dollars a month. They bought only a few pieces of furniture, making boxes and cartons do as substitutes. Lilian made muslin curtains for the windows.

To provide an income, Carl got a job as advertising manager for a Milwaukee department store, but in order to do this full-time work, he had to resign from the Socialist Party position. In his new capacity, he wrote the advertisements so well that he landed a job as a reporter and feature writer with the *Milwaukee Journal*. He later wrote editorials for the *Milwaukee Daily News*. The following one, in observance of Lincoln's birth, attracted some attention:

LINCOLN ON PENNIES

The face of Abraham Lincoln on the copper cent seems well and proper. If it were possible to talk with that great, good man, he would probably say that he is perfectly willing that his face is to be placed on the cheapest and most common coin in the country.

The penny is strictly the coin of the common people. At Palm Beach, Newport and Saratoga you will find nothing for sale at one cent. No ice cream cones at a penny apiece there.

"Keep the change," says the rich man. "How many pennies do I get back?" asks the poor man.

Only the children of the poor know the joy of getting a penny for running around the corner to the grocery.

The penny is the bargain-counter coin. Only the common people walk out of their way to get something for 9 cents reduced from 10 cents. The penny is the coin used by those who are not sure of tomorrow, those who know that if they are going to have a dollar next week they must watch the pennies this week.

Follow the travels of the penny and you find it stops at many cottages and few mansions.

The common, homely face of "Honest Abe" will look good on the penny, the coin of the common folk from whom he came and to whom he belongs.

—Carl Sandburg

It is not strange that this was always one of Sandburg's favorite pieces of money. Partly as a result, he caught the attention of Mayor Emil Seidel of Milwaukee who hired him as his secretary, and Carl held this position for about two years. Meanwhile, he sold a story on the public recreational facilities of Milwaukee to a woman's magazine for $50 which gave him a sort of shot in the arm of encouragement. In 1912, he joined a new liberal daily named the *Milwaukee Leader* and syndicated a column in the labor press called "Bunts and Muffs." On the staff of this paper was also E. Haldeman-Julius, who later was to become the publisher of many popular miniature books about the American scene.[3]

The Sandburg home in the suburbs of Milwaukee has been described as being so plain it was almost shabby, with no carpets and little furniture. On the covered rear porch of the cottage was a large tray of sprouting wheat, which Sandburg said he liked as a diet. A good part of the daily food seems to have been black bread and beer. Lilian was seen as gracious and charming, "with a soft, misty light in her beautiful blue eyes."

The sequence of Milwaukee activity ended in the same year when a newspaper strike in Chicago seriously affected the dailies there, all except the *Chicago Daily Socialist*. Its name was changed to the *Chicago Daily World* and Sandburg, Julius, and others answered its call for reporters. But when the strike was over, the circulation of the new paper was virtually over also, so Sandburg along with others was out of a job. This would not have been of much consequence back in his freewheeling days, but now Carl Sandburg had a wife and new baby, Margaret, born in 1911, and there was no money in the family till. He did not want to leave Chicago. It seemed to be the city for him. So he tried hard to get work, walking the streets in search of it, sitting in the offices of employment agencies, and reading the want ads in the newspapers. Finally, he landed a spot on a small Chicago tabloid, the *Day Book,* owned by E. W. Scripps, the future journalistic tycoon. Carl remained here only two months, then switched over to *System: The Magazine of Business* for which he wrote his articles on labor so dexterously as to change somewhat its viewpoint.[4]

Vincent Starrett, who knew Sandburg at the time, recalls that the latter did not care a "hoot in hell" about rare books, even though both men often haunted the Chicago bookshops. Sandburg was described as then being gaunt and gray and seeking books in the old stores "as if he were seeking diamonds in a dust heap, as indeed he was." At Payne's shop one day, while searching through a pile of volumes, Sandburg came upon one that caught his attention. He took it up and suddenly ripped out the first thirty pages. The horrified clerk started to remonstrate but then Sandburg paid him for the whole book. He told Starrett that he only wanted the part he tore out and that he would never mutilate a valuable book.

The Sandburgs lived in Maywood, a suburb, at this time and Carl liked to stroll in Oak Park "where no saloons were allowed and in Forest Park where there were more saloons than churches." It was in a barroom in Forest Park that Starrett first heard some of the delightful children's stories that Sandburg was planning to write, after he had sufficiently tried them out on his children. As the two companions sat and nursed beers beside a big pot-bellied stove, Sandburg described Henry Hagglyboogly who played the guitar with his mittens on, and Bimbo the Snip whose thumb got stuck to his nose when the wind changed.

As for the critics of his poems, Sandburg told Starrett, "A man was building a house. A woodchuck came and sat down and watched the man building the house."

At night he was continuing his writing of poetry. Here he was to write the *Chicago Poems* and start on those entitled *Cornhuskers.* He had written much poetry but had sold none of it. This situation changed, at least for a breakthrough, in 1914 when

Carl Sandburg won the Levinson Prize of $200 offered by *Poetry* magazine. The prize was for a series of poems including the Chicago ones, and Harriet Monroe was editor. At last, the voice of Sandburg was heard through a respectable medium.

> Hog Butcher for the World,
> Tool Maker, Stacker of Wheat,
> Player with Railroads and the Nation's Freight Handler;
> Stormy, husky, brawling,
> City of the Big Shoulders.[5]

These lines from *Chicago* shocked many readers who were accustomed to more elegance. Some of those who perused the new type of poetic expression were outraged by Sandburg's use of slang and the earthy idiom of the common man. But with his increase in output there came also acceptance by most readers, although there were some, including critics, who were never to receive his poetry as such.

More of the startling new poet was revealed in such paeans to the people as the following:

MASSES

Among the mountains I wandered and saw blue haze and red
  crag and was amazed:
On the beach where the long push under the endless tide maneu-
  vers, I stood silent;
Under the stars on the prairie watching the Dipper slant over the
  horizon's grass, I was full of thoughts.
Great men, pageants of war and labor, soldiers and workers,
  mothers lifting their children—these all I touched, and
  felt the solemn thrill of them.
And then one day I got a true look at the Poor, millions of the
  Poor, patient and toiling; more patient than crags, tides,
  and stars; innumerable, patient as the darkness of night
  —and all broken, humble ruins of nations.[6]

Sandburg seemed to possess an affinity with the element of water, even if it were represented only by Lake Michigan. That lake mirrored for him the local human misery:

THE HARBOR

Passing through huddled and ugly walls
By doorways where women
Looked from their hunger-deep eyes,
Haunted with shadows of hunger-hands,
Out from the huddled and ugly walls,
I came sudden, at the city's edge,
On a blue burst of lake,
Long lake waves breaking under the sun
On a spray-flung curve of shore;
And a fluttering storm of gulls,
Masses of great gray wings
And flying white bellies
Veering and wheeling free in the open.[7]

Perhaps Sandburg never loved the city. At least, after many toilful years, he fled from it, even as he had fled from his small-town home on the prairies to wander the country and finally come to a restless stop in the metropolis. Surely he detested what he saw at times:

THEY WILL SAY

Of my city the worst that men will ever say is this:
You took little children away from the sun and the dew,
And the glimmers that played in the grass under the great sky,
And the reckless rain; you put them between walls
To work, broken and smothered, for bread and wages,
To eat dust in their throats and die empty-hearted
For a little handful of pay on a few Saturday nights.[8]

Beneath the ground where ran the roaring trains, he saw a symbolic comparison to the depths of human endeavor:

SUBWAY

Down between the walls of shadow
Where the iron laws insist,
   The hunger voices mock.
The worn wayfaring men
With the hunched and humble shoulders,
   Throw their laughter into toil.[9]

Yet there could be a good side to the city of the big, cruel shoulders, the noisy town that so often crushed and bent its victims. From his daily experience with even less fortunate human beings, Sandburg could see that there were worse things even than Chicago:

A TEAMSTER'S FAREWELL
SOBS EN ROUTE TO A PENITENTIARY

Good-by now to the streets and the clash of wheels and locking
   hubs,
The sun coming on the brass buckles and harness knobs,
The muscles of the horses sliding under their heavy haunches,
Good-by now to the traffic policeman and his whistle,
The smash of the iron hoof on the stones,
All the crazy wonderful slamming roar of the street—
O God, there's noises I'm going to be hungry for.[10]

But Carl Sandburg did find some happiness existing in Chicago, although it apparently took him some time to find it and longer to realize just what it was. Alternately he was to find the bitter with the sweet; almost regularly, it appears, he swung on the pendulum from tears to laughter. What was to remain most in his heart, only he could know:

HAPPINESS

I asked professors who teach the meaning of life to tell me
   what is happiness.

> And I went to famous executives who boss the work of
>   thousands of men.
> They all shook their heads and gave me a smile as though
>   I was trying to fool with them.
> And then one Sunday afternoon I wandered out along the
>   Desplaines river
> And I saw a crowd of Hungarians under the trees with
>   their women and children and a keg of beer and an
>   accordion.[11]

In 1913 Carl left *System* because its viewpoint, he felt, was too conservative. For a short time, he worked on the *National Hardware Journal,* then he went back to *Day Book* for $25 a week. After all, he and his family had to live. The tiny Scripps paper was only 8 by 10 inches in size, carried no advertising, and usually consisted of twelve pages. Among the events Sandburg covered was the fifteen-week strike of the Amalgamated Clothing Workers' Union led by Sidney Hillman, who, during the struggle, was ill in bed most of the time. Sandburg visited him frequently and felt the strong influence of this active union leader. Many examples of workers who were adversely affected by the practices of business at that time were dug up and printed, and Sandburg solidified his attitude against abuse of the lowly.

It was during this time that Carl Sandburg wrote one of the most quoted poems of his lifetime. It contained only twenty-two words, and although they may not hold the historic significance of some of his passages on Lincoln, they do carry a world of meaning as far as he himself and life are concerned. They were written while he was sitting in the anteroom of a juvenile-court judge, waiting for an interview:

Fog

The fog comes
on little cat feet.

It sits looking
over harbor and city

on silent haunches
and then moves on.[21]

Here was something all could understand yet not all did appreciate. It was short and simple like the lives of the simple people of America. It was plain and moving, yet fleeting. It was the inner melody in a new poetic symphony by Sandburg.

In a way the poem was Sandburg himself, active, shifting, then going on to something new yet ever old. In it there was a freedom like that of working on the newspaper that carried no advertising—writing what he wanted to write without regard to the sacred cows of the common journalistic media. He wrote, for example, about how two girl clerks in a large department store in Chicago were arrested for stealing food. But he did not stop at this point. Sandburg went behind the story to show that these girls, like many of their kind, could not buy enough out of their meager salaries to sustain themselves; therefore they were reduced by hunger to take what they felt they must have.

A momentous event occurred in 1916. Sandburg's salary was raised to $27.50 a week.

But this affluence was short-lived. The next year, the *Day Book* closed down because of World War I, but not before Sandburg had written for it an astute editorial on the role of the Negro in race riots, in which he foresaw many aspects of similar situations which have developed in recent years. Always he showed a warm and sympathetic understanding of the condition of the colored people, just as he did those of the less fortunate whites.

For three weeks, Sandburg worked for the National Labor Defense League whose purpose was to help striking union members protect their rights. Then he made a trip to Omaha during which he wrote the poem of that name about its raw midwestern atmosphere. Back in Chicago, the roving writer received a call from the editor of the *Evening American*, William Curly, who explained that it and the other Hearst newspapers had tried to employ Professor Charles E. Merriam of the University of Chicago, a civic reformer, as an editorial writer. He had refused the offer saying, "Carl Sandburg can do a better job than I can." With this promising introduction, Sandburg went to work for Hearst for $100 a week, but he stayed only three weeks because he felt he did not fit in.

The next step in his ever-growing variation of endeavors probably marked the real start in his journalistic career. He joined the staff of the *Chicago Daily News* and seemed to have found his niche at last, a welcome haven after long, hard years of wandering about our rugged hinterland. Harry Hansen, an associate on this newspaper, is the one who is always called upon to recount what Sandburg was like then. Hansen remembers that the newcomer had the same unruly shock of hair over his forehead, the same attitude of leaning forward to catch a significant remark, and the same deliberate manner of winding up a sentence with an explosive laugh at the end that Sandburg retained until the end of his long life. When Hansen first met him, he was greeted with the remark, "My name's Sandburg. What kind of a Scandihoovian are you?"

Hansen observes:

> The warmth that Carl had for people was something that you never forgot. He was from the beginning a newspaperman and he had the qualities of a newspaperman. He had awareness. A newspaperman somehow knows what is going on around him. He doesn't live in isolation. Carl had a keen sense of justice. He hated injustice and it runs all through his career, runs in his poems. Carl also had a great sense of proportion. He enjoyed humor. He found all sorts of amusing things in clippings and his pockets were always full of clippings in those days at the *Chicago Daily News* and at any time, he would take one out and read it and expect you to chuckle just as much as he did.[13]

Hansen remembers that as book editor he came close on one occasion to falling out with Sandburg. "He gave me something which had nothing to do with book reviewing," Hansen said, "and I didn't want it, and he came in one day and said:

" 'Are you going to run that piece I gave you?'

" 'Well, we've only got this much space and I don't think I'll run it,' Hansen replied.

" 'If you want to lose a good friend, then don't run it,' snapped Sandburg."

Hansen states that he did not run the article, but fortunately did not lose the good friend. He added:

> Carl was always noseying in to see me because I got the books for review, and he used to filter through these to see if there was something he was interested in and that is how we got more or less in contact—through books. Once he left a little note on my table, which read something like this: "Harry, why are you never in? Why are you always out? We shuffle in. We shuffle out. Why do we never find you in and yet never find you out?" [14]

Hansen may have been "out" at times in this respect, but the poetry of his friend was beginning to be "in." Knowing Chicago itself, the editor was profoundly affected by the poem of that name. "I had found expressed something I had dimly apprehended," Hansen said. "As a statement of the fact of existence, the basic impulses of a vast, confusing city, *Chicago* is incomparable. It made a tremendous impact on my emotions. It made me hear the hootings of tugs on the river, the grinding wheels of the elevated trains, the slam-bang of trolley trucks on the streets."

While Sandburg's poetry dealt with the city in general, his reporting for the newspaper was mainly about labor activities. He would attend a convention and stay there for days because he was given a fair amount of leeway in his schedule. He worked directly with the news editor, Henry Justin Smith, who was called the "principal of the Chicago school of writers," which included Ben Hecht, John Gunther, and Lloyd Lewis. Smith encouraged Sandburg in his writing of poetry and thus had a helpful influence upon the development of the latter's artistic side.

This was the time when Carl Sandburg really began to write about Abraham Lincoln. He would mention to Hansen or some of the other writers discoveries he had made about Lincoln, some information from a book or from a document he had seen in the great collection of Oliver Barrett in Chicago. When Sandburg went to other cities to lecture—and he was able to do this from time to time—he would take the opportunity to look at local Lincoln collections and to meet and talk to men who had first-hand knowledge of the martyred President. Hansen said:

> Carl dealt in specific incidents, not abstractions. This trait came into full use in the final volumes of the Lincoln biography. The heaping up of incident, the use of anecdote and the casual remark as a key to inner motives, sidelights out of a letter—the use of all this material as illustration is characteristic of Carl's biographical manner. It is also characteristic of his intense interest in all phases of human behavior.[15]

That the behavior of Carl Sandburg, however, was not often consistent is indicated by one of Hansen's experiences with him. A New York magazine writer came to Chicago to study midwestern writers, and Hansen told him how informal Sandburg was in performing before audiences, especially in not wearing a dinner coat, as did so many of the Europeans who were at that time appearing before American groups. That night the New Yorker heard Sandburg lecture at the University of Chicago, and later, much to Hansen's surprise, wrote in a magazine article that while Midwesterners boasted that they were of common clay, even Carl Sandburg, their most characteristic spokesman, sang folk songs in a dinner coat. The only explanation Hansen could figure out was that Sandburg, as was his habit, had worn a dark suit and a little black bow tie, which from the twentieth row of seats where the writer sat, resembled formal clothes.

In Hansen's recollections, the following picture of Sandburg emerges:

Carl was a commoner. He never lost the common touch. In all the years that I knew him, from his days as a reporter to the time when he was sought out by Presidents, Carl did not change his attitude toward people or his basic judgments about life. His humanity made him the champion of the underdog, but he argued for no specific political plan to remedy abuses. Yet he could always be found on the side of those for social betterment. Carl liked to be helpful and sometimes his kindness was abused. But if he had made a promise, he kept it. At times he was exploited by enterprising persons who capitalized on his distinction. Carl was good copy, and many who had no comprehension of his depth, exploited the opportunity to use him. He did not complain but sometimes these activities were a drain on his vitality. Occasionally he would fend off irritants with a sharp remark. Usually it was cryptic, and those addressed took it for a compliment.

I have memories of the doings of a peculiar galaxy with which Carl was familiar and of which he was a part. A galaxy that had John Gunther and Ben Hecht and all those interesting people of the time and which had a lot of people like Sherwood Anderson running in for lunch. It was a wonderful period. And the most interesting man among them was Carl Sandburg and everybody recognized it and everybody knew there was something coming. Carl worked for very little. I remember one time a group in Milwaukee wrote me and said, "We've got $25. Will you come up and talk to us?" And I replied, "Well, I can't come up and talk to you." But I gave it to Carl and said, "Carl, do you want to go to Milwaukee and talk for $25?" He said, "Yes, why not?" [16]

Chairman of the occasion in Milwaukee was S. D. Stephens, now a retired professor of English from Rutgers University. It was in the spring of 1925, he recalls, and the gathering was a dinner meeting of high school teachers. Stephens's reactions toward the substitution were mixed. He did not know how well this would work out. So he tried to telephone Sandburg in Chicago but did not locate him at first. Then he finally was notified, "Greetings! I shall be on the North Shore train at 7 P.M."

This would mean close connections, because the dinner meeting started before this hour. So Stephens left the old City Club where it was being held and met Sandburg at the nearby North Shore station. He urged the visitor to come promptly, since his dinner was waiting for him. But Sandburg was in no hurry. He asked to eat some "lunch" at the counter in the station. "He quizzed the waitress about the pastries," recalls Stephens. "She assured him that they were good for what ailed him, with a look as if she wondered what did ail this queer codger with the Windsor tie and guitar. He chose two pastries and when the waitress appeared, he surprised her by taking both. Finally, I got him to the lobby of the banquet room."

There Sandburg decided he wanted to telephone a local woman poet—her name is not recalled—whom he had known when he lived in Milwaukee. She was not at home and, after wondering at length why she was not, he made a second try. He next asked a lobby attendant for a drink of water and was told there was water on the speaker's table.

"But," said Sandburg, "you wouldn't want me to drink in front of all that audience, would you?"

"Would you like me to bring it to you?" replied the attendant.

"I'd be very happy if you would," was the response.

So the attendant did.

During this time, sporadic handclapping could be heard in the dining room, and now and then a guest was seen to depart.

"Do you think, Mr. Stephens," asked Sandburg, "that that applause is for us?"

"Yes, Mr. Sandburg, I'm afraid it is."

"Well," he replied, "We'll just let them wait. That's one thing the American public hasn't learned, to wait."

So they waited.

At last, Stephens got Sandburg to the speaker's table and he was duly introduced. Stephens recalls:

There were all the handicaps a speaker could have. He was a substitute for the advertised speaker, he was late, he was at that time little known to a general audience. He sang some songs from the material which he had collected for the *Songbag,* he read the fable of the two skyscrapers who produced in marriage the transcontinental express train, he did all sorts of things which made his hearers wonder when to laugh. I was interested in the audience, which I had to live with, and when after fifteen minutes they were sitting forward in their seats, and when after an hour and fifteen minutes they applauded him loudly, I realized that he had overcome all his handicaps.[17]

Later when Stephens and his wife accompanied Sandburg back to the railroad station, he was able to enjoy the visitor in a more relaxed way. Sandburg showed them the galley proofs of *The Prairie Years* which he had been reading on the train and he discussed the nature of the work.

"It's a biography of Lincoln," he explained, "made up of material which only a newspaper man would realize the importance of. When I take it to New York, it will have been the biggest manuscript ever taken there by an author who knows it is going to be published."

Sandburg cited a few bits from the book, giving one story—in which Lincoln as a young lawyer defended a man for committing a nuisance in his front yard—that Sandburg was afraid the editors wouldn't appreciate. They didn't.

Stephens himself, when teaching in central Illinois, had met several people who had attended the Lincoln-Douglas debates, including the one at Galesburg. He and Sandburg exchanged pleasant correspondence about the matter, Stephens finding this a pleasant contrast to his struggle to deliver Sandburg to the lecture audience. At that time, when he gave him the $25 fee allotted to Hansen, Stephens had been somewhat apologetic, but Sandburg had said, "Oh, this is fine. This is all velvet, you know."

"Industry, persistence, and patience have played a large part in the flowering of Carl Sandburg's genius," Hansen believed.

> No matter how hard he had to work, there was always a singing inside of him. When he wrote poems he expressed the emotional side of American social history. When he sang folk songs, he demonstrated the oral tradition by which simple events are recalled. In small talk, he put things in a new way. I have known him to have plenty of time for talk and because he has worked hard, he has always had something to say.[18]

He had something to say about Frederic Babcock of the *Chicago Tribune* who was a newcomer in that city at the time, and who wrote a scathing article for the *Nation* in which he attempted to hold up for sarcastic ridicule a leading national figure. Writing in the *Daily News*, Carl Sandburg said of the article: "Babcock writes like a gargoyle, not knowing whether to laugh or weep." Then Sandburg sent Babcock an apology. The latter replied, thanking him for his note, saying it was deeply appreciated, even though unnecessary. Months later, the two sat together at a dinner for the Walt Whitman Fellowship and became lasting friends.

Sandburg may have been some kind of celebrity in those days, but his income did not indicate it. His annual salary on the *Daily News* for years was $2,500 and this was hardly enough for a family that now numbered five, two more daughters having been born—Janet in 1914, and Helga in 1918. Poetry then, as at any time, did not bring in much money, and he netted only about $400 a year additionally from that. His singing-speaking engagements brought in some more cash but not much, counting the expense of traveling, etc. He noted that people wanted to see a poet but that they did not want to hear poetry alone for a whole evening. So he spiced it up with music. Once he complained to an associate, Bruce Weirick, that he had to limit himself to fifteen cents for bean soup for lunch, while Ben Hecht and Charlie MacArthur could spend a dollar and a half for theirs at a restaurant called Schlogi's. For this revealing remark, Carl received the possibly consoling answer that, anyway, he was not digging his grave with his teeth.[19]

Weirick also noted that Sandburg's appearance was usually sloppy and his suit unpressed, but that this had its advantages. For example, the two used to leave the newspaper and walk down Madison Street, through a neighborhood that was dark and grim, to catch the "owl train" for Elmhurst. Sandburg often walked this street alone and when asked if he thought it wise to do so in the darkness, he replied that there was not a bit of danger—he had been doing it for years and had never been held up. Weirick, who was always nattily dressed, felt that one would not be safe; but when he looked at the almost shabby attire of his companion who resembled a working man of the factory more than he did a writer, he could better understand Sandburg's feeling of security.

In the Sandburg house at Elmhurst, there was a quiet and homey quality like the serenity of many traditional New England homes. The young ones of the family cavorted in a style that showed them to be quite happy, reflecting both the mother's busy attentiveness to them and the childlike nature of their father. At times, Mrs. Sandburg called Carl "My Buddy," reminiscent of a popular and appealing World War I song. Her devotion was constant, in rain or darkness. There is little doubt that her encouragement helped him keep at his task of writing poetry when none was expected, and she was a competent listener to his work as well as an affectionate friend. When he did not show up for dinner at times, she did not complain as some women would have done; she felt he had a reason to be absent, that he had secreted himself in order to work out some part of his writing or to brood over a poem or visit some workingman's home, learning there the realities of poverty so that he could portray even better such existence in his books.

Sandburg and Weirick would sit together with others of the news staff and talk, and sometimes Carl would play his guitar and sing ballads about the Civil War or the West or the railroads or the stockyards. Now and then Harry Reeves, a specialist in balladry, would hum one that Sandburg did not know but the poet would immediately commit it to memory and add it to his already large repertory. Between ballads, the men would discuss such topics as politics, money, and making a living. Weirick realized that Sandburg had had a hard time in his impoverished youth—he was twenty before he entered college, thirty before he married, and thirty-eight before his first little book was published. As the son of a workman at the turn of a century that had its twelve-hour days, twelve-and-one-half-cents-an-hour pay, and sometimes a seven-day week, he symbolized, somehow, the slow and hard struggle of labor to wrest from employers a fair share of the profits they made.

The fact that Carl Sandburg had come up in this environment always remained in his poems and his heroes were the heroes of the people: Eugene V. Debs, Clarence Darrow, and John Peter Altgeld. But Carl would treat with equal deference an obscure editor of a little railroad magazine whose views he admired, or even a nameless workman just doing his job. One of the poems through which he expressed such sentiment is the following:

CHILD OF THE ROMANS

The dago shovelman sits by the railroad track
    Eating a noon meal of bread and bologna.
        A train whirls by, and men and women at tables
        Alive with red roses and yellow jonquils,
        Eat steaks running with brown gravy,
    Strawberries and cream, eclaires and coffee.
    The dago shovelman finishes the dry bread and bologna,
    Washes it down with a dipper from the water-boy,
And goes back to the second half of a ten-hour day's work
Keeping the road-bed so the roses and jonquils
        Shake hardly at all in the cut glass vases
        Standing slender on the tables in the dining cars.[20]

Sandburg's fight for the rights of labor seems to have been only a part of his personal commitment at that time. In the summer of

1918, he went to New York City to cover a labor convention. The war fever was at its peak and in this day of cooperation between government and labor, led by Woodrow Wilson and Samuel Gompers, the gathering appeared rather tame and lacking in news interest. Down at the Hudson River piers, however, the ever curious Carl saw a big troop ship getting ready to leave for Europe, filled with noisy American "doughboys." His heart went out to them, in the typical fashion of a veteran who, having served in the Spanish-American affair, was always to retain that peculiar camaraderie which military men experience in their common service.

It was also a time of celebration in New York. Our country had not yet learned the horrors of war at first hand. So we were facing a glorious adventure. Here was a romantic challenge: a fracas far overseas which demanded our attention and help. And whether it demanded it or not, we wanted to go in, most of us, and get into the thick of things. Thousands of bright American flags were flying across Manhattan, bands were playing martial and patriotic songs as the young recruits marched in parades down Fifth Avenue and along lower Broadway. Girls lined the sidewalks as soldiers and sailors filed past, leaning over to kiss their heroes who were going off to make the world "safe for democracy." It was a heyday of war fever and Carl Sandburg was caught up in it like so many others.

He wanted to go, too. But being then forty years of age, he was old for military service, and besides he wanted to write about the war. It so happened that the Newspaper Enterprise Association, a feature organization serving 350 newspapers and having special correspondents, had, without his knowledge, decided that Sandburg could do a good job for it in Scandinavia.

The request was for him to go to Sweden and was in the form of a letter to Sandburg dated July 11, 1918, from S. T. Hughes of the newspaper organization. It stated:

As you know, Stockholm is next door to both Germany and Russia. The very latest and best German news gets to

Stockholm faster and better than it gets to either Berne or Amsterdam. . . . I am convinced that the Russian news is going to be just as important, if not more important than from any other part of the world. I know you are better fitted than most newspapermen, mentally, temperamentally and otherwise, to cover this particular place and that section of the world. Of course I am not offering you the Stockholm thing as a temporary assignment. I want you to be a regular and fixed member of the Scripps institution. You know our ways and our ideals. We know you and we like you. We would not look on you merely from the standpoint of exploiting your brains. We are in sympathy with men of your kind. When the war ends, or when this Stockholm assignment ends so far as you are concerned, we want you in the office here.

To this Sandburg immediately replied: "It is a go. On hearing from you that you can finance the stunt, I will begin packing for Stockholm, and looking up Chicago ends that have connections in Europe. I was more than glad to get your letter. It goes both ways."

The two wishes were joined and in the middle of October, 1918, the new foreign correspondent sailed, his specific assignment being to look for people who were leaving the war zone and interview them for inside news of the war, especially if they came out of Russia. So Sandburg went to Stockholm and remained for five months. His knowledge of the Swedish language was a help to him, but he found that the whole project turned out to be of less importance than had been expected. People back home wanted to read war stories rather than background articles, and he had arrived late in the conflict for any such purpose as that, even if he had gone into the fighting sectors. There was something going on, however, that much interested Sandburg. This was the collectivist movement of the Bolshevists. Being not far from Russia, he talked a great deal to Michael Borodin, a Lenin agent in Stockholm, who had lived in Chicago when Sandburg did. Another companion was a former fellow-Socialist editor, Per Albin Hansson, who had much in common with Borodin and Sandburg.

Though Sandburg did not participate actually as a war correspondent, he evidently developed an appreciation of these men and women, for some twenty years later he wrote a tribute to them which was read at a memorial dinner to him at the Overseas Press Club in New York not long after he died in 1967. In part, his tribute to the 110 foreign correspondents who lost their lives in the performance of their duty ran as follows:

> In a time of world storm, more vast than before known to mankind, those who print and publish for readers, those who broadcast for listening millions have a responsibility beyond calculation. This holds true for the new and strange breed of men and women who in war gather the round-the-earth news. The meaning of this deepens in us when we look at the multiple mirrors of the changing war: facts, plain rumors, official communiqués, guesses, probabilities and possibilities, weaving crazy and dizzy patterns. . . . A French marshal of the First World War said, "The control factor in war is the unknown." In all weather, the overseas correspondent seeks the controlling factor, centers and hunts the dark unknown from winding and tortuous paths where the known faded into the cogs of the unknown. They did their best to discover what was happening from day to day. Valor is a gift. Those having it are never sure whether they will have it till the test comes. No one knows better than the tested overseas correspondent how a brave man can be so rash and take such chances that he goes down and never lives to file what might have been his greatest story. The toll of those who took death, wounds, disease, suffering in rain and cold and heat and foul prisons—their names have a definite sounding majesty. What some of them did is far past flowers and tribute or weeks of verbal salutation. . . . After calling the roll of their names, let them have remembrance and the relevance of silence. Let them sleep, deep among the never-forgotten.

Back in Chicago, Carl Sandburg oversaw the operations of the Newspaper Enterprise Association for a short time, but this kind of work did not suit him so he hied himself in May, 1919, back to the editorial fold of the *Daily News*. Here he was to remain for thirteen years. And why not? He was allowed to pick his own writing assignments, most of which turned out to be labor stories and interviews; some of the latter he wrote without even seeing the persons concerned, because he knew them so well that personal contact was not necessary. After writing the story, he would telephone the subject of it and read it in order to obtain approval. In such work, Sandburg, of course, met all kinds of people, especially those from the harsher side of life. He was at home with bums, job-seekers, starving men, and members of the IWW as well as contrasting figures in the better economic brackets.

One whom he definitely was not at home with, however, was the flamboyant evangelist, Billy Sunday, a dynamic "reformed" professional baseball player who electrified audiences by his gymnastic antics in the pulpit and who called on people to "hit the sawdust trail" for Christ, as the aisles of his speaking places were called. Carl Sandburg thought Billy Sunday was a kind of bombastic imposter who preyed more than he prayed, and felt he was misleading the people through fervent and high-pressure appeal to their emotions. The fact that most Americans did not agree but felt that Sunday was a benign and needed influence did not deter Sandburg. This proved another revelation of his unorthodox religion; but some religion he undoubtedly did have.

In the meantime, Sandburg had met a man who was to play a vital part in the future of his literary output. He was Alfred Harcourt, a book salesman for Henry Holt & Company of New York, who had read in *Poetry* magazine some of Sandburg's poems which "stirred" him greatly. The next time Harcourt was in Chicago he tried to find Sandburg but without success. But he did find Alice Corbin, assistant to Harriet Monroe, editor of *Poetry*, and asked her to steer Sandburg his way when he had enough poems for a book.

It was in the fall of 1915 that Miss Corbin took into the New York office of Henry Holt & Company a manuscript from Carl

Sandburg entitled *Chicago Poems*. Harcourt saw at once that it was of first importance and quality but his colleagues were not so perspicacious. They felt, because of the somewhat conservative traditions of the Holt firm, that the poems with their midwestern flavor and their strong subject matter were rather too raw for their imprint. But Harcourt would not relent and finally Henry Holt himself agreed that they should try the book.

Chicago Poems was published the next year and Carl Sandburg went to New York and met Alfred Harcourt, the start of a long literary and personal friendship. The new book received considerable attention from the critics, and Holt and Company soon became proud of their discovery. Harcourt later recalled that for almost ten years after that, his association with Sandburg was mainly by correspondence

> . . . and what correspondence! Every letter he wrote, even of humdrum details, seemed to sing. Everything Carl writes is music and full of wisdom. He had a regular job on the *Chicago Daily News* so he couldn't get to New York, and when in 1919 I started my own firm, Harcourt, Brace & Company, I was too busy to get to Chicago. I did drop in on him once in Elmhurst where he lived. I found Eugene Debs there, just freed from a Federal penitentiary where he had been serving a sentence for trying to keep the United States out of the First World War. Debs was recovering his health and spirits in the warmth of the Sandburg home. I then heard Carl sing for the first time. Debs had been teaching him some of the songs he had heard his fellow prisoners sing.[21]

So it was natural that Sandburg was the friend of the down-trodden and these of course included the Negroes. In Chicago, after World War I, returning white soldiers found many of their jobs filled by southern Negroes who had come to that city during their absence. Apparently this group of migrants had become so numerous that the political bosses and many white residents came to fear their growing strength. Eventually, a Negro boy was killed by a rock someone had thrown, and the police seemed to ignore any real investigation. The incident helped to bring on the Chicago race riots of 1919 and Sandburg did a series of articles on the subject for the *Daily News*. These stories showed a strong sympathy for the Negroes and some of the accounts could have a ringing reverberation in the racial disturbances of today. They were gathered together in a paperbound book that was published in the first list of the newly formed Harcourt, Brace in the autumn of 1919. Significantly, on page 2 is mentioned the Emancipation Proclamation of Abraham Lincoln.[22]

In the articles, Sandburg pointed out that the race riots started in Chicago during the last week of July, 1919, on a Sunday at a bathing beach. A Negro boy swam across an imaginary segregation line and some white boys were said to have thrown rocks at him and knocked him off a raft. He was drowned. Colored people rushed to a policeman and asked for arrest of the boys throwing rocks, but the policeman refused. More rocks were thrown on both sides, fighting spread to the Black Belt of the city, and at the end of three days, twenty Negroes and fourteen white men were recorded dead and several Negro houses burned.

Three conditions marked this violence, according to Sandburg: First, the Black Belt population of Chicago, which had been 50,-000, doubled during the war, but no new houses or tenements were built to take care of the great increase. So under pressure of war industry, the already overcrowded slum district was compelled to hold twice as many people as before. Second, the Black Belt was probably the strongest effective unit of political power, good or bad, in the United States. It connected directly with a city administration which refused to draw the color line, and a mayor whose opponents failed to defeat him even by circulating the name of "nigger lover." This was the kind of place to which the black soldiers returned from France and cantonment camps. Third, thousands of white men and thousands of colored men cooperated during the riots, and officials of the Stockyard Labor Council issued statements asking the public to take note that they were shaking hands as brothers and could not be counted on as sharing in the mob exploits. Poles, Negroes, Lithuanians, Italians, Irish, Germans, Slovaks, Russians, Mexicans, English, and Scotchmen proclaimed unprecedented and organized opposition to violence between union white and black men.

In any American city where the race situation is critical, Sandburg perspicaciously observed, the radical and active factors probably are housing, politics and war psychology, and organization of labor.

At this time in Chicago, barber shop, cigar store, and haberdashery windows ironically displayed helmets, rifles, cartridges, canteens, and haversacks as well as photographs of Negro regiments which had served in France. Sandburg walked around the Black Belt and found that the black folks responded, when asked about their future, that they had made the supreme sacrifice and no work-or-fight laws were needed for them. "Like Old Glory, the flag we love because it stands for our freedom, our record hasn't got a spot on it; we 'come clean'; now we want to see our country live up to the Constitution and the Declaration of Independence."

It was pointed out that the black people of Chicago had the largest single Protestant church membership in North America in the Olivet Baptist Church at South Park Avenue and East 31st Street; it had more than 8,500 members. The local of the Meat Cutters and Butcher Workmen's Union at 43rd and State Streets claimed over 10,000 Negro members. Chicago then had the reputation of being the most liberal city in the nation in this respect and the constitution of Illinois, the most liberal of all state constitutions, according to Sandburg.

But for the black families which came up from the South in large numbers the problems of adjustment were formidable. Five such families, for example, lived in a big brownstone house on Wabash Avenue. All were from Alabama. At first they were said to have thrown their dinner leavings from the back porch. Next, they sat on the front steps and ate watermelon and threw the rinds out into the street. Soon, said the Sandburg account, they learned what garbage cans were for, under the local urgings that anything they did might reflect credit or discredit on their whole race and therefore they should be careful.

Leaders of the black community in Chicago reminded Sandburg that the only great source from which the United States could develop a new power of labor at that time was the 12,000,000 Negro workers. They stated spiritedly that when orders for goods came from France and Belgium and Central Europe and South America and Africa to American factories, it did not matter an iota what was the color of the skin of the man whose hand or brain produced that product.

But many Negroes still found it difficult to obtain employment in Chicago, Sandburg revealed. Some of the returned men of the 8th Infantry Regiment went to see about getting places as Pullman car porters. They found that they would have to stand an initial fee of $35 for uniforms, and since they had no money, they gave up the idea. On the other hand, the People's Gas Company broke a precedent by employing four black meter inspectors at salaries of $100 per month and four special meter readers, boys of sixteen years of age, at salaries of $55 dollars a month. The gas company's experiment proved so successful that the Commonwealth Edison Company soon followed suit by hiring six Negro men in its meter installation department.

Hundreds of letters, it was learned, written to the newspaper *The Chicago Defender* and to the Urban League, gave certain causes for the migration of individual Negroes from the South to the North. Charles Johnson, an investigator for the Carnegie Foundation, and formerly a lieutenant with overseas service in the 803rd Infantry, found the principal motive was economic.

> There are several ways of arriving at a conclusion regarding the economic forces behind the movement of the colored race northward. The factors might be determined by the amount of unemployment or the extent of poverty. These facts are important, but may or may not account for individual action. Except in a few localities of the South,

there was no actual misery or starvation. Nor is it evident that those who left would have perished from want had they remained. Large numbers of Negroes have frequently moved around from state to state and even within the states of the south in search of more remunerative employment.

The migrations to Arkansas and Oklahoma were expressions of the economic force. A striking feature of the northern migration was its individualism. Motives prompting the thousands of Negroes were not always the same, not even in the case of close neighbors. The economic motive was foremost, a desire simply to improve their living standards when opportunity beckoned. A movement to the West or even about the South could have proceeded from the same cause.[22]

During the influx of black people from the South, Sandburg reported, the Chicago Urban League issued a creed of cleanliness aimed especially at the women concerned, as follows:

For me! I am an American citizen. I am proud of our boys 'over there,' who have contributed soldier service. I desire to render citizen service. I realize that our soldiers have learned new habits of self-respect and cleanliness. I desire to help bring about a new order of living in this community. I will attend to the neatness of my personal appearance on the street or when sitting in the front doorway. I will refrain from wearing dustcaps, bungalow aprons, house clothing and bedroom shoes when out of doors. I will arrange my toilet within doors and not on the front porch. I will insist upon the use of rear entrances for coal dealers and hucksters. I will refrain from loud talking and objectionable deportment on street cars and in public places. I will do my best to prevent defacement of property, either by children or adults.[23]

Regarding neighborhood conditions, it was disclosed that a

prominent Chicago club woman sold an apartment house on Wabash Avenue for $14,000 when it had cost her $26,000. Her agent had advised her to make the sale because, he said, the colored people were coming into the neighborhood and the property surely was going to slump. Yet in this very apartment building, rent of each apartment jumped from $35 to $50 a month because black persons were willing to pay more than whites to live in this location. Twenty years earlier [c. 1909], fewer than fifty Negro families in Chicago owned homes. When Sandburg wrote, thousands did, their purchases ranging from $200 to $20,000, from tar paper shacks in the steel district to brownstone and graystone establishments with wealthy or well-to-do white neighbors.

A pamphlet published at the time and written by Lieutenant Charles S. Duke, a black Harvard graduate and civil engineer, set forth proposals under two headings. One was in regard to "things that Chicago owes her colored citizens":

1. The privilege of borrowing money easily upon real estate occupied by colored citizens living on the south side, and in the same amounts as can be borrowed upon property in other parts of the city.

2. Better attention in the matter of repairs and upkeep of premises occupied by colored tenants.

3. Making an end of the neglect of neighborhoods occupied principally by colored people.

4. Abandonment of all attempts at racial segregation.

5. Prohibition as far as possible of the commercializing of race prejudice in real estate matters.

6. Recovery from hysteria incident to the advent of the first colored neighbors.

7. Fewer indignation meetings and more constructive planning.

8. Better schoolhouses and more modern equipment in schools in districts where colored people live in large numbers.

9. More playgrounds and recreational centers on the South Side.

10. A beautiful branch library in the center of the colored district.[24]

After reporting the race riots, Sandburg filled in for the motion picture editor of the *Daily News,* William K. Hollander, who was then on a vacation. The latter soon decided to quit his job and Sandburg was asked to replace him, which he did with much pleasure. One reason he leaped at the new duties was the extra time the work would give him for his own writing. He worked out a schedule so that he left his suburban home on Sunday mornings, saw three new movies from 11 A.M. on, and then went to the office and wrote his reviews. He would then stay overnight in Chicago, see three more new movies the next day and write them up, as well as his column on "Thoughts for Saturday." By Monday night, his work week was finished and he had Tuesday through Saturday to work at home on his poems and children's stories. His movie criticism turned out to be a disorderly hodgepodge of everything —lectures to the public, observations on the state of the times, admonitions about social conditions—a regular soapbox presentation of Sandburgisms tied loosely to the peg of comment on the cinema.

Such liberties naturally caught the attention of the trained newsmen on the paper who were accustomed to writing stories on the assignments they were given, not on whatever topic happened to interest a subjective, poetic, sometimes cantankerous writer. Some of them felt that Sandburg did not show enough of the straight journalistic qualities which a reporter ordinarily conforms to. But this was no ordinary reporter, and Henry Justin Smith knew this so well that he would not let the copyeditors change any of the Sandburg copy before it went to press.

If the atmosphere of the newspaper office had not before been Sandburgian, Carl made it so.

Asked to fill out a form for keeping his name on the payroll, Carl Sandburg submitted the following:

THE CHICAGO DAILY NEWS COMPANY

Order to Cashier for Entering Name on Pay Roll
                    Date: Saturday, Ruck & Rayner's

To the Cashier:
Please put on the *Egghead* department
Pay Roll beginning *Discreetly*
Re-employed *Frequently*
Name *Carl Hjalmar Sandburg*
Address *courteous*
Employed in capacity of *145 pounds*
Salary $ *medium*   Age   *pliocene*
Married? *Experimentally*   Schooling—where and how
long? *Dill Pickle Club—Miss Starrett's Academy*
Where last employed? *not yet ascertained*
What Capacity? *More than two fingers daily*
What salary? *Piece Work*   Why Disengaged? *the
      word is inadequate*
References and remarks:
References: *Amy Lowell, H. L. Mencken, Christian Science
      Monitor, Michael Kenna, Arthur Burrage Farwell,
      U.S. State Dept., J.B. Forgan, Barney Bertsche, God
      Almighty*
Remarks: *See this author's poem "The Space Killer"*
                    Signed

                              Carl Sandburg

Walter Yust remembered visiting the office and finding Sandburg sitting in a noisy, cluttered room beside a cluttered desk where he did most of his work. The floor was paper-strewn and the desks were dusty. "Outside the thundering elevated drove away any vision I might have had of a lonely poet dreaming in his lonely room." Sandburg remarked that what he wrote took a long time to finish; it might be two years before a poem was ready for publication, because he first penciled it and then carried it around in his pocket, reading and rereading it until he felt it was fully ready. For example, he explained that he rewrote "Prairie," which opens *Cornhuskers,* fourteen times before it reached print.

Asked what he read, Sandburg told Yust that it was mostly the Bible, Ibsen, Chinese poetry, and Scandinavian and Negro melodies. Yust commented:

> Sandburg's poems are not an expression of eccentric individualism but are an honest attempt to express a richly developed personality. That is why they are authentic poems. That is why Sandburg must discard rhyme and conscious meter; that is why he must use living 'common' words. Sandburg's poems are Sandburg. They are powerful, live, brutal, gentle, and humorous—and so is he.[25]

In 1920, Sandburg published a third book of poetry, *Smoke and Steel,* which contained poems of roughly vivid realism about men who worked in the fields and factories. Carl Sandburg knew these men. He had worked with them and shared their hard lives. But the poems also hold tenderness, romance, and adoration. The book begins with a poem of the same name, part of which is given here:

SMOKE AND STEEL

Smoke of the fields in spring is one,
Smoke of the leaves in autumn another.
Smoke of a steel-mill roof or a battleship funnel,
They all go up in a line with a smokestack,
Or they twist . . . in the slow twist . . . of the wind.

· · · · ·

A bar of steel—it is only
Smoke at the heart of it, smoke and the blood of a man.
A runner of fire ran in it, ran out, ran somewhere else,
And left—smoke and the blood of a man
And the finished steel, chilled and blue.

> So fire runs in, runs out, runs somewhere else again,
> And the bar of steel is a gun, a wheel, a nail, a shovel,
> A rudder under the sea, a steering-gear in the sky;
> And always dark in the heart and through it,
>   Smoke and the blood of a man.
> Pittsburgh, Youngstown, Gary—they make their steel
>   with men.[26]

From the time they came down from Milwaukee until 1919, the Sandburgs lived at 4646 North Hermitage Avenue in a suburb of Chicago called Maywood. They occupied the second-floor flat of a wooden house shaded by tall elms and cottonwoods, owned at that time by Harry S. Moniger. As has been observed, here the Chicago poems were written, here the poet had formed his impressions of the Clark Street Bridge, Maxwell Street, the skyscrapers, a boat lost in the fog, teamsters, working girls, shovel men, and picnic boats. But finally the family moved to a better home in Elmhurst, farther out in the suburbs.

Regardless of where they lived, the Sandburgs always seemed to be happy. According to Margaret,

> I don't know anyone who has been happier all these years. My father would go off on trips, but he felt they were necessary to make money to support his growing family. When one was in his place and was offered so much for a lecture, it was hard to turn it down. Contrary to some impressions, he did not just go off and wander around aimlessly. That was before he was married and when he roamed around with hoboes. But he was never affected, with any kind of people. Just independent minded.[27]

No matter where they lived in Chicago, the family felt the current dynamism of the city. It was in a day when Edgar Lee Masters wrote his great *Spoon River Anthology* and Sherwood Anderson his *Winesburg, Ohio*, exposing more of the foibles of the small town. It was a day when Harriet Monroe fought to keep her *Poetry* magazine alive and this inspired Carl Sandburg who,

it seemed, was himself always fighting for some cause. When Miss
Monroe died some years later, she had been so impressed by him
that she requested no funeral services except a few remarks from
him—which he duly gave.

Chicago was then called by H. L. Mencken "The Literary Capital of America." "Big Bill" Thompson was the colorful mayor;
Samuel Insull, the utilities magnate, was creating the Chicago
Opera before his own financial demise; and the notorious gang-
ster Al Capone reigned in tyrannical splendor over the huge
bootleg system of the city and the nation. The *Chicago Tribune*
styled itself "The World's Greatest Newspaper." Truly, this was
a "city of the big shoulders."

So it was with verve and natural artistry that Sandburg appeared before audiences out of town. His first college speaking
engagement was at Cornell College at Mount Vernon, Iowa, in
1920. Meantime, he had shared the Poetry Society of America
prize twice and this evidently gave him at times too much *élan*.
Bruce Weirick has told how Carl Sandburg

> chose to be difficult. He refused, though he had already
> consented to the arrangement, to dine with the large group
> of ladies who were sponsoring him, and who had charged
> the guests a nice sum for the privilege. We hastily arranged,
> at his suggestion, a table for six at the Faculty Club. Then
> he relented, and consented just to appear at the banquet
> and greet the ladies. Once there, he liked them and told
> them all with dubious diplomacy that but for our "drag-
> ging him off to the club," he would have been charmed to
> dine with them. A remark, needless to say, that put those
> of us who were trying to look after him right behind the
> eight ball. . . . This was bad enough, but more was to
> follow. We were late getting to the club and Carl was
> sulky. Didn't like the excellent dinner that was ready, in-
> sisting on only a large bowl of breakfast food. Conversa-
> tion was desultory, and he snubbed Garreta Busey when

she ventured some literary query as to the relative difficulty of writing prose and poetry. At seven-fifteen, with the lecture forty-five minutes away, he went upstairs for a nap with instructions to wake him in half an hour. I did so, finding him cozy in long red underwear. About eight, he discovered that he had none of his books to read from. He doesn't remember his own poems as he does the ballads. I made a dash home for my copies, and at eight-thirty he began the eight-o'clock reading and song fest and quite charmed everybody.[28]

Enter Father Abraham

SANDBURG WAS NOW increasingly busy with a new and encompass-
ing project. The Lincoln material which he had been collecting
since Galesburg days began to take shape. In 1923, Sandburg
went to New York and had lunch with Alfred Harcourt at the
Chatham Hotel. He asked the latter what he thought his next
book should be. Harcourt knew of his interest in Lincoln and knew
that he loved to write for children, so he suggested a life of Lincoln
for teen-age boys and girls. It must have been comforting to
Sandburg to know that he was now an established author with
his publisher; anyone who has gone through uncertainty from
one book to another with different publishers appreciates the

good fortune of the author who has found a home and goes from one book to another with the same firm.

Sandburg told Harcourt how his interest in Lincoln began when he worked on a milk wagon in Galesburg, Illinois, his home town, and on his way to work cut across the Knox College campus, past a building on which was a tablet stating that this was the scene of one of the Lincoln-Douglas debates and giving a quotation from that debate. Sandburg had learned this quotation by heart and it led him to read the entire series of debates and then on to other material connected with Lincoln. The publisher and author talked of a book of around 400 pages, although Harcourt perspicaciously thought it might be a little longer. So Sandburg agreed to try his hand at a boy's life of Lincoln.

Two years later, Sandburg went to Harcourt with a manuscript that had grown into two volumes. Into this life of Lincoln, Sandburg had poured himself. In it he gave a picture of the poor whites in Kentucky, Indiana, and Illinois from 1805 to 1855, of Lincoln growing up as a product of this environment and of his own destiny. The manuscript ended with the departure of Lincoln from Springfield to take the oath as President of the United States. It did not have a title. At that time Van Wyck Brooks, the author and critic, had an office next to that of Harcourt and was acting as a special adviser to the publishing firm. He read the manuscript and was greatly impressed by it, so, in a vein characteristic of his own rich literary style, he suggested the title: *Abraham Lincoln: The Prairie Years.*

In those days there was an excellent magazine for women entitled *The Pictorial Review* and it became interested in using parts of the manuscript. But the editors offered only $3,500 for the right to select materials from it. Alfred Harcourt, already full of enthusiasm for the project himself, was not satisfied. He informed the editors that he felt *The Prairie Years* would rank as one of the greatest biographies in the English language and indicated that about ten times their offer would be more suitable to him. They were taken aback, but finally agreed to pay $30,000.

Carl Sandburg was in Texas at the time on one of his lecture tours. Harcourt telegraphed him the good news, and the reply was:

> Dear Alfred:
>
> This is the first time I've understood something about the emotions of holding the lucky ticket in a lottery. Professor Armstrong of Baylor College at Waco wired your telegram to me at Commerce, saying, 'I have received the following telegram. Does it mean anything to you?' I replied "Thank you for sending a telegram with news equivalent to falling heir to a farm."
>
> Carl

Even while pursuing every bit of information about Lincoln he could lay his hands on, Sandburg still went on around the country acting the troubadour. He carried a guitar, read his own poetry, and sang folk songs. This travel enabled him to meet men who remembered Lincoln. Sandburg's figure became familiarly symbolical—tall, lean, and stooped, with deep lines in his face, white hair parted in the middle and hanging low over his temples, his eyes piercing above a big nose. He wore a blue serge, baggy suit, frayed shirt, and shoes that needed a shine. His voice was low and pleasant but his showmanship was better. He knew how to "put a song across," even if it was not so well performed, and he selected songs he knew his audience would like.

As a sort of prelude to his big effort, Sandburg wrote a poem about Lincoln which he entitled:

Fire Logs

Nancy Hanks dreams by the fire;
Dreams, and the logs sputter,
And the yellow tongues climb.
Red lines lick their way in flickers.
Oh, sputter, logs.

Oh, dream, Nancy.
Time now for a beautiful child.
Time now for a tall man to come.

When asked by Louis Untermeyer what he planned to write, Sandburg replied, "I aim to write a trilogy about Lincoln some day, to break down all this sentimentalizing about him." On his manuscript he had done much polishing and had searched for what he called "picture words" such as the Indians and Chinese used. He found them.

His work on Lincoln has been called the greatest study of an American ever written by another American. It is treated not only historically but, in the Sandburg manner, poetically. *The Prairie Years* was described in *Current Biography* as "like a lyric prologue to the greatly written human tragedy of *The War Years.*" His publisher did not depend on the publicity given to the new book by the *Pictorial Review* alone, but carried out a promotional campaign, part of which was a forty-page pamphlet that included a part of the preface by Sandburg and part of the introduction to the magazine version by Harry Hansen. This was sent to 2,500 book dealers around the country. Hansen stated that Sandburg was as much at home with tales of Lincoln as the latter was with the "boys" around the courthouse or country store. As for Carl himself, he admitted that his first book on Lincoln ran much longer than he had thought it would, but that he had found the martyred President a more companionable personality than he had expected, that Lincoln had never lived up to the great-man theory, and Carl summed it up with the classic comment, "The son-of-a-gun grows on you."

Even though his absorption with the serious, enigmatic Lincoln held him most of the time, children also had their claim on him. When his children's stories began to be popular, his little daughters gathered around him whenever they had the chance; and always the great comfort and solace of a welcoming feminine committee at home sustained and inspired him to the end of his long life. The sources of his rich fund of children's stories are not too clear, but he did read Hans Christian Andersen's fairy tales and these helped to fire his already vigorous imagination. His *Rootabaga Stories* appeared in 1922 and at once stamped him as a master teller of juvenile tales. The stories are full of gay and lovable characters, fantastic perhaps, but still human enough to be remindful of human foibles and desires that themselves defy reality.

His children's stories concern such things as the Zigzag Railroad, the Valley of Cream Puffs, and Pigs with Bibs On. The rutabaga is described in the dictionary as "a Swedish turnip with a large yellow root." Sandburg apparently misspelled it deliberately for his own poetic purposes. The titles of some of the stories are revealing: "How They Broke Away to Go to the Rootabaga Country"; "The Wedding Procession of the Rag Doll and the Broom Handle and Who Was in It"; "The White Horse Girl and the Blue Wind Boy"; "Slipfoot and How He Nearly Always Never Gets What He Goes After"; "How Bozo the Button Buster Busted All His Buttons When a Mouse Came"; "How Deep Red Roses Goes Back and Forth Between the Clock and the Looking Glass." The stories are just as fantastic as their titles suggest, taking the appreciative reader—and Frank Lloyd Wright was one of the most devout—out of the world of reality and transporting him into a sweet never-never land of living-happily-ever-after.

Sandburg started writing children's stories in the 1920s for his daughters, Margaret, Janet, and Helga. He would spin yarns for them and they loved it, so it was decided to submit the stories for publication. The tales touch gently on those mysteries of human life that mingle fun and pathos. He dedicated the stories to "Spink," "Skabootch," and "Swipes," his nicknames for the three beloved children.

Frank Lloyd Wright wrote to Sandburg about one of the volumes, *Rootabaga Pigeons:*

> It is a beautiful book, issued in a unique style befitting its contents, and I shall have this to add to my collection of literary treasures and to serve as a precious and beloved

companion to me always. No one but you could have produced this wonderful volume. It required your peculiar
genius and your marvellous imagination to conceive and
execute this striking original and appealing production.[3]

One reader suggested that a trip to Rootabaga Country should
be an annual pilgrimage if one wants to keep his spirits young
and buoyant. There is no journey to compare with this one,
through the land where balloons are harvested by balloon pick-
ers on stilts, where circus clowns are baked in ovens and are
pumped alive with living red wind, and where one wanders over
the zigzag railroad tracks and into the stories' fable land where
the tracks run off into the sky.

In the heart of Rootabaga Country sits the wise blind man,
Potato Face, with his accordian. He peers over the top of his
glasses and tells Blixie Bimber, "Tomorrow will never catch up
with yesterday because yesterday started sooner." This kind man
loves the precious things that are cheap such as the stars, the
wind, pleasant words, the time to be lazy, and fools. He realizes
that young people are young, no matter how many years they
live, and that a young heart keeps young by a certain measure of
fooling as the time goes by.

It seems remarkable that Carl Sandburg could write so many
kinds of things, this capacity inspiring the comment that he could
write anything. Yet he said that his children's stories were harder
to do than anything he ever wrote. "If the people who read books
don't like these stories there is no joy left in the world," he
rightly said. And this work was a relaxation to him, a joy in his
own life that many readers shared.

Again a tribute from Frank Lloyd Wright:

> I read your fairy tales nearly every night before I go to
> bed. They fill a long felt want—poetry. . . . O man! the
> beauty of the White Horse Girl and the Blue Wind Boy.
> And the fairies dancing on the wind-swept corn. The
> Wedding Procession of the Broomstick and the Rag Doll—
> the Skyscrapers that decided to have a child. All the chil-

dren that will be born into the Middle West during the
next hundred years are peeping at you now, Carl—
between little pink fingers—smiling, knowing that in this
Beauty they have found a friend.[4]

An unusually remunerative opportunity now presented itself
when the Hearst newspapers offered him $100,000 for two years
of editorial writing. That his career had reached a kind of ma-
turity was evidenced in the fact that he declined this offer,
explaining that he had three or four more books to write.

Writing to Alfred Harcourt on December 23, 1927, Sandburg
exulted:

> I have had to turn down an official invitation to be the
> main speaker at the Lincoln Dinner, February 13, of the
> National Republican Club of New York City. In doing so,
> I had to recall our common thought (it hit both of us at
> about the same time) that the Lincoln book would make
> us 'respectable.' However, I have accepted an invitation
> to deliver the Poem before the Phi Beta Kappa Chapter
> of Harvard University next June. They pay $100 and
> board you for two days. Somehow, I have to laugh about
> it rather than take it solemnly. There is something Roota-
> baga about it. Please don't say anything about it; let any
> announcement come from Harvard.

In twenty years, Sandburg traveled from coast to coast a dozen
times. Included in his itinerary were the Poetry Society of South
Carolina in Charleston, and he appeared before audiences in all
the former Confederate states except Florida. As he stood before
the students of Washington and Lee University, he had solemn
thoughts of Robert E. Lee, a founder, whose tomb is nearby. In
San Antonio, Texas, the troubadour was presented with a $200
bond of that state after it had left the Union. When Sandburg
showed up in Athens, Georgia, he was presented with a check
signed by Alexander H. Stephens, Vice President of the Confederacy, by the latter's niece. In Colorado Springs, he met the

granddaughter of Jefferson Davis, and at Chicago, he met a son of Gideon Welles. A great-niece of General Abner Doubleday drew a charcoal sketch of Sandburg at Bennington College. While he was in a newspaper office in Palm Springs, California, he met a lady whose grandfather had played with the sons of Abraham Lincoln in the White House, and on the same visit, he also met a niece of Stephen A. Douglas. On a plantation in South Carolina, Julia Peterkin showed Sandburg the descendants of slaves.

During the Chicago days, Sherwood Anderson described Sandburg thus:

> He comes into the room where there is company heavily and slowly, staring about. His eyes are small and blue-faded. Everyone knows a personage has arrived but there is no swagger to him. He is not a physically strong man although he looks like the stuff out of which champion middleweights are made—a fighter who has given up fighting, gone out upon another road, out of condition for fighting. His eyes are not strong and he reads little. He is an eternal sitter-up o'nights drinking quantities of black coffee.[5]

Anderson went on to say that when Sandburg talked of labor and poetry, his two favorite subjects, he was unsure of himself. The former also recalled that a Frenchman was at his house one night and wanted to meet Sandburg, so Carl was invited over. The two guests just sat and stared at each other. Then Sandburg gave the Frenchman some statistics about how much coal was mined in Illinois each year, the mileage between Chicago and Dallas, etc., and the Frenchman still stared. Then Sandburg sang and the Frenchman melted, became friendly, and later told Anderson it was one of his finest experiences in America. Coincidentally, during the same evening, a robber crawled in at the window and made off with the Frenchman's clothes, money, and luggage, "this giving him, in addition to his evening with Sandburg, a strikingly true picture of what Chicago is like. I've a notion," concluded Sherwood Anderson, "that he went home to France inclined toward the suspicion that Sandburg and I were in league with the robber."

A producer of the National Broadcasting Company program "Believe It or Not," by Ripley, asked Sandburg for a definition of a kiss. He got short shrift, for Carl replied on April 14, 1938,

> Regret that I have no definition of a kiss which could figure in your Ripley program. It is one of the better programs and I shall try not to miss your evening. To try to write such a definition would be much like trying to write a poem on an assigned topic: you should allow a fellow a year or two of time on the mystery of osculation. Ibsen said, "There is no word that has been soiled with lies like the word love." And the movies, the slicks and the pulps and much else culturally, now almost permit the substitution of the word "kiss" for that of "love" in the Ibsen quote. If you have thousands (no less) of kiss definitions, why not when in New York, stop in and see Harcourt, Brace & Company? [6]

Publication of *The Prairie Years* brought a long-sought circumstance: now Carl Sandburg was in a position to give up his job with the *Chicago Daily News*. The book was a huge success, 48,000 sets being sold in the year of its publication. He began to travel more and more, taking along his guitar as insurance, but wherever he went he delved into the libraries that might contain valuable Lincoln material. He not only met men and women who had known the Civil War President, but their sons and daughters who had close contact with the martial drama. Although his research was not that of a Ph.D., it was painstakingly thorough as befits the trained newspaper man who has learned to check all angles of a story before it goes to press. He found the *Official Records of the Union and Confederate Armies*, all 133 volumes, invaluable, as well as the files of the *Congressional Globe*. Said he about the two valuable sources: "In these two wildernesses of words, I have picked my way carefully, sometimes drearily and with hope and patience, or again fascinated and enthralled by the basic stuff of indisputable great human action in play before my eyes."

In following Lincoln through every step of his trip to the inauguration, Sandburg tends to invent some phases, which caused Edmund Wilson to criticize him adversely for treating historical fact with poetic license; yet what biographer has not had to resort to similar devices for filling in gaps that inevitably crop up in the recorded lives of his subjects.

The Prairie Years showed a vivid parallel between the lives of Abraham Lincoln and Carl Sandburg, especially in their boyhood days. Although many critics found flaws in the facts presented and complained of the elaborate description, they almost always agreed that they did not really know enough about the subject to be too positive. The critics did admit that here was a picture of a man being tested by the growing pains of a new nation, and through the great mass of detail, the earlier life of Lincoln emerged from a fog of sentiment and legend into that of a real human being. Writing in *The New York Times,* Robert E. Sherwood, the renowned playwright who was later to bring Lincoln so dynamically to the stage, said:

> In *The Prairie Years,* with fewer documents and many more myths at his disposal, Mr. Sandburg gave greater play to his own lyrical imagination. Anyone can indulge in guesswork about the raw young giant who emerged from the mists of Kentucky, and Indiana, and Sangamon County, Illinois, and Mr. Sandburg's guesses were far better than most.[7]

For not only had Sandburg been gathering information about Lincoln from all over the United States—the first time this had been done so diligently by a single biographer—but he had also been absorbing it into his own mind and spirit and coloring it with his own poetic imagination. All his writings are inevitably a part of his own distinctive personality. The story of Lincoln's growing up was so heavy with details that at times it appears to be simply a catalog of facts, as indeed some of it is. Sandburg's great mass of information and legends sometimes seems to overwhelm the reader; but if it does, it also impresses and, like the repetition of a melody, finally embeds itself in the consciousness. Not only did Sandburg compile a myriad of names of things, but he reveled in their vividness, their euphony, and their attunement to his great subject. He knew he had hold of a monumental subject about which too much could hardly be said, and he acted accordingly. His object was to convey the image of Lincoln from innumerable angles, and in this he greatly succeeded.

Yet with all the material he presented, Sandburg omitted many things which could have been told about Lincoln. Following his poetic bent, he inevitably included the most colorful and emotionally inspiring details, but for some reason, perhaps his own, omitted others that might have been present in the dissertation of a Ph.D. candidate who had no literary axe to grind or who was as yet mercifully unconscious of royalties. Sandburg's biography was therefore said to have been the truth as he saw it but not the whole truth. This charge stems from the theory that the biographer should include everything, whether or not it contributes to his purpose of portraying the whole man. It must be recalled, however, that the times of which Sandburg was writing were among the few greatest crises in the history of our country; and these times and the man who dominated them were alone of such significance that any fresh treatment of them was important to a proper impression of the period.

Withal it did seem that Sandburg had given his readers a biography of Lincoln's earlier years that was appropriate, satisfying, and rewarding, up to its chosen terminal point. To the scholar who was accustomed to thick accumulations of footnotes either at the bottom of the pages or less formidably arranged in the back of the book, the lack of such was a cardinal omission. Yet even those most demanding of this scholarly apparatus did not appear too unhappy about the end result, for the material which they saw for the first time in these pages gave them the correct impression that here was a researcher who had taken his own way to seek out the answers, and had formulated them with his own kind of authority. Sandburg was obviously not set on finding definite answers to the disputed issues in the Lincoln biography—although he did set to rest some popular misconceptions such as the overly romanticized roles of Ann Rutledge and Nancy Hanks in the life of his hero. Neither was he trying to introduce a wealth of new information. He was correcting in a colorful and satisfying way the inconsistencies in the American myth which was apparently destined to live on forever. At the same time, he was far from being a debunker; no, he was much too devout an admirer of Lincoln to try to tear him down from his pedestal.

The Prairie Years naturally contained errors, as do most books gleaned from secondary sources and not always carefully checked against original documents. But when the one-volume edition came out in 1954, many of the errors were corrected. It had been noted by Sandburg that the Lincoln family had neither a cow nor horse when they moved from Kentucky to Indiana. Later scholarly research has brought out that they did have both horses and cows. Although this was not a crucial point, it does show that the early Sandburg method was not as meticulous as it might have been, indeed not as careful as it was later. Other doubtful passages dealt with the deathbed scene of Nancy Hanks as she spoke to her children, overdramatized in the Sandburg version, and the author's perfunctory appraisal of John Quincy Adams as a "sweet, lovable man" which hardly tallied with the actual personality of this son of a President who strove rather vainly to achieve his somewhat startlingly progressive ideals of what made a good United States. Perhaps Adam's unrelenting stand against slavery influenced Sandburg to the extent that he gave undue weight to the other aspects of the man.

The critics picked up such errors as: placing Crawfordsville, Indiana, on the Wabash River; locating the shipwreck in which Shelley was drowned in an Italian lake rather than on the Ligurian Sea; attributing a quotation to de Toqueville when he meant Montesquieu; and citing a letter of Lincoln to his wife as hitherto unpublished when this was not the case—all these slips were grist for their mill. But despite such revelations, which often help bulk out a reviewer's article, the biography stood up more than well. Sandburg accomplished what he set out to do—to present the unique figure of Abraham Lincoln during the years when he was ripening for the presidency, set against the unprecedented background of his rough and seemingly patternless environment. This setting included so much of national significance that the figure of one man, even that of Lincoln, could have but little import compared to the problems of a new nation bursting out at its western seams—nurturing pioneer settlements that tested the mettle of humans who dared to plant them, and embracing the still greater problems of the drastic agricultural revolution, the coming of industry which even in its primary stages was pregnant with the issues of today, and the economic growth which was to start our modern Hamiltonian nation on its way to bigness never even dreamed of by its founders.

Whenever there is an awkward gap in his narrative, Sandburg fills it with a diverting anecdote. He uses these anecdotes frequently to set forth not only the philosophy of Lincoln but his own as well. For example, Bill Greene, a lawyer friend of Lincoln's, when once asked on the witness stand who were the principal citizens of New Salem, had replied, "In New Salem every man is a principal citizen." But Sandburg takes pains to point out, as in the case of the idealized Nancy Hanks, that some of the stories are apocryphal. Even so, he evidently felt that they were significant and entertaining enough to be included and perhaps believed that, like the cherry tree story about George Washington, they were at least to a considerable extent characteristic of their subjects. The author does not spend much time in interpretation. Rather he is content to present the facts and then let the readers find their own way by the light of his new information. Still, by his choice of facts, by the vividness of their presentation, and by the emphasis he places upon some of them, he makes clear what he believes about the life of Lincoln and its place in our history.

Running through the early pages is a manifest sympathy with
Lincoln, who, like Sandburg, as an extremely poor boy, grew up
in the prairies and lived to conquer his environment. The social
life was hard and, though it had its rewards, there was much sor-
row mixed with the pleasant side. Sandburg rightly attributes
Lincoln's humor to the necessity for escaping at times the severe
realities of the frontier. Later, when he was in the White House,
Lincoln explained that if he did not laugh he would have to
weep. The book disposes of the effect on Lincoln of the death of
Ann Rutledge, his sweetheart, as follows:

> It was to come to pass that 30 years later New Salem
> villagers soberly spoke and wrote that Lincoln went out of
> his mind, wandered in the woods mumbling and crazy,
> and had to be locked up, all of which was exaggeration
> and reckless expansion of his taking Ann's death "very
> hard." Woven with the recollections of his "insanity"
> were also the testimonies of what a deep flaming of lyric
> love there had been between him and Ann. A legend of
> a shining, deathless, holy and pure passion arose, spread,
> grew by some inherent vital sheen of its own or the need of
> those who wanted it. . . .[8]

Whether Sandburg approved of the Lincoln marriage, so different from his own, is an unanswered question in *The Prairie
Years*. Lincoln and Mary Todd had rough going, separating while
engaged, quarreling and making up, finally taking the vows;
while Sandburg and his wife met, were drawn to each other from
the start, were married without any significant disagreements,
and lived in unusual happiness from that time on.

The volume describes warmly the event that probably first
drew the attention of young Sandburg to Lincoln:

> On October 7, [1858] in the intinerary, came Galesburg,
> in Knox County. Twenty thousand people and more sat
> and stood hearing Lincoln and Douglas speak while a raw
> northwest wind tore flags and banners to rags. The damp

air chilled the bones of those who forgot their overcoats. For three hours the two debaters spoke to people who buttoned their coats tighter and listened. They had come from the banks of the Cedar Fork Creek, the Spoon River, the Illinois, Rock and Mississippi Rivers, many with hands toughened on the plow handles, legs with hard, bunched muscles from tramping the clods behind a plow team. With ruddy and wind-bitten faces they were of the earth; they could stand the raw winds when there was something worth hearing and remembering.[9]

It was about this time that Lincoln is credited with saying the famous words which Sandburg loved to quote: "You can fool all the people part of the time, and part of the people all the time but you can't fool all of the people all of the time." Also, Sandburg points out that Lincoln was a clipper of newspaper items. This habit probably inspired Sandburg in practice which he followed most of his own life. With careful scissoring, Lincoln cut out his own speeches and those of Douglas in the 1858 senatorial campaign—his own from the friendly *Chicago Press* and the *Tribune* and those of Douglas from the *Chicago Times*—which later he compiled neatly for publication as a book.

If Sandburg was not the first to discover the sources of Lincoln's growth, he was, it has been well said, a masterful interpreter of the concept that the wellsprings were peculiarly American. He realized that Lincoln was a product of influences and forces which make America what it is. True, others had previously seen this; but Sandburg did the outstanding job of translating it. He saw Lincoln as sensitive to the words and ways of the people around him. These people with their homes and occupations, songs and sayings, were portrayed in that continual transition that accompanied pioneer life. They were the backdrop of the life of Lincoln.

Sandburg has been likened to Lincoln in appearance, as a tall, gaunt man, stooped from hard work in his young days and from bending over a typewriter. His face was lined and wrinkly and

his expression kind and quickly humorous. He had two unruly
locks of stiff, white hair which he constantly pushed back and
which just as often fell forward again. When he worked, he wore
thick glasses and in his teeth clutched a small cigar which
usually was cold and unsmoked.

The New York Times found *The Prairie Years* "as full of facts
as Jack Horner's pie was of plums." Mark Van Doren remarked
in *The Nation,* "Here is God's plenty indeed." The *New Statesman* considered it "a masterpiece which suits its subject" and
Bookman regarded it as a "veritable mine of human treasure
from which to read aloud or to pore over by oneself." John Drink-
water, the Lincoln dramatist, had already read a dozen Lincoln
books and never thought anyone could get him to read another
thousand pages about Lincoln. But he did read *The Prairie Years*
and found it "a quite sincere and cumulatively very touching
reversion of a mind, closely disciplined in an almost savage
candor, to a natural grace and leniency of sentiment."

Sandburg himself said: "Among the biographers, I am a first-
rate poet. And among the poets, a good biographer; among singers, I'm a good collector of songs and among song collectors a
good judge of pipes." But always the poet shone through his
writings. As Allan Nevins has said,

> He was always primarily a poet, even when he was writing
> prose, and always something of an evangelist, even when
> his utterances were apparently tinged by cynicism. He
> had a vein of deep religious feeling which he concealed
> rather than paraded. As a newspaperman, he was highly
> skilled, and as an historian, he showed fine artistry. But
> whether he was writing a review of a movie or an account
> of an election or a characterization of Lincoln, he was,
> above all, a poet with a strong sense of the values of
> democracy.[10]

In describing the Mexican War in the book, Sandburg utilizes
his experience in the Spanish-American War to good advantage
and affords a colorful picture of the conflict. He depicts the war

in Kansas fairly but vividly and sets the violent forces off against each other in a novel manner. Although he shows sympathy for Harriet Beecher Stowe and her part in moving against slavery, he shows her faults as well as virtues and relates the reaction of Lincoln to her propaganda in an analytical rather than an emotional way. He accuses her of playing up a "black Christ" and describing this country as divided into two parts, one desecrated and the other sacred. For John Brown, Sandburg showed little sympathy, pointing out through the reaction of Lincoln that no matter what the cause, law and order should be observed.

Throughout the book, Sandburg tries hard to keep Lincoln the central and overriding figure, and in the main succeeds, but often is hard put to maintain full attention on him. Even so, out of the immense amount of relevant material and anecdote, as well as some that is irrelevant, the gaunt and mystical figure of Abraham Lincoln does emerge clearly. The President is pictured as the product of the Midwest, which at that time constituted mainly our extreme western borders. His character, as Frederick Jackson Turner has contended about Americans as a whole, was molded by his environment more than anything else. It grew from the soil and its people, the raw problems and hard challenges which most people have met but from which many have recoiled. From out of the struggle with the climate and other natural difficulties, there emerged the characters not only of Lincoln but of his biographer as well. That they survived that environment and rose far above it, whereas the majority were flattened by it and passed into oblivion, is a tribute to their strength of will. Why these two gathered strength and rose to fame in a somewhat similar manner has still an element of mystery about it. Sandburg in his first book on Lincoln strives hard to explain the phenomenon. He has come closer than anyone else; but the mystery of the Civil War President remains.

The biographer has shown the development of the young Lincoln who gave no obvious promise of becoming a dedicated genius in the White House during a fratricidal conflict. Sandburg hoped to make it clear that the raw material was here, and from this the reader could judge for himself what was to come and why and how. Awkward and bashful as he was, Lincoln nevertheless made a tremendous impact on those with whom he came in contact, whether favorable or not. What this impact was to amount to, it was not for his contemporaries to judge; nor can it be judged from Sandburg's narrative unless one chooses to read hindsight into the story. Lincoln was almost without formal education; yet deep inside of himself there appeared to be an innate wisdom which might have come from the fountain of knowledge which he found in his few books. The Emancipator remains simple and natural throughout; but one is led to believe that behind this disarming facade of rural plainness, is a mystic power which is only awaiting its destined opportunity to mount onto Olympus.

As humble as Lincoln is pictured—in our histories as well as in the Sandburg biography—he came from respectable stock. Virginia gentry, Pennsylvania Quakers, and Massachusetts Puritans all go into the making of the unique Chief Executive. But despite this, Sandburg, who was of common and alien stock himself, chooses mainly to ignore hereditary factors and associate Lincoln with the stark forces of his raw environment. The circumstances which surrounded Lincoln would have discouraged men of lesser determination from trying to get even a rudimentary education. But the force that Sandburg considered to be driving Lincoln toward his great place in history impelled him forward into a kind of self-education that at least fitted him for the halls of government.

Ordinary schools were unavailable; therefore Lincoln had to seek other channels. In his studies, he grew familiar with Aesop and John Bunyan's immortal *Pilgrim's Progress*, which along with the dictionary and the Bible were the pioneer's indispensable books. Lincoln, like Sandburg, even wrote verse, although most of it has fortunately disappeared. He was discerning enough to recognize even then the greatness of the orations of Daniel Webster, and perhaps knowledgeable enough to distinguish between the real greatness of Webster and his sad weaknesses. He analyzed the sources of Webster's brilliance, and although he never became an eloquent orator in the sense of Burke, Webster, Clay, and Calhoun, he evidently absorbed their gems of expression and used them in his own quieter but effective way.

More than these early American orators and statesmen ever were, Lincoln was close to the people. He reveled in the daily contact with the common man; though he was not a common man himself, he drew from that fellowship something that Sandburg recognized and fused into his own personal philosophy, strengthening his affinity with Lincoln. "To walk with kings, yet have the common touch" was a bond between subject and biographer that shows throughout the lengthy writings of the poet from Galesburg.

In his biography Sandburg shows that while Lincoln sought the respectability of polite society, he also enjoyed the off-color stories which men tell to each other—or at least such as were once so confined. Sandburg did this too. In some of his informal moments, he told yarns with four-letter words and one of his favorite private expressions was "son-of-a-bitch." But the stories told by both Lincoln and Sandburg in these "closed sessions" were clever and therefore perhaps somewhat justified as media of entertainment.

As Sandburg wrote:

> When Mary Todd, twenty-one years old, came in 1839 to live with her sister, Mrs. Ninian W. Edwards (Elizabeth Todd) she was counted an addition to the social flourish of Springfield. They spoke in those days of "belles" and Mary was one. Her sister told how she looked. "Mary had clear blue eyes, long lashes, light brown hair with a glint of bronze and a lovely complexion. Her figure was beautiful and no Old Master ever modeled a more perfect arm and hand." Whatever of excess there may be in this sisterly sketch, it seems certain that Mary Todd had gifts, attractions and was among those always invited to the dances and parties of the dominant social circle. Her

sister's husband once remarked as to her style, audacity or wit, "Mary could make a bishop forget his prayers."

Such was the woman Lincoln gathered in his arms some time in 1840 when they spoke pledges to marry and take each other for weal or woe through life. For two years Mary Todd haunted Lincoln, racked him, drove him to despair and philosophy, sent him searching deep into himself as to what manner of man he was. Some time in 1840, probably toward the end of the year, Lincoln promised to marry Miss Todd and she was pledged to take him. It was a betrothal. They were engaged to stand up and take vows at a wedding. She was to be a bride; he was to be a groom. It was explicit.[11]

Abraham Lincoln, as Sandburg so well shows, was a living paradox of the gregarious and the lonely. He was one of the most companionable men in the world; yet when he was alone, he often fell into a dreadful melancholy that at times seems to have bordered on psychological instability. He naturally had a long face, it is pointed out, and he enhanced the solemnity of his physiognomy by a dire and intense preoccupation with personal and world problems. Often he burst into tears to relieve the painfulness, an understandable and welcome relief to all who suffer so. Yet Lincoln, like Sandburg, yearned for distinction. They both courted the public favor in a way which could not be denied. They both had an ambition possessed by few notable figures in all our history, and each brought this ambition to fruition in an overwhelming way.

In *The Prairie Years,* Carl Sandburg shows a Lincoln who was sometimes a clown—devoting whole chapters to anecdotes true and otherwise—and at the same time pictures a profound philosopher who must have sprung full-blown from the brow of one of the Greek pundits. Wise, humane, and attuned to the lowly in life, Lincoln fashioned himself into an image of the downtrodden and a defender of the faithful poor. He made a fetish of trying to raise the lowly into higher places, yet he himself never quite rose above his early level; despite all of his fine philosophy and achievements, Lincoln was always the commoner; and Sandburg himself chose to adopt this position, even after he had become so affluent that he had no material need to do so. How sincere both were, no one can tell. Both were admirable in their positions.

In the book, Lincoln emerges as a constant contradiction, simple and yet wise in the ways of his world and even beyond. He seemed to hear the beat of the distant drum of humanity from an innate standpoint drawn from some mystic inner source that leaves us yet marveling. Why was he so solicitous about his fellow man? Why did he have little compunction about the lowly status of the slaves, then later cry out against the inhumanity of slavery? No doubt, he grew in stature, especially later when he occupied the White House. But Sandburg shows that there was something more than political ambition that motivated Lincoln. Part of it may have been a strange, enigmatical identity with the fate of man as the rail splitter understood it.

Sandburg does not depict Lincoln as unblemished. His admiration shows through but he depicts the warts as well as the smooth skin. Lincoln is described as the self-serving lawyer who would not hesitate to use legal tricks when they were necessary, although he was generally ethical. When he entered politics, he knew it was an opportunistic game and he was willing to play it to the hilt. When he did not choose to answer a question directly, he always seemed to have a good, down-to-earth story with which to counter the questioner, and which usually left him in stitches of laughter or qualms of disgust. Lincoln, like his discerning biographer, was shrewd. Only seldom did the President-to-be waver from his course, although he was repeatedly beaten at the polls until he came almost to the last big contest.

Yet with all his enterprise, Lincoln is portrayed as he really was, at heart a conservative but one who was willing to take liberal chances. He was a believer in the democratic principles of the nineteenth century but adapted himself to the growing consolidation of the country. His heart was with the rural life of the nation; his brain often went beyond this. His was not only a voice crying in the wilderness; it was a clarion call to those within the wasteland to move in the right direction.

To an
Advanced Retreat

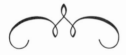

THE PUBLICATION OF *The Prairie Years* in 1926 enabled the Sandburgs to move out of the "windy city" to a place more secluded but equally windy. It was at Harbert, Michigan, a crossroads town about sixty miles east of Chicago across the lake. To get there, the family went through the shabby scenes of South Chicago and through Gary, Indiana, where at night the iron furnaces shot a fiery glow against the sky, and then on through Michigan City. From there, they made their way along Lake Michigan behind a row of massive sand dunes. The Sandburg house was atop one of these huge dunes, about a mile from the post office at Harbert. On its land side, it was a triple story structure, with the top deck open and blessed with the sun on pretty days, swept by the snow in winter. From the front porch the family could see along ten miles of beach dotted by tall pines.

The house at Elmhurst had not been adequate to hold all the research material which the father now needed to have at hand, and he had been moving things around so much to make room for his work that he became irritated at times.

"Just make up your mind," he told his wife with unusual asperity, "whether you would like to live in Illinois or Michigan. I don't want to keep moving this stuff around." After some reflection, she chose Michigan.

The Sandburgs already had a summer home at Harbert and they liked it there. So they enlarged the house and put in storm windows because of the awful wind from the lake, but they found in time to come that the putty had to be replaced many times.

In the large, comfortable attic of the house, Sandburg placed a stove, a cot, some chairs, and several book shelves. Over by a window in the corner, he put his typewriter on an old box which was about the right height for his work. His explanation of this was that if Grant and his generals could conduct their war from cracker boxes, a cracker box was good enough for him. The author called this his Lincoln Room; eventually it was so full of books that it was like a store. Here Sandburg began his great work on the sequel to *The Prairie Years,* the two-volume work which was to be succeeded by four more volumes on Lincoln, titled, *The War Years.* Their Michigan home, the Sandburgs named "Chickaming," in memory of its first Indian settlers.

One visitor noticed that the attic workshop had a bare, unpainted floor, no ornaments except a life mask of Lincoln beside the desk, and on the wall an old top hat from Lincoln's day. Rows of books stood on open shelves made from rough timber around the four sides of the room, while other volumes lay in piles on boxes and tables, bins and cases. From the wood stove in the center of the room, a stovepipe zigzagged up to the roof. Nearby was a worn woodbox with kindling beside it. Just in case, a fire extinguisher reposed near the top of the stairway.

Regarding his Michigan retreat, Sandburg wrote to a friend in 1935 that when he "went away in February, they decided a goat herd, hens, ducks, geese and rabbits were not enough, and took on a horse. When I left in April for ten days they took on two pigs. The horse can live on what the goats reject. And the pigs get by on leavings no others will touch, though like very ancient farmers we cannot begin to get God's intention in curling the tails of the pigs."

Helga Sandburg, the daughter who showed promising literary talent, recalls that their father's jokes did not seem very funny to the family at first. He would sit and tell one of his "long jokes" and they would sit obediently and listen. For example, how Pat and Mike were at a wake when they grew thirsty and decided to carry the corpse across the street to a saloon and prop it between them. There they left the stiff for a few moments at the bar in care of an innocent customer. Sandburg described minutely how the customer tried to become friendly with the corpse, until finally, in anger, he knocked it over. Then came the familiar ending: Pat and Mike rushed over and sobbed out, "You've killed him!" And then the retort, "I had to. The son-of-a-bitch pulled a knife on me!"

Mrs. Sandburg, in lightening Carl's life, reared the children with the impression that their father was a genius with unique faculties. Still under this impression after she had learned to type, Helga began to type his manuscripts, and worked especially hard when they lived on Lake Michigan. When Sandburg was working, his wife would admonish the children to be quiet —sometimes he added to this with his own stentorian voice from upstairs—and when he was sleeping, often at odd times, the same directions were given. He would usually arise in late morning and work until dawn. Although this was important from his standpoint, it hampered considerably the household work where the women were at such chores as cleaning and cooking, trying meanwhile to keep the ordinary noises at a minimum.

Mrs. Sandburg was a fancier of goats, so in some barns behind the rambling house on the dune, she began to raise blooded dairy goats. And this was not just a hobby. She became one of the leading goat raisers of the country and regularly marketed them at state fairs. This brought in needed money too. Alfred Harcourt admitted that he felt Carl could not have written his books without the help of his wife; and the writer himself praised her as being more able than he in several ways, including artistic talents and good business sense. She was ever to be his faithful and understanding helpmeet.

Bernard Hoffman, who was a photographer for *Life Magazine* for some years, called on Sandburg at his Michigan home in order to do a story. The weather was so cold that even the goats were virtually freezing outside, recalls Hoffman. Whereupon, Sandburg called them into the house and about fifteen of the shivering animals crowded into one of the rooms. Sandburg did not stop with this hospitality. He took up his guitar and played for the visiting goats. "They listened politely," said Hoffman.

Like his friend, the late Douglas Southall Freeman, Sandburg made no engagements from April to October each year. The two shared a mutual admiration. Both wrote monumental biographies about great men; both knew the value of time and used it accordingly; both had been newspapermen; and both received acclaim for their prodigious work which, coming later in life, was all the richer and more appreciated.

Sandburg wrote to Freeman on September 27, 1938:

> You don't have to be modest—yet it is inconceivable that you could be anything but humble. . . . Lee was not a Union man—and he was. Lincoln didn't love the South— and he did. The paradoxes are terrific. Much of that war runs into the imponderable and the inarticulate. From the way you delineate Lee as an executive, I would judge you handle men on your staff [Freeman was editor of the *Richmond News Leader*] much as did my old chief, Henry Justin Smith on the *Chicago Daily News*. . . . I am now doing the last chapter of the only American biography equaling yours in length (though not footnoted with the fine fidelity that goes with yours) so perhaps we

should meet as the only two biographers in the Western Hemisphere who have written a million-word portrait.[1]

In his turn, Freeman said, upon presenting Sandburg with the Gold Medal for History and Biography awarded by the Academy of Arts and Letters on May 28, 1952,

> Carl Sandburg embodies something happily identifiable and gratefully cherished in American life. He is more than a poet or musician or biographer or philosopher or historian. He is all of these combined in the second generation of the living Lincoln tradition. His is the happy fortune without a single imitative touch to personify the spirit of the man of whom his greatest prose work was written.[2]

In his commemorative address about Freeman exactly two years later, Sandburg said, "He could have said, had there been time, 'So this is you, Mr. Death. I've been walking and talking for years with men and women well acquainted and familiar with you, Sir. You are no stranger, and since you say so, I'll go with you.'"

Sandburg figuratively chained himself to his cracker box and struggled with the greatest task of his life. He was fifty years old when he began *Abraham Lincoln: The War Years* and he realized that this was to be his biggest challenge; indeed in some ways it was perhaps the biggest that any American writer had faced, this highly ambitious life of the man who had been most dramatic in the history of the United States, a martyr by any definition and a mystic figure who had perplexed the best of the historians and utterly confounded others.

And after all, who was Carl Sandburg to presume to write the definitive biography of Abraham Lincoln? Like him, I am a son of the prairie, Sandburg reasoned, a poor boy who wandered over the land to find himself and his mission in life.

He would do the gigantic task at night, when the world was quiet and the wind sang more musically and when even his devoted women were asleep. Lincoln would come back to him then as he would not in the daytime; the records would read better and shape up better as his own. So he wrote from midnight until dawn as a rule, retiring only when the sun looked over the lake to find virtually all of the inhabitants of the Sandburg home still in slumber. It is not known when Sandburg's thick hair first turned white, probably it did gradually, but the strain of night work, one can readily surmise, did much to hasten this process.

Books were of course only one of the media of information that Sandburg utilized. Journals, letters, diaries, documents, and especially newspapers came under his scowling scrutiny. He had the orderly but sharply inquiring sense of the reporter, and from this viewpoint he sifted out the fact, as he saw it, from fancy, trying to separate the man from the myth. This did not mean that he was not, like any conventional biographer, devoted to his hero. Sandburg stood at the shrine of Lincoln but he saw his faults as well as his virtues and proceeded to put down all that he felt he judiciously could. Big boxes were used to hold the materials and in separate envelopes the different facets of his subject's character were described. When he could literally tear out portions of books, he had done so, and had thrown the rest of the volumes away. These parts went into individual sections of his research material.

The biographer's own background became more and more helpful. Coming appropriately into play was the tow-haired boy from Galesburg, his father an emigrant Swede, who listened as old-timers talked of Lincoln and the Civil War; then the migrant laborer, the short-time soldier in the Spanish-American War, and the embryo newspaper man in Milwaukee and Chicago who learned the hard way about business, labor, and the inside workings of politics. His innate sympathy for the working man, the tender spot always in his heart for the underdog—these two entered into his interpretation of the material he had gathered. He felt the naked isolation of the Midwestern hinterland and also projected the powerful pulsation of its cities. In his description of Lincoln there ran a poetic strain, engendered not only by his native background but by acquaintance, either personally or by correspondence, with such figures as Vachel Lindsay and Edgar Lee Masters; Ben Hecht, whose desk was near his at the *Chicago Daily News;* William Allen White, the small-town editor of Emporia, Kansas, who also thought in a universal manner; Governor Henry Horner of Illinois; and Oliver R. Barrett of Chicago, whose collection on Lincoln proved to be a mighty adjunct to Sandburg's own collections.

Like Douglas Freeman, who believed that the first requisite of a successful biography was "choosing a large subject," Sandburg had now settled on something which was already large in proportions before he even started on it. The job of making the huge project come alive was up to him and he was fortunate in having chosen, unlike Lindsay and Masters, a living subject of universal and eternal appeal. The style of the material he found doubtless influenced him, made him more careful in his own writing, and inspired him with its somber quality. From all of the bits and pieces, he fashioned his own style, a lucid, simple, poetic approach. At times it even seems staccato. But so were the events. At times, the style appears to be a patchwork; but so was much of the life of Lincoln. As the writing progressed, Carl Sandburg became, on paper, more and more Abraham Lincoln.

The monumental task was truly devastating; no one could stand the pace of it for twelve months a year. Sandburg, knowing that he did not have to hurry, did not do so. He was already successful as a writer and felt that his publisher would not let him starve, come what may. So he added to the diversity of his program by taking off a few months each year for a routine he loved, as did those who were more and more numerously becoming a part of it. He now owned six guitars, none of which he could play very well, but he periodically grabbed up one of these and took to the road again. The money helped too; he received good fees. And in addition to relief from the grueling writing, these tours gave him an opportunity to visit local libraries and private collections containing Lincolniana. To lend variety to his platform programs, Sandburg alternated his singing with reading of his poems. By the dexterous use of his mellow voice and his smart showmanship, he made the two parts of his performance blend so well that many of his audience hardly seemed to realize they were listening to literary creations. Sometimes his reading of poetry sounded almost as musical as his singing. He included the ditties and ballads that he had already collected in his *American Songbag*, which was published in 1927.

Thus Carl Sandburg became known to new thousands because of his popular and colorful performances. He had a pleasant baritone voice and seemed to sense quite correctly the mood of his audiences with whom he quickly developed a dreamy kind of rapport. His haunting jigs and songs of loneliness appealed to the common folks just as they always do, and to most folks considered uncommon. His unique use of words, giving emphasis to syllables where such had never been done before, his lilting delivery coupled with a wide grin under his tumbling hair led numerous admirers to believe that this was all that Sandburg was capable of doing—that is until they read his works.

These traveling intervals also rested Sandburg's eyes. Straining over the various kinds of materials in his attic, some of them dimly written or printed, would have placed a burden on anyone's vision and was especially fatiguing for a fifty-year-old man who had already used his eyes for reading and writing more than the average person does in a lifetime. In addition to writing his manuscript, he had to carry on an extensive correspondence in order to bolster, supplement, and correct his research. This rigid requirement led to a kind of antipathy at times to answering mail and telegrams. Once in the presence of this writer, Sandburg received a telegram asking why he had not replied to a letter sent some time before. Squeezing the telegram in his big hand, he grinned impishly and commented, "Hell, I didn't ask him to write the damned letter in the first place!"

Sitting on a stool at the folk-music concerts and looking as lonesome as some of the ballads he sang, Sandburg intoned often one of his favorites:

WANDERIN'

My daddy is an engineer,
My brother drives a hack,
My sister takes in washin'
An' the baby balls the jack,
An' it looks like I'm never gonna cease my wanderin'.
I been a-wanderin'
Early and late,
New York City
To the Golden Gate,
An it looks like
I'm never gonna cease my wanderin'.
Been a-workin' in the army,
Workin' on a farm,
All I got to show for it
Is the muscle in my arm,
An' it looks like
I'm never gonna cease my wanderin'.[3]

The recent revival of folk music among young people of the United States and elsewhere was spurred by Carl Sandburg more than is generally realized. He was a folk minstrel who brought to life the haunting beauty of the songs of the people. Not only did he collect and get published many songs which had long lain dormant except perhaps in the more or less private renditions of the people, but he himself performed them to such extent that more and more Negro songs and songs of laborers and convicts, plains and mountains were brought to the attention of music publishers and radio and television media. Sandburg appeared not only before staid audiences and college groups but also at hootenannies and such.

According to Carl Haverlin, ex-president of Broadcast Music, Inc., and also a collector of Lincolniana:

It has long been recognized that Sandburg is the father of the current interest in American folk music. The upsurge started with the appearance of his great *Songbag* in 1927 and his recitals have continued to stimulate composers, publishers and singers alike. . . .

I did not know him while he was writing *The Prairie Years* or *The War Years,* but those who did say he worked then as intensely as he did later on his *New American Songbag*—tirelessly and with a singleness of purpose a little terrifying to the undedicated; as though the words he [wrote] were a daily service at the altar of some personal deity. Though we sometimes shared my office, most of the time he spent with us he worked alone in a big room, at a long table covered with notes and manuscripts and photostats, with a third of a cigar clutched firmly in his teeth, a shawl around his throat, a cap on the back of his head, a pencil stub dwarfed in his strong fingers. Pondering over an old scrap of paper covered with his unique system of musical notations, he would lean back with his eyes closed to hear it played. We learned to wait before knocking at his door if we heard his guitar being touched hesitantly as he sought for a missing phrase, or strongly as his amazing memory brought the song swirling back up from the time of its first hearing. Sometimes he would sit in front of a microphone and the boys would tape some songs to be transcribed later. . . . And all the time all of us felt good because here in our offices [in New York] for a little while was a man who had heard America sing.[4]

Sandburg himself said in his introduction to *The American Songbag:*

A wide human procession marches through these pages. The rich and the poor; robbers, murderers, hangmen; fathers and wild boys; mothers with soft words for their babies; workmen on railroads, steamboats, ships; wanderers and lovers of homes, tell what life has done to them.

> Love and hate in many patterns and designs, heart cries
> of high and low pitch, are in these verses and tunes. . . .
> With more people than ever taking to folk songs, some
> believe these songs have a relation to faith in the people,
> that there is involved an instinct or feeling related to the
> importance of songs arising out of the people.[5]

Bing Crosby echoed this idea in a handwritten foreword to the 1950 edition of the book: "American music lovers owe Carl Sandburg a great debt for the ceaseless research which has rediscovered so much authentic American music for their enjoyment. This here songbag is just loaded with old goodies."

For example, in connection with the song, "Old Abe Lincoln Came Out of the Wilderness," Sandburg comments: "Torchlight processions of Republicans sang this in the summer and fall months of 1860. The young Wide Awakes burbled it as the kerosene dripped on their blue oilcloth capes. Quartets and octettes jubilated with it in packed, smoky halls where audiences waited for speakers of the evening. In Springfield, Illinois, [Lincoln] heard his two boys, Tad and Willie, sing it at him."

Men of note in America learned early to appreciate the musical and melodic in Sandburg. From Emporia, Kansas, William Allen White, the small town but eminent editor, wrote to a New York man, "The Carl Sandburg entertainment is more than a lecture. It is a concert, grand opera, philosophic pabulum and dramatic entertainment all in one. I have never enjoyed an evening's entertainment more. I can recommend it to the highbrow or the lowbrow, if any, without stint, let or hindrance."

And Robert Frost bowed to at least one Sandburg superiority. He wrote the guitarist:

> I shall never be able to resist the flattery of being treated
> as if I knew anything about music and could sing chan-
> teys. Neither will I that of being treated as if I had been
> an athlete and could still play tennis. Either form simply
> strikes me dumb with rapture and caution. You can see
> the need of caution. If I said much, I might give myself

away; if I tried to sing at all, I might lose the cheese out of my mouth the way I did when I was a crow in the time of Aesop. You may remember. You were possibly there in the capacity of the fox. When the fox finally said, "Hence with denial vain and coy excuse." [7]

Musicians knew that Sandburg was not a good guitar player; in fact, he concentrated on two or three chords. Marge Braye told a story of when she and a group were at a dinner at Alicia Patterson's. Carl Sandburg was near the head of the table and John Steinbeck was sitting near Miss Braye. After a while, Sandburg got out his guitar and began to play. It seems that Steinbeck always wanted to play the guitar but never had learned. He sat there looking at Sandburg and after a little while said, "Carl has hair. He plays the guitar. He has a wonderful voice. He writes wonderful books. I hate him!"

In the midst of the New Deal days, Sandburg made no excuse for his country. He felt it needed none, even in such throes. Appearing in Washington, D. C., as a troubadour, he reported in 1936 that the outlook was fine for a good pawpaw crop in Michigan and that his goat, Gladys, had three kids. "Mr. Sandburg," wrote the columnist, Lemuel F. Parton,

> is America's favorite minstrel, gleaning songs from levees, hobo jungles, cotton patches, work camps, ranches, mines, cities and deserts; he is more hopeful about everything than worried statesmen and journalists who work only in prose. . . . He's worried about one thing, though. Everywhere he goes, toting his big guitar and singing his songs, interviewers ask him what he considers important in these days of uncertainty, and when he tells them, he can't get his story into print. They skip it and print his views on literature and art. What he wants the world to know is that at an Indiana crossroads, he has discovered a young Negro ball-player who is pitching no-hit games left-handed and underhanded. He is afraid that indiffer-

ence to this story indicates some kind of decadence in journalism.[8]

Asked to report on the state of the nation as he attuned his guitar to its pulse beat, Sandburg remarked:

> Working through this Lincoln stuff all these years has made me feel better about this country. I don't think we're going to crack up. In my opinion, Sinclair Lewis was all wrong in that book, "It Can't Happen Here." That's a defeatist attitude which I think is nothing short of poisonous. There's a whole lot going on in America that the intelligentsia don't know anything about. You'll begin to catch it if you'll just take twenty or thirty years off and peek around the country and do a lot of listening. We pick up a word like Fascism, for instance, too carelessly. . . . It's hard to put into words without making it sound like whistling in a graveyard, but what I mean is that, when you know a few thousand real American songs, you begin to understand that there is something unique and mysterious in this country that's going to make it come through all right.[9]

Yet Lewis and Sandburg had much admiration for each other. The latter said of Lewis, "This great big husky fellow—he's got something stirring inside him; George Horace Lorimer wanted him to be one of his trained seals, like Irwin Cobb, but he kicked over the traces; I wouldn't be surprised if, in ten years or so, he gathered up all that is in him, Main Street and all, and came out with something big." [10]

In such gatherings, Sandburg sang tunes like "Casey Jones," "Frankie and Johnnie," "Whiskey Is the Life of Man," "Blow the Man Down," and "Noah's Dove." Many of his songs he took down from the singing of odd characters from coast to coast. Professor John Lomax of the University of Texas gave Sandburg a number of songs he had discovered. These folk songs originated among men who chanted them in lumber camps, on timber lands, plantations, and cattle ranches, in railroad yards, and among cowboys and hoboes all over the country. One of these was about the sinking of the *Titanic,* sent to Sandburg by an inmate of the penitentiary in Atlanta, Georgia. Once when Sandburg was visiting his brother-in-law, Edward Steichen, the photographer, in New York City, he got to know a couple who stayed in the same house. It happened that they were from Oklahoma and had retained a number of folk songs chanted by the earliest settlers there who had crossed the Indian lands in covered wagons. In Nebraska, Sandburg came upon an old Civil War song about "the Linkun gunboats," and in Montana he discovered a woman who had once lived in the Kentucky mountains and who recalled for him some ditties she had learned there as a girl.

While visiting in New York on another occasion, Sandburg was asked to pose for a picture in the lobby of the Royalton Hotel, a quaint hostelry on East 44th Street where he liked to stay. Having revealed that he had recently had a guitar lesson from the famous musician, Andrés Segovia, the folk singer was asked to hold a guitar while he was being photographed. He replied that he had none with him and suggested that he and the photographer go to some nearby pawnshop and get one. They did. It was a battered and worn old instrument from the window of the shop, and when he learned who was holding it, the pawnbroker said to Sandburg, "I won't even charge you the $1 rental fee."

In reviewing *The New American Songbag,* Carl Carmer said about the author, "Because he himself has within him the whimsey and the humor, the horse sense and the moonshine that have characterized our national fancy since its inception, his choices from the storehouse of American folk materials are amazingly revealing, ever unerring."

As for his famous pupil, Segovia commented,

> I admire Carl Sandburg for the many rays of his talent. As a historian, he is firm and profound like the roots of a sequoia. As a poet, he is light and iridescent as a cloud.

His soul is always humming the songs of the soil. Sometimes they overflow and then he tunes his voice to the voice of the guitar—but his fingers labor heavily over the strings and he asked for my help in disciplining them. . . . To play the guitar as he aspires will devour his three-fold energy as a historian, a poet and a singer. One cause of Schopenhauer's pessimism was the fact that he failed to learn the guitar. I am certain that Carl Sandburg will not fall into the same sad philosophy. The heart of this great poet constantly bubbles forth a generous joy of life —with or without the guitar.[11]

Another noted guitarist, Sophocles Papas of Washington, D.C., was fond of Sandburg and felt an affinity for his music. Papas felt that Sandburg's "conversation was studded with humor," and he recalled one joke which Carl delighted in telling over and over again: "After the deluge, Noah opened the gates of the Ark. As the pairs of animals made their exit, he blessed them with 'Go forth and multiply.' Presently two snakes came along and as Noah gave his blessing, they hissed at him. When Noah asked why, they replied, 'We are adders.' "

On a balmy night years later Sandburg appeared at Carnegie Hall to narrate Aaron Copland's composition, *A Lincoln Portrait*, the orchestra being conducted by André Kostelanetz. The poet-biographer had just had a birthday and was asked by newsman Joseph Wershba what advice he had for people. "Just because I've gone past eighty five," was the reply, "I don't go around giving people advice on how to live long." His wife, Lilian, who had accompanied him—an unusual occurrence for he ordinarily traveled alone—added that when he was one hundred ten, he then might be entitled to pass along some advice. By this time, however, Carl was ready with some.

"My advice," he pronounced, "reduces itself to this: watch out about stumbling into a coal hole. And it's always safer to walk upstairs than down."

The rehearsal for the concert had proved to be more than that.

As Sandburg walked out on to the stage with a big grin, all of the orchestra arose and applauded him. Lilian remarked that this had happened to him all over the country. He tried out the microphone and Teleprompter and nodded to Kostelanetz. Soon the soaring music of the Copland *Portrait* swept up, to be followed by the voice of Sandburg speaking Lincoln's lines in his address to Congress in 1862: "Fellow citizens, we cannot escape history. The fiery trials through which we pass will light us down in honor or dishonor to the latest generation." Again there was applause.

Irving Kolodin wrote about him in the *Saturday Review:*

> Sandburg is the least affected, the most eloquent, the closest in identity with the martyred President and his thoughts. Seated though he was, and protected by a robe across his knees from chill of the air-conditioning, Sandburg nevertheless made a towering presence at least equal to the six-feet-four attributed to Lincoln in the text. He was greeted by a standing applauding audience in tribute to past accomplishments; the equivalent, in greater numbers and louder volume, after his performance was a testimonial to an achievement equally impressive on its own.[21]

Afterward at a nearby table, Lilian told him, "You were good, buddy, but tomorrow night I want you to wear your lower incisors so that your voice will be clear as a bell." He protested that he could not find them. "I have them right here in my pocket," she replied.

Backstage, this writer joined the principal performer and reminded him that we had invited him for a little get-together that evening. He remembered and was about to go when a young man approached him and spoke earnestly. Sandburg must have liked the fellow, for I heard him say, "You stick around and we'll open up a keg of nails."

Which must have been some kind of a verbal record for Carnegie Hall.

He joined a small group of us and we went to the Park Avenue home of Mrs. O. O. McIntyre, widow of the late New York columnist. It was a magnificent sixteen-room apartment and one was reminded of the $150,000 a year McIntyre made when income taxes were low. As she was a Christian Scientist, no liquor was served, but instead, some of the most delicious ice cream and cake her guests had ever tasted.

I had "framed up" with Frank Warner, the folk singer, friend of Sandburg, and Y.M.C.A. executive, to bring along his banjo and try to get Sandburg to play it, although he had said he was through with playing stringed instruments.

So, as Carl sat comfortably in a lounge, Frank went over to him and in seeming innocence showed him the banjo. Sandburg took it, fondled it affectionately and slowly began to pluck its strings, then to strum it and this started him humming. Soon Sandburg was playing and singing and his small audience was enthralled. Frank Warner looked at me and winked. "Mission accomplished," he said.

Warner had first met Sandburg when the former had sung at an author's luncheon in New York just after the publication of *The War Years.* He had with him a new banjo of wood, made by a North Carolina mountain friend, and Sandburg became intrigued by it and autographed it. Later, Warner acquired some 150 additional signatures, mostly from celebrities, but he always remembered gratefully the one who first inscribed his name. Warner has a good but not sensational voice, as Sandburg wryly noted when he told him, "It is easy to see your voice has not been ruined by a conservatory." The Warners and Carl had occasionally visited at their apartment in Greenwich Village, which was on the ground floor of an old brownstone house where there were young children, a fire in the fireplace, a cat, a pot of coffee always ready, and a shared interest in people that seemed to mean for Carl an escape from the crowds and adulation that surrounded him elsewhere. 'This isn't New York City,' he often used to say when he was there. "At first we considered his visits an honor," they said, "but soon these became just a joy. We often recall with amusement and pleasure the benediction with which he frequently left us after a great evening (even though we know he said it to many other people of whom he was fond, including Marilyn Monroe): 'Anne and Frank Warner are not what is wrong with this country.' "

The Warners have recalled proudly that Sandburg read to them the following fitting lines from his novel, *Remembrance Rock:*

> When we say a patriot is one who loves his country, what kind of love do we mean? A love we can throw on a scale and see how much it weighs: a love we can take apart and see how it ticks? A love where with a yardstick we record how long, high, wide it is? Or is a patriot's love of country a thing indivisible, a quality, a human shade and breath, beyond all reckoning and measurement? These are questions. They are old as the time of man. And the answers to them we know in part. For we know when a nation goes down and never comes back, when a society or a civilization perishes, one condition may always be found. They forgot where they came from. They lost sight of what brought them along. The hard beginnings were forgotten and the struggles farther along. They became satisfied with themselves. Unity and common understanding there had been, enough to overcome rot and dissolution, enough to break through their obstacles. But the mockers came. And the deniers were heard. And vision and hope faded. And the custom of greeting became "What's the use?" And men whose forefathers would go anywhere, holding nothing impossible in the genius of man, joined the mockers and deniers. They forgot where they came from. They lost sight of what had brought them along.

In the songs of Sandburg was an interpretation of American history. He felt in the folk songs the musical pulse of the American frontier as it slowly extended its inevitable way from the east to the west of our continent. To him, the songs he sang and collected were part of this history, a folk poetry told in music which reached the hearts of even the simplest people. In this music was the struggle of the American Revolution, the saga of the Civil War, the sadness and the joy of the birth and development of a new nation. And just as the English ballads had served as a rhythmic pattern for early local life, so did the American folk songs reach out across our plains and mountains as they became more populated. Around the campfires and cabins, the banjo and guitar rang out, accompanied by the intoning of the pioneers, then of their descendants; and the voice of Carl Sandburg repeated this music on the stage as his white, bushy-haired head bent over his "lonesome gittar."

Nor was it only the simple people who had loved these songs. Abraham Lincoln liked them, Theodore Roosevelt gave encouragement to their preservation, and Woodrow Wilson sang them. The fine folk-music collection of the Library of Congress in Washington attests today the official reverence which has come to this important medium of our national expression. In the 1920s, Sandburg had begun collecting such music, and as he traveled around the country, he set down in a kind of musical shorthand the songs he heard. So when his *American Songbag* was published, it contained the words and music of some 300 ballads, along with his own personal explanation of them. In the volume, as its author says, are dramas and portraits that express the diversity of the United States: love tales told in song, colonial ditties, pioneer memories, black-face minstrel melodies, Mexican border songs, ballads from the southern mountains, Great Lakes songs, and mighty spirituals. Truly, a great human procession marches through these pages.

Yet the only singing lessons Sandburg ever had were a few from a choir singer in Galesburg. A far cry indeed from the eventual achievement of the man whom Allan Nevins termed "the nearest approach to the minnesinger America has ever produced."

The War Years

SANDBURG'S WORK ON *The War Years* went on apace. He turned in chapters to Alfred Harcourt as they were completed and on the basis of this work, the magazine *Redbook* contracted to publish portions of the book in eight of its issues. Four appeared in 1936, one each in 1937 and 1938, and the final two sections in March and May of 1939. Harcourt, Brace was excited about the forthcoming book. The publisher even went so far as to imprint on all its metered mail the arresting words, "The War Years Are Coming"; this worked effectively until complaints began to arrive, pointing out that the situation in Europe in the late 1930s made the message all too poignant. The slogan was discontinued but the outbreak of war in Europe made it seem prophetic.

Charles A. "Cap" Pearce, later the noted editor-partner in the publishing firm of Duell, Sloan and Pearce, was then managing editor of Harcourt, Brace. He recalls that Sandburg came to New York occasionally and was under a great strain while writing *The War Years*. Sandburg would drop around to the office and Pearce would send out and get a pint of liquor which diverted the biographer and relaxed him.

"Sandburg always felt for the essence of things," relates Pearce. "He tried to evoke the ghost of Lincoln, who, like him, was a melancholy dreamer of the Midwest, which meant that they believed in no El Dorados but just hard work. So Sandburg drank hard liquor, smoked too many stogies, and did not take very good care of his health in those days."

Once Pearce invited Sandburg out to his home in Tarrytown, New York. The guest had a cold, so he tried to cure it by smoking and drinking.

"He reveled in the local scene of Washington Irving," Pearce said, "and he also was grimly amused by the fact that in the local cemetery, Andrew Carnegie and Samuel Gompers are buried near each other. Sandburg was very interested in the remains of the redoubt on the Hudson River there, from which the American patriots had shelled British ships during the Revolution. He enjoyed such history more than the local residents. But now and then, Mrs. Pearce had to open the windows of our house to let out his cigar smoke."

On April 6, 1937, Sandburg received a letter from President Franklin D. Roosevelt to whom he evidently had written. FDR thanked him for his letter, invited him to the White House, and said that he had long wanted to talk to him about Lincoln and other things. "You have reconstructed so well the picture of the executive duties and life in Lincoln's day that perhaps you will be interested in seeing at least the same relative problems at first-hand in these days," the Chief Executive added.

Three years later, he wrote Sandburg thanking him for making a radio broadcast in behalf of his candidacy. "You are such an understanding soul," FDR said, "and can make allowances with such fairness for the weaknesses and frailties of human nature that you are one of the few people who can truly understand the perplexities, the complications, the failures and the successes of what goes on in Washington."

On September 7, Sandburg wrote to Lloyd Lewis regarding the Lincoln project, "A writer I consider great, picturesque, vital and versatile, should be detached from doing in history and biography what cannot be so well done by others while he fills a job that it would be no great loss if someone else did. . . ."

As publication date of *The War Years* approached, Sandburg came to New York for a while to be near the scene of operations. He worked with the editors in selecting and arranging the illustrations for the ponderous work, and during part of the summer and fall of 1939 lived in the Brooklyn house of the copyeditor, where he read the galleys and page proofs. Each day a batch of these were sent to the publisher in Manhattan, thence to the printer in New Jersey. Copies of the book, as soon as they came off the press, were wrapped in gold paper and sent to reviewers along with relevant preliminary information. Now the "boy's life, about 400 pages" had grown, counting *The Prairie Years* and *The War Years,* into six bulky volumes of about 650 pages each.

Said Sandburg to Harcourt: "This has grown into a scroll, a chronicle. There's one thing we can say for it: it is probably the only book ever written by a man whose father couldn't write his name, about a man whose mother couldn't write hers."

Alfred Harcourt at once ordered 15,000 sets printed. Sandburg happened to be in the office and learned of this. "Fifteen thousand sets?" he exclaimed to the publisher in disbelief. "You mean sixty thousand books?"

That is what Harcourt did mean. In fact, when he saw the advance orders, he directed that an additional 14,000 sets be printed for Christmas and Lincoln's birthday. All of the 29,000 sets of *The War Years,* four volumes each, sold out within a few months at twenty dollars a set. Harcourt was presented with a gold-paper crown by his staff "in recognition of the crowning point of his publishing career." In appreciation of the excellent job the printers had done, Sandburg himself made a visit to their Rahway, New Jersey, plant and gave the personnel samples of his songs and readings "in token and appreciation of their fellowship, craftsmanship, anxiety and zeal in connection with the making of *The War Years* from a manuscript of 3,400 typewritten pages into the finished book of four boxed volumes that has had from everywhere high praise as to typography, presswork, illustrations, binding." Sandburg referred in addition to "the ancient and natural partnership that exists between authors and printers, how neither can effectively get along without the other."

The theme of his *Lincoln* might be summarized in his earlier lines from *The People, Yes:*

> He was a mystery in smoke and flags
> saying yes to the smoke, yes to the flags,
> yes to the paradoxes of democracy,
> yes to the hopes of government
> of the people, by its people, for the people.[1]

With the completion of this monumental work, Carl Sandburg gained a permanent place in American historical biography. So closely did he live with Lincoln in the years of hard and continual writing, that he achieved a tapestry of detail in some ways unparalleled. Here was not only the story of a great man but the account of a free people in a new democracy, struggling to remain free. In so embodying the man in a lasting, verbal framework, Sandburg became—as he was termed when he received a Civil War Round Table award from the hands of this writer—"the Lincoln of our literature."

For America viewed Sandburg as an integral part of this new land and its human occupants. As Lincoln was in a special sense a rare representative of his age in America, so was Sandburg a symbol of the twentieth century in its more traditional form. Both Lincoln and Sandburg were products of early hardships and both spoke to the people in the people's voice. There was hardness, there was earthiness, and there was pathos in these voices; but both were heard and their meaning was unmistakable. Both men grew through age and experience to heights of greatness at the apexes of their lives. Sandburg faced a changing America a hundred years after Lincoln, yet it was still emerging as the most important nation on earth—waiting to be expressed. Although both Lincoln and Sandburg were extremely American, the latter remained so, while Lincoln, through his martyrdom, became a universal symbol. But both men have become symbols of democracy and this is perhaps their greatest distinction.

Just how well Sandburg understood Lincoln is impossible to state. How well can anyone appraise Lincoln's record as a country lawyer, crisscrossing the prairies in pursuit of his practice; his shrewd understanding of human nature as evinced by his homely anecdotes and speeches; his highly unsuccessful course as a political candidate in his earlier career; his record as state legislator and Congressman; and his transformation into a sort of genius when he became President and Commander of the Armed Forces of the United States during its most excruciating war? Carl Sandburg could not relive these phases of Lincoln's life. But he has come closer to it than anyone else.

As James G. Randall said,

> One must put together the statements of men all over America to have even the beginning of an appraisal of what Sandburg means in poetry, in the journalism of reporting, in the journalism of the column, in history, in biography, and in the vibrant world of American song. There occasionally arises among us one who embodies the fulfillment of American democracy, while at the same time he is the spokesman of democracy. Such a man was Lincoln, and such a man was Sandburg. In his life and achievement he stands as the proof, the very certificate of democracy.[2]

Panegyrics from reviewers included the eloquent one from Robert E. Sherwood, himself a magnificent dramatic writer about Lincoln:

In *The War Years*, Sandburg sticks to the documentary evidence, gathered from a fabulous number of sources. He indulges in one superb lyrical outburst at the conclusion of the chapter in which is described the dedication of the cemetery at Gettysburg; and in the last volume, after John Wilkes Booth has fired the one bullet in his brass derringer pistol, Mr. Sandburg writes with the poetic passion and the somber eloquence of the great masters of tragedy.[3]

Lloyd Lewis writing in the *New York Herald-Tribune Books* said:

There has probably never been such a summoning of witnesses before in American literature or law, no such marshaling of incident, such sifting of rumor, such collecting of evidence, eye-witness and hearsay, as the author here produces. In the thirty-odd years across which he has been collecting Lincolniana, Sandburg has gone everywhere that he heard a Lincoln letter or an observation on the man might be stored. And his product is, like his poems, a singularly eloquent use of contemporary anecdote and language. What people did about Lincoln, what they saw him do, what they heard he said and did—it is all here, as detailed as Dostoievsky, as American as Mark Twain.[4]

Allan Nevins, in customary generous evaluation, commented that *The War Years* was "a gargantuan work of four stout volumes and two thousand five hundred pages which appeared in 1939, thirteen years [after] the publication of his two-volume study of the prairie rail-splitter, storekeeper, lawyer, Congressman, debater and Presidential candidate." Nevins told of the vague reports which had come to the world of history about the task in progress at Harbert, Michigan:

of the attic workroom, the shelves of books, the growing hillocks of notes and excerpts, the copyists tap, tapping downstairs, the biographer himself ceaselessly toiling through long spring and summer days at his cracker-box-

typewriter. Everyone who knew of Sandburg's rich, if unconventional equipment for his task—his poetic insights,
his mastery of human nature, his power of selecting the
vital human details from a mass of arid facts, his command
of phrase and imagery, and above all his feeling for the
mingled humor, pathos, shoddiness and grandeur of democracy—expected a remarkable work. To history he
brought just the faculty that the *London Spectator* had
detected in Lincoln himself, "a mind at once singularly
representative and singularly personal." No one, however,
was prepared for the particular kind of masterwork that he
laid before the country.[5]

Here was a book, according to this scholar, that was beautiful
in its simplicity, yet in its sweeping but detailed panorama was
unlike any other biography or history in the language. Its hero
was a folk hero and its story a folk war. This work created a convincing picture both of the Lincoln who belonged to the people
and of the people who belonged to Lincoln. In it, while Lincoln
himself holds the center of the crowded stage, Sandburg, like
Nevins, filled in pages about other interesting people and things
of the times.

When Sandburg was not focusing on Lincoln, he discussed the
strutting but well-meaning General Winfield Scott; John Pope
who could not make good all of his boasts; the colorful and enigmatic John C. Fremont; the obstreperous and bothersome Ben
Butler; the eccentric but able Stanton; the ambitious but generally judicious Salmon P. Chase; the obdurate and egotistical
Charles Sumner; a great soldier but vulnerable political leader,
Ulysses Simpson Grant; the effective but cruelly relentless, William Tecumseh Sherman; the courageous David Glasgow Far-
ragut; the cautious but still admired George Brinton McClellan;
the tardy but generally competent George Gordon Meade; the
sharply observing reporter and author, Noah Brooks of the *Sacra-
mento Union*. Or when he was not concentrating on some other
prominent figure, his subject was bound to be the plain people

who milled around the President, for they were the ones both the martyred leader and his recent biographer loved best.

Nevins liked the book when it first appeared. Twelve years later, he read it again and still liked it. He pointed out that at first there were many critics who were so awed by the mass of detail in the million and a half words that they felt there was a lack of system in the work. "We can now see," observed Nevins in retrospect,

> that a vigorous selective talent had been exercised upon the multitudinous facts, anecdotes, conversations, reports, documents and other materials; that those chosen were relevant to a few central ideas. As Sandburg put it, "the teller does the best he can and picks out what to him is plain, moving and important. We can also see that while seemingly unsystematic, the tremendous narrative really has a careful underlying plan. It is a presentation of all that touched Lincoln immediately or remotely in 1861–1865, set down chiefly as he saw or heard of it, and so arranged as to depict these years with the greatest possible verisimilitude.[6]

The decade of the thirties was timely for Sandberg's project. Our world was seeing a resurgence of interest in Lincoln and the Civil War. Sandburg knew this. As an old newspaperman, he was conscience of timing, of deadlines, of getting out the story at the proper time for people to read it. Most of the information for a great new version of Lincoln had been assembled. Ida Tarbell, who had given us such a vivid if one-sided account of the Standard Oil Company, had turned her vast energy to Abraham Lincoln and had come up with much valuable material on every facet of his complex nature. For four decades a flow of studies about the fascinating but elusive character had been produced: the *Diary of Gideon Welles,* the *Letters of John Hay,* the *Diary of Orville H. Browning* as well as that of *Edward Bates,* the *Letters* collected by *Gilbert A. Tracy* and *Paul M. Angle,* and many other relevant contributions. So the time for Sandburg's book was ripe.

Carl Sandburg at the age of 38. (Courtesy of the New York Public Library.)

Sandburg in a pensive mood.

Carl Sandburg and his wife not long after their wedding.

Carl Sandburg relaxing with his beloved wife Lilian, at their home, Connemara, at Flat Rock, North Carolina. (Photograph by Charles Clark courtesy of the Travel and Promotion Division, Department of Conservation and Development, Raleigh, North Carolina.)

Amid discerning and appreciative souls at Connemara. (Photograph by Dan McCoy courtesy of Black Star.)

Carl Sandburg, Edward M. Seay, and Beatrice Lilly in New York City.

In a moment of musical meditation. (Photograph by Editta Sherman.)

Carl Sandburg with his wife and daughters, Helga, Margaret, and Janet, near their home on Lake Michigan in 1930.

"The most distinctive qualities of the Sandburg work," said Nevins, "are three":

> first, its pictorial vividness, a product of his graphic style, love of concrete detail, and ability to recreate scenes imaginatively in a few sentences; second, its human quality—its feeling for men and women, great and small, with all their frailties and heroisms; and third, the cumulative force of its detail in building up, step by step, an impression of the crowded, discordant times, with problems rising in endless welter—and, by the same means, an impression of Lincoln learning to endure the storm, patiently developing his powers, and finally mastering all the adverse forces. These are the qualities of a great historian who is also a finished artist.[7]

Such qualities are revealed in the mosaic of details gathered from long, patient search, pieced together into an awesomely impressive whole. From this, readers gain the correct impression of a difficult, chaotic era, the one in which Lincoln lived, and hardly less, Sandburg's too. As Abraham Lincoln struggled against his environment and his destiny, so did Carl Sandburg strive to master the wealth of material left in the record. It was as if Sandburg was Lincoln again come to life, reproducing in sweat and toil the ordeal of the sixteenth President. Yet the book is not characterized by hero-worship, for it often shows Lincoln's lack of organization, errors of judgment, his indecisiveness, and especially his fits of melancholy which at times appear to be almost pathological. At the same time, the excruciating struggles which Lincoln had to make against great odds are depicted so vividly that due credit is thus given him for his valiant endeavors.

As in classical tragedy, Abraham Lincoln is shown caught up in a dire dilemma. His was the lot to lead a peaceful nation in an internecine warfare that threatened to destroy it and for which it was unprepared. In order to achieve victory, Lincoln had to make himself a kind of dictator. Sandburg shows that the President did not desire to be a tyrant but he knew that at times he must exercise almost tyrannical powers and at other times stoop to low politics to attain his ends. Some of the vital decisions during the war required the talents of a genius, but Lincoln felt himself often to be wholly inadequate. Yet out of the chaos and confusion, out of the indecision and disloyalties, the wartime leader fashioned a great military machine which was finally turned over to men who could run it successfully.

Right in Washington itself, Lincoln faced meddling groups of rival army and government men who tried to thwart him at every turn. Representatives of the states flocked to the capital and harried him in their efforts to gain local advantages and curry favors. Greedy and ambitious politicians egged on by lobbyists were worrisome and obnoxious. Even in his own cabinet, Lincoln found jealousy and disloyalty as well as downright opposition and attempted sabotage of some of his war efforts. When Congress fell under the leadership of the radicals, they turned on the President with ferocious hostility until he hardly knew whom to trust. Some of them so ridiculed and vilified Lincoln that he swayed under their assaults, often breaking into tears. Abolitionists criticized him for not freeing the slaves sooner; Copperheads criticized him for leaning too far in the other direction. Here was a leader caught in a mighty maelstrom of opposition. Here was a country lawyer facing what turned out to be not only a national crisis but one with world-wide dimensions as well. It would now appear that the more historians delve into the course of the Civil War, the more they relate its conduct and outcome to the part which Lincoln himself played. He was in a sense personally behind the military moves of the North, behind the political trends, and behind the freeing of the slaves in the midst of the conflict.

This was "Mr. Lincoln's War" in so many ways that, when doing his life, Sandburg found himself becoming a military historian as well as biographer. However, the author has wisely withheld judgment on military strategy and tactics, confining himself mainly to the personal part that Lincoln played, his almost mystic guidance of the principal currents when they seemed to falter in their flow, and the effects which the war and its people had upon

Lincoln himself. His story turned out to be an Olympian drama unsurpassed in history. This first modern war of movement made such an impact upon the military mind that it is still being studied in the academies of the world in their training of officers. A lesser man than Lincoln would have become embittered at the South instead of sadly impatient; and a lesser biographer than Sandburg might well have stressed the victory of the Union generals at the expense of the Southern leaders. But Sandburg gave due credit to Lee and Jackson just as to Grant and Sherman and their associates. In this he seems to have some of Lincoln's magnanimity. The President is shown to be, in at least several respects, "for the ages" as much as he was for his time.

Standing out on the broad verbal canvas is the pathos of Lincoln. But alongside of it is painted the stubborn refusal to break down. In the Congressional elections of 1862, for example, Lincoln was faced with a persuasive group of defeatists led by the eccentric Horace Greeley, a movement that would have forced backward a weaker man. In his Cabinet there were antagonisms worse than those between Hamilton and Jefferson, some of which Lincoln was able to resolve, others which never yielded to the light of reason. As if this were not enough, the war was going so badly that many in the North, including government leaders, were ready to throw in the sponge in discouragement and disgust. The growing casualty list, the demands of Congress that the Cabinet be remade in its own image, the fiscal problems, foreign relations and the pressure of the restive Negroes, all combined into what seemed insurmountable obstacles. Opposition of the fickle part of the press, distortion of news and draft riots here and there, the deflation of the greenbacks and inflation of commodity prices merged into an ominous wall of resistance. So Sandburg had the conflict of his narrative cut out for him. No Greek drama had a more consistently ascending line of action, no more dramatic crescendo and climax, and then the quiet like that of "the cool tombs" which came in the tragic aftermath.

It was not so much that this was new in fact, Nevins points out, but the way in which Sandburg handled it that made his great work so distinctive. He went at the Herculean task of amassing hundreds of thousands of details about Lincoln and did not let up until he had distilled his pages from tens of thousands of sources. These materials he sorted, classified, selected, and rewrote into readable form as no one else had done before. Here is not only the story of a man. Here is a miniature drama of American life played out against its most tragic background. Although civil war had been predicted by some of our Founding Fathers and the country had been warned by later prophets that conflict, particularly because of the slavery problem, was inevitable, the fact remained that for some seventy years of the existence of the new republic, no real armed disruption of the national life had yet occurred. George Washington and Andrew Jackson, especially, had seen to that. Perhaps their overriding wisdom was needed now. But Lincoln was in command.

Yet with all the terrible tragedy in the unfolded story, there is as much comic relief as in a Shakespearean play or a Sandburg platform recital. Humor graced the sad heart of Lincoln and burst forth when he was most disheartened. Lincoln himself explained that this was necessary to preserve his sanity. Sandburg, through his anecdotes, sidelights, and portrayal of the reactions of other people, demonstrates what the results were in the grand performance of Lincoln on the national stage. Nor does the earthiness of the Lincoln humor fail to appear, although Sandburg did know that some dirtier yarns testified to by auditors were confined to private talk fests with friends. And although he wisely does not inject four-letter words into his dignified project, Sandburg does include enough examples of the salty stories told by Lincoln to show that, at times, his jokes were distasteful. At least they appeared to be to sedate people such as Seward and Chase who scowled at the anecdotes told by Lincoln as if they felt the humor belonged more in the back house than it did in the White House.

There is joy in the book, even if some of it is unrefined. Our nation was too ebullient to be wholly presented as a somber multitude of striving souls. Against the serious side, Sandburg brings out not only the light quality of much of Lincoln's humor but the happiness of the people themselves. They had a vitality in their struggle to preserve the nation which is irrepressible and which is contained in the pages of the biography. The people had much to lament, much to cry over, but, as is shown in Sandburg's poem, *The People, Yes,* which he said was his "footnote to Lincoln's Gettysburg Address," their clarion shouts of gladness are also heard.

Humor even entered into the writing of *The War Years.* Recalled by Isaac Don Levine, former Hearst foreign correspondent and member of the staff of the *Chicago Daily News,* John Steinbeck wrote of a prank played on Carl Sandburg when he was working on the biography at Harbert, Michigan:

> He lived on the shore of Lake Michigan, and every morning he would put his mind in rhythm and discipline for the day's work. He walked on the sand at the edge of the lake, head down, mop-hair flying. His hand gestured privately and his lips moved, trying on the words for size and stability. The time never varied; it was the hour after sunrise, whether the sun rose or not. People who lived on the bluff behind the beach would see Carl far below, shambling along the water's edge, and they said you could set your watch by him. No one ever did, but you could. Those same people on the bluff knew all about Carl and how he was writing *The War Years.* The two volumes of *The Prairie Years* were already published and nearly everyone had read it, and besides, Carl was not a secret man; if you asked what he was working on, he would tell you.
>
> Once the great joke was hatched, it had to be carried out. Quite a few people living nearby were involved in the arrangements and a good many more wanted to see it work out. The plan was simple, clean, and inexpensive. A committee went into Chicago and hired a long, lean actor for a one-day stand. They bought a beard for him and costumed him in a frock coat, a stovepipe hat, and a shawl.

Then one morning, the jokers and their friends gathered
at the top of a bluff to see it work. You could set your watch
by Carl, and from the top of the bluff, you could see him
a long way off, loose-jointed, shambling, keeping to the
water's edge where the footing was firm.

When Carl was about a quarter of a mile away, the tall,
top-hatted actor was signaled to walk toward him. He
had been instructed to meet Carl just below the place
where the gallery had settled to watch. The tall, black
figure was made enormous by the two feet of hat on top of
him. The beard was a masterpiece and the shawl flapped
in the wind.

Carl, as always, wore his disreputable hat which framed
rather than covered his light-colored hair. As usual, his
head was down, studying on the unmarked wetness of the
beach the cadences of the words which he would write
that day. The two figures drew slowly together and then the
jokers saw them pass. Carl looked up for a moment and
then his head was down again as he moved on, studying
the sand.

The majestic, tall dark actor, on the other hand, looked
over his shoulder, and then he broke and ran up the steep
path to the bluff. He was winded and his beard had slipped
by the time he made it. The gallery of onlookers quickly
surrounded him.

"What did he do?"

"Nothing. He just looked at me for a moment."

"Didn't he do anything?"

"Yes, he bowed."

"Well—didn't he say anything?"

The actor was still getting his breath and his eyes were
a little crazy.

"He said . . . and that's all he said."

"Said what?"

"It was just after he bowed. He said, 'Good morning, Mr.
President.'"

On one of his New York visits, Sandburg gathered with some friends at an uptown apartment and waxed convivial. One of those present recalls some of the remarks made by the visitor: "I've written poems I can't understand myself. . . . As a boy, I wondered what life was—so many things were happening and nobody explained why. I wondered what America was all about."

In jovial banter with another guest who asked him just what he was anyway, Sandburg replied with gusto, "I'm a son-of-a-bitch without discount!"

Then he recalled a story about Abraham Lincoln when the President was visiting a military hospital during the Civil War. Also with him were Kate Chase Sprague, daughter of the Secretary of the Treasury, and some friends. While Mrs. Sprague was at one end of a ward of wounded men, she noticed that Lincoln was down at the other end talking animatedly to a soldier lying in a bed. When he again joined the party, she asked him what he had found so interesting about the patient that made him look solemn and then laugh intermittently. The President looked at her intently, then said with a chuckle, "Mrs. Sprague, if you had been standing in the position that soldier was when he was wounded, you would not even have been hit."

So in Lincoln's life, as well as in Sandburg's, there was humor. But for the most part, writing this life was a taxing assignment. Thumbnail sketches of heretofore little known but interesting and important people dot the pages like small stars. These vignettes, along with the countless other obscure data, emphasize the old adage that truth is stranger than fiction.

Probably the two greatest elements in the biography are Lincoln and the people. How to blend these two entities in narration and show their relationship properly at the same time was Sandburg's task. He succeeded. The people were there and they were in the turmoil of conflict. Lincoln was there, leader of most of them, though never actually President of all of the United States—some one has called them "the disunited states." Being so much one of the common people, having had close contact with crowded streets, hobo camps, boisterous political conventions, the cause of laborers striving to be heard, and a brief period of military service, Sandburg was equipped to tie Lincoln and his seething environment together. In an extended and rhapsodic way, he is saying, "Lincoln and the People, Yes."

How familiar Sandburg was with a kaleidoscope is not known. But it is certain that he used kaleidoscopic methods in his depiction of Lincoln. Through his unique way of putting bits and pieces together, many markedly symmetrical patterns appear. Though at times one seems bogged down in the abundance of detail, there eventually emerges a clearer Lincoln, a more lustrous figure—and the great mystic of his time slowly comes to radiant life. Had Carl Sandburg followed Abraham Lincoln around the White House and elsewhere during his crucial years, he could hardly have had more information than he actually did gather later. And then it would have been mainly through the eyes of the biographer and not from many divergent viewpoints, such as are employed in the book.

It is this virtue of the biography that keeps the writer in the background and his subject paramount. Sandburg, instead of issuing many pronunciamentos on what kind of man Lincoln was, is constantly inclined to present the facts and the observations of other people, and then let the reader judge the subject for himself. This method alone shows the confidence of Sandburg in his readers: give them light, he paraphrases, and they themselves will find the way. The author does not choose to stand high above the story and direct the manner and result of its impact. He literally lets the chips of information fall where they may and is willing to be judged accordingly.

By such means, the Sandburg story shows in the fullest way the almost miraculous transformation of Lincoln from an ordinary lawyer and Congressman to the remarkable leader he became after he entered the White House. We still wonder just what happened here. More than any other of the great number who had tried, Sandburg shows the steps of this transformation and lights the stage from all angles so that his audience can see Lincoln from inauguration to assassination.

"The tale is not idle," wrote Sandburg—and this is as great an understatement as one is apt to find anywhere. It is a tale like that described by Shakespeare, "full of sound and fury," and accepted in the Sandburgian manner, it can be read aloud and much of it will sound like poetry—as much of it is. While all six volumes of the biography, as well as the condensed one-volume edition, will probably endure as long as history does, *The War Years* is probably Sandburg's greatest work. It is biography, history, poetry, drama, and a kind of background music that can be heard by those who have known the author and who appreciate his subject.

Filed in the dusty morgue of the late *New York Herald Tribune* was a writer's comment: "After its publication, Mr. Sandburg said he would take a rest, but men like Carl Sandburg don't rest. They are too much a part of life and of America."

In the book section of the same newspaper, Lloyd Lewis had written:

> Lincoln was in himself so large a mirror of mankind that every biographer finds in him the thing he admires most, hence lawyers think Lincoln's legal side the thing that made him great, soldiers think his education in handling soldiers the main thing in his fame, preachers say it was his exalted moral sense, and Sandburg the writer, while giving the most catholic of evaluations to date, would seem, by his emphasis, to feel that it was as a user of words that Lincoln shone the brightest. And the evidence goes far to support such a view. To read Sandburg's detailed description of how Lincoln wrote his most renowned papers, speeches and letters, of what was in the air at the moment, is as absorbing as it would be suddenly to come across the revelation of just how Shakespeare wrote *Hamlet*.[9]

An example of the atmosphere which Sandburg poetically recreated in depicting the course of Lincoln's life is found in the chapter in which the President-elect is preparing to leave for

Washington: "The sunshine and the prairie summer and fall
months would come sifting down with healing and strength;
between harvest and corn-plowing there would be rains beating
and blizzards howling; and there would be the silence after
snowstorms with white drifts piled against the fences, barns and
trees."

Not less lyrical was the description that Sandburg's friend,
Stephen Vincent Benét gave in the *Atlantic Monthly*.

> In *The War Years*, Carl Sandburg carries on and com-
> pletes his life of Lincoln, through the turmoil of Civil War
> to the burial at Springfield. He has done so on the grand
> scale—it is a mountain range of a biography. The four
> volumes comprise well over two thousand pages of text,
> four hundred and fourteen half-tones of photographs,
> two hundred and forty-nine reproductions of letters,
> documents, cartoons. To review such a work in brief is
> rather like trying to take a picture of the Lincoln Memorial
> with a miniature camera. In the first place, this is a biog-
> raphy, not only of Abraham Lincoln, but of the Civil
> War. The great, the near-great, the wretched, the com-
> monplace, the humble, the shoddy—dozens, hundreds of
> men and women, known or little known, who played their
> part in those years—generals, civilians, office seekers, Con-
> gressmen, cranks, soldiers of the North and South, traitors,
> spies, plain citizens—appear and disappear like straws
> whirled along by a torrent. . . . The scares, the fears, the
> indecisions, the whole getting under way of the huge,
> creaking, war machine of the North, the false alarms and
> dashed hopes, and yet the gradual, growing devotion
> between President and people—these Mr. Sandburg has
> done and done superbly. He has shown the worry and
> chicken scratchings of 'the best minds' when confronted
> by a new phenomenon, the hate of the scorners and the
> impeccable growth of greatness. . . . For the man who
> was Lincoln—the great, complex, humorous, melancholy

figure—Mr. Sandburg shows him in certain sections of this biography as clearly and as fully as he has ever been shown. The slow growth is there, and each ring on the tree is counted.

But Benét's comments are not all applause. He adds:

Now and then it is hard to see the wood for the trees; now and then Mr. Sandburg's principles of selection and omission strike one oddly. . . . There are places where Mr. Sandburg's style touches genuine poetry, there are others where it descends to bathos. And now and then, he permits himself a sort of rhetorical broodiness which is neither poetry nor prose. But when all this is said, the book remains. To chip at it with a hammer is a little like chipping at Stone Mountain.[10]

What about the political viewpoint of the author? Was it sectional or not?

Charles A. Beard, who could be impartial on hardly anything, says about *The War Years:*

The scene is viewed mainly from the Northern standpoint. The weight of emphasis is on Northern events and personalities, despite the passages on campaigns and battles. . . . And, although Mr. Sandburg cites freely many adverse Southern judgments on Lincoln, he sees that strange figure in the White House undamaged by the animadversions. After all, just what is *the* Southern view of the war years or anything else? Moreover, who, North or South, is fitted to tell the truth, the whole truth and nothing but the truth?

Yet Lincoln is not portrayed in these pages as the mighty hero, the great wise man who foresaw things perfectly and moved with unerring wisdom to the great end. He is shown as a poor limited mortal, of many moods, tempers, and distempers, stumbling, blundering along, trying this and trying that, telling jokes, bewildered, disappointed, grieved by his fractious wife, weeping now, laughing then, ordering this, canceling that, trying to smooth ruffled personalities, looking upon mankind, like Marcus Aurelius, as composed of little creatures playing and loving, quarreling and fighting, and making up again, all without much rhyme or reason—Lincoln steadfast in his purpose of saving the Union, and, if possible, reducing the area of slavery or getting rid of it entirely.

There may have been men around Lincoln who were greater (whatever that may mean); many of them at least imagined themselves greater; but I am convinced that Mr. Sandburg's pages will dispel any illusions on this score.[11]

Perhaps Beard could discern some obscure meaning in the words of Sandburg which pointed to the Northern viewpoint. Although he was born in what is ordinarily thought of as "Yankee Country," Sandburg, it appears to this writer at least, maintains a fair and middle-of-the-road approach as far as sections are concerned. At times he goes out of his way to bring in instances of Southern heroism or compassion, such as the description of the speech of Horace Maynard of Tennessee in the Republican National Convention of 1864, when he brought tears and applause to the crowd by his impassioned account of the plight of the people in the South. Also at this time, Andrew Johnson was nominated for Vice President, and Sandburg spares no words in setting forth the homely virtues of this man who was to succeed Lincoln in the White House. And it has always seemed an indication of impartiality that Sandburg eventually moved with his family, not only to the South, but into the old home of the one-time Confederate Secretary of the Treasury.

To present a full picture of the Lincoln saga, Sandburg had to consider well both sides in the Civil War. A good part of his research digging was in Southern records and he visited every part of the country in his quest. For eleven years he "read more Lincoln material than any other man living or dead": mountains of newspapers, cascades of letters, diaries, pamphlets, posters, proclamations, pictures, handbills, and cartoons. One of the most difficult sources he examined—and probably one of the dullest—was the Congressional Record, which represented all parts of the nation. Too, Sandburg had a rare poetic sympathy for the underdog and he was too much of a dramatist to lose sight of how important as well as touching was the inclusion of much in his work about the South. He explained that the reader, seeking Lincoln would have to endure in imagination what Lincoln went through in reality.

What lifts the book above mere stupendous anecdotage is the thoughtful, searching comment of the collector. Each anecdote and incident is fastened to the growing pyramidal monument by the cement of Sandburg's particular feeling for the form of words and of Lincoln's character. This method allows the author to compile, along with the monument to Lincoln, another—one to the people of the time. As in *The Prairie Years,* Sandburg seemed to have transposed himself back to an earlier day; to have lived with a man of that day until both the man and the times came alive in his mind.

Here one sees Lincoln guiding when he can, biding when he knew that he must do so. He tried everything: coaxing, persuading, even beating on the heartstrings of his people. He is more often disappointed than pleased and is usually shown as harassed and beaten down. Though Lincoln is confused and beset at times, he sticks to his purpose in the realization that here he is being tried by fire. He is a kindly soul who can ease the burdens of the lowly just as he can endure the cruel barbs of the arrogant. Lincoln is depicted as one who hates war yet feels that it is his only means to the big end. He pardons so many accused that one wonders if he overdoes it, giving generously of his power to both friend and enemy. Although he is excoriated and assailed, he is as patient as Job and shows, according to his biographer, more tolerance and forgiveness than any other national leader in history.

While Lincoln assumed the sorrows and sufferings of his people, he still retained his undying faith in them in the long run. One of Lincoln's qualities which annoyed and even upset his associates was his lack of observance of social customs. He was plain and unpretending and was one of those rare individuals who honestly felt that he was above certain mere formalities, although these were observed by most of the people. He could make his own rules as well as those who had set themselves up as arbiters of our society. Though at times he was undoubtedly crude, his sincere simplicity usually won over in the end those who might at first have been offended.

Initially Lincoln seemed and was unsure of himself. Then, as Sandburg lets us know, as time went on and his Presidential policies proved themselves to be right and effective, he gained faith in himself, perhaps even in God, and took up the middle course of great leaders. At intervals Lincoln was the true mystic, communing with another world that was remote from those who scoffed at his communication. He evidently saw a divine Providence working by means mysterious its wonders to perform, and bringing about reform through the blood shed on the field of battle. He has been said to have combined the true independence and freedom, the humor and philosophy of the plains, with the strength of the mountains. By word and colorful illustration, Sandburg shows in *The War Years* that the very face of Lincoln mirrored the hard tragedy of his life, albeit now and then softening over some humorous tidbit. In that face there was a solemn sensitivity, whether reflecting mirth or melancholy. It was a face lined by the storms of early life on the frontier and now become more wearied by the conflicts with the more cruelly subtle ways of the East and North. Of course the factor that gave it the aspect almost of a death mask was the war itself and its heavy responsibilities. Only the face of Robert E. Lee could be compared to that of Lincoln after the battles were over.

There is naturally more characterization of Lee and such major figures in the biography than there is of minor ones. But the little ones get their share too. Here is a great panorama of humanity, interspersed with anecdote and incident, and over all, the looming outline of Lincoln himself standing massive and solitary. The aim of Sandburg was to restore Lincoln to the common people, for he belonged to them. Equally important is the objective he attained of showing what happens to a democracy when it goes to war. In the words of Allan Nevins, "It is not merely a biography; it is a magnificent piece of history, an epic story of the most stirring period of national life and a narrative which for decades will hearten all believers in the stability of democracy and the potentialities of democratic leadership." [12]

Not only a sense of its significance but the ability to endure physical strain, as Lincoln did, was required of Sandburg in finishing the monumental task. His mind was at times so tired, as well as his back from eighteen-hour stretches over the cracker box, that he implored the Lord to spare him until he could complete the great job. But he did not consider shortening the work to fewer volumes; he stuck with his objective and saw it through, feeling no doubt the sinewy spirit of his subject helping him. Sandburg had said, "Lay me on an anvil, O God. . . . Let me lift and loosen old foundations." Now he had done just that. He had altered the conventional foundations of writing biography. From the sweat of the harvest fields where he had labored, the cold he had suffered while delivering milk and newspapers in his prairie town, the handling of heavy cakes of ice, all had brought him physical power to endure. And he needed it all, for writing is the hardest and loneliest work in the world. His mind had been bolstered by his contact with so many people; and his poetic imagination aided him in soaring above the clouds.

On one of these flights, he glorified, as had not been done before, the Gettysburg Address of Lincoln. Yet the biographer did not omit the details of the preparation of the memorable speech; he shows that it was not scribbled out on the train en route to the battlefield. He makes Lincoln's efforts more ordinary than this but shows the effect of the speech to have been superb. Yet, the general on the other side of the battle comes in for adequate treatment—that Sandburg sincerely admired Robert E. Lee is shown in his magnanimous comments. The biographer wished that Jefferson Davis might have escaped from the country before the Northerners could capture him—something which, of course, did not come about. Lincoln himself had an innate affection for the South and did not want his house divided. Long before the war ended, the President was making his plans to bind up the wounds of the nation and to care for its widows and orphans. Lincoln, as well as Sandburg, lamented the scorched-earth policy unnecessarily carried out by General Sherman in his cruel march through Georgia, and by Sheridan in his devastating raid through the beautiful Shenandoah Valley of Virginia.

But again Sandburg would turn from such weighty matters to draw upon the President's boundless stock of stories. There is the tale about the man who gets to the theater just as the curtain goes up. So interested is he in what is happening on the stage that he puts his tall silk hat, open side up, on the seat next to him, not noticing that just opposite is standing a very stout and near-sighted woman. She sits down. There is a crunching noise and the owner of the hat reaches out for it as the stout woman arises. Then he looks at his hat, and at her: "Madam," he said, "I could have told you that my hat wouldn't fit you before you tried it on!"

Such humor did not sit well with all who heard it. His friend Isaac N. Arnold visited Lincoln one day after the bloody battle of Fredericksburg. Lincoln started reading aloud from Artemus Ward, one of his favorite humorists. The visitor was so shocked that he actually criticized the President for such levity. Whereupon, Lincoln threw down the humorous book, and with tears streaming down his wrinkled cheeks, his slender body quivering as he spoke, said, "Mr. Arnold, if I could not get momentary respite from the crushing burden I am constantly carrying, my heart would break!"

One of Sandburg's original observations was that the conflict between the states was semantic in nature. "The Civil War," he wrote, "a bloody time that claimed more than a half-million of the living, actually was fought over a verb. Before the war, this country was referred to in all the treaties as 'The United States *is*'—and it is still the same now!" [13]

This spirit was reflected in the comments of many reviewing readers who saw in Sandburg a counterpart of Lincoln. So much of Lincoln's outlook, so much of his personality and philosophy and purpose, were absorbed into Carl Sandburg that he seemed to become like Lincoln in his recapitulation of the tragic saga. Both had a warm way of seeking both sides of a question before giving it a definite answer—if there was one. Both thought of all people as being worthy of dignified consideration as human entities. Deep sympathy was shown the defeated, true patriotism was respected as it should be today. There was something fundamental in Lincoln and Sandburg which the world sorely needs now they are gone.

Yet if such a message is not conveyed, it is not the fault of the author. In *The War Years* there are about 1,175,000 words, more than in all of Lincoln's printed speeches and writings, while in the whole Bible, including the Apocrypha, there are only 926,-877 words. By comparison, the complete works of Shakespeare total 1,025,000 words.

For at least a fourth of his long life, Sandburg had lived with his hero, Lincoln, and their association had been perhaps without precedent in the history of a biographer. So saturated was he with his subject that he talked and looked like him, thought like him, and expressed himself on paper much as did the martyred President. This identity Sandburg caught as essential, way back when he began the work. Although it grew on him, as he said, he came to know more and more that to reproduce creditably the person of such an important man, it was necessary to put himself insofar as possible into the man's place. After *The War Years* had come off the press and the mountainous burden had somewhat lifted from his big shoulders, Sandburg was asked what he intended to do next.

"I must first find out who this man Carl Sandburg is," he replied, with more meaning than even he must have known. For it was hard for him to lose his identification with Lincoln; in fact, he never really did. Nor did he, in this opinion, want to.

Sandburg had found that he was not the kind of a man who

leaves things unfinished. He had even planned, after finishing
The Prairie Years, to cover the rest of Lincoln's life simply in an
introduction. He actually wrote one called "A Lincoln Preface"
which began at the death of Lincoln and worked back to the day
he left Illinois. The reader could then turn to the book and begin
with his birth. But this was not the Sandburg way. No makeshift
measures would do. So, discarding the idea, he worked on *The
War Years* and considered throwing away the introduction.
Thirty years later, however, he decided he could let it be published. It is such a revealing and fitting distillation that it is set
forth here virtually in full:

> In the time of the April lilacs in the year 1865, a man in
> the City of Washington, D.C., trusted a guard to watch at
> a door, and the guard was careless, left the door, and the
> man was shot, lingered a night, passed away, was laid in a
> box, and carried north and west a thousand miles; bells
> sobbed; cities wore crepe; people stood with hats off as the
> railroad burial car came past at midnight, dawn or noon.
>
> During the four years of time before he gave up the
> ghost, this man was clothed with despotic power, com-
> manding the most powerful armies till then assembled in
> modern warfare, enforcing drafts of soldiers, abolishing
> the right of habeas corpus, directing politically and spirit-
> ually the wild, massive forces loosed in civil war.
>
> Four billion dollars' worth of property was taken from
> those who had been legal owners of it, confiscated,
> wiped out as by fire, at his instigation and executive direc-
> tion; a class of chattel property recognized as lawful for
> two hundred years went to the scrap pile.
>
> When the woman who wrote *Uncle Tom's Cabin* came
> to see him in the White House, he greeted her, "So you're
> the little woman who wrote the book that made this great
> war," and as they seated themselves at a fireplace, "I do
> love an open fire; I always had one to home." As they were

finishing their talk of the days of blood, he said, "I shan't last long after it's over."

An Illinois Congressman looked in on him as he had his face lathered for a shave in the White House, and remarked, "If anybody had told me that in a great crisis like this the people were going out to a little one-horse town and pick out a one-horse lawyer for President, I wouldn't have believed it." The answer was, "Neither would I. But it was a time when a man with a policy would have been fatal to the country. I never had a policy. I have simply tried to do what seemed best each day, as each day came."

"I don't intend precisely to throw the Constitution overboard, but I will stick it in a hole if I can," he told a Cabinet officer. The enemy was violating the Constitution to destroy the Union, he argued, and therefore, "I will violate the Constitution, if necessary, to save the Union." He instructed a messenger to the Secretary of the Treasury, "Tell him not to bother himself about the Constitution. Say that I have that sacred instrument here at the White House, and I am guarding it with great care."

When he was renominated, it was by the device of seating delegates from Tennessee, which gave enough added votes to seat favorable delegates from Kentucky, Missouri, Louisiana, Arkansas, and from one county in Florida. Until late in that campaign of 1864, he expected to lose the November election; military victories brought the tide his way; the vote was 2,200,000 for him and 1,800,000 against him. Among those who bitterly fought him politically, and accused him of blunders or crimes, were Franklin Pierce, a former President of the United States; Horatio Seymour, the Governor of New York; Samuel F.B. Morse, inventor of the telegraph; Cyrus H. McCormick, inventor of the farm reaper; General George B. McClellan, a Democrat who had commanded the Army of the Potomac; and the *Chicago Times*, a daily newspaper. In all its essential propositions the Southern Confederacy had the moral support of powerful, respectable elements throughout the North, probably more than a million voters believing in the justice of the cause of the South as compared with the North.

While propagandas raged, and the war winds howled, he sat in the White House, the Stubborn Man of History, writing that the Mississippi was one river and could not belong to two countries, that the plans for railroad connection from coast to coast must be pushed through and the Union Pacific realized.

His life, mind, and heart ran in contrasts. When his white kid gloves broke into tatters while shaking hands at a White House reception, he remarked, "This looks like a general bustification." When he talked with an Ohio friend one day during the 1864 campaign, he mentioned one public man, and murmured, "He's a thistle! I don't see why God lets him live." Of a devious Senator, he said, "He's too crooked to lie still!" . . .

While the luck of war wavered and broke and came again, as generals failed and campaigns were lost, he held enough forces of the Union together to raise new armies and supply them, until generals were found who made war as victorious war has always been made, with terror, frightfulness, destruction, and valor and sacrifice past words of man to tell.

A slouching, grey-headed poet, haunting the hospitals at Washington, characterized him as "the grandest figure on the crowded canvas of the drama of the nineteenth century—a Hoosier Michael Angelo."

His own speeches, letters, telegrams, and official messages during that war form the most significant and enduring document from any one man on why the war began, why it went on, and the dangers beyond its end. He mentioned "the politicians," over and again "the politicians," with scorn and blame. As the platoons filed before him at a review of an army corps, he asked, "What is to become of these boys when the war is over?"

He was a chosen spokesman; yet there were times he was silent; nothing but silence could at those times have fitted a chosen spokesman; in the mixed shame and blame of the immense wrongs of two crashing civilizations, with nothing to say, he said nothing, slept not at all, and wept at those times in a way that made weeping appropriate, decent, majestic.

His hat was shot off as he rode alone one night in Washington; a son he loved died as he watched at the bed; his wife was accused of betraying information to the enemy, until denials from him were necessary; his best companion was a fine-hearted and brilliant son with a deformed palate and an impediment of speech; when a Pennsylvania Congressman told him the enemy had declared they would break into the city and hang him to a lamp post, he said he had considered "the violent preliminaries" to such a scene; on his left thumb was a scar where an ax had nearly chopped the thumb off when he was a boy; over one eye was a scar where he had been hit with a club in the hands of a Negro trying to steal the cargo off a Mississippi River flatboat; he threw a cashiered officer out of his room in the White House, crying, "I can bear censure, but not insult. I never wish to see your face again."

As he shook hands with the correspondent of the London *Times*, he drawled, "Well, I guess the London *Times* is about the greatest power on earth—unless perhaps it is the Mississippi River." He rebuked with anger a woman who got on her knees to thank him for a pardon that saved her son from being shot at sunrise; and when an Iowa woman said she had journeyed out of her way to Washington just for a look at him, he grinned, "Well, in the matter of looking at one another, I have altogether the advantage."

He asked his Cabinet to vote on the high military com-

mand, and after the vote, told them the appointment had
already been made; one Cabinet officer, who had been
Governor of Ohio, came away personally baffled and frustrated from an interview, to exclaim, to a private secretary, "That man is the most cunning person I ever saw in
my life"; an Illinois lawyer who had been sent on errands
carrying his political secrets, said, "He is a trimmer and
such a trimmer as the world has never seen."

He manipulated the admission of Nevada as a state in
the Union, when her votes were needed for the Emancipation Proclamation, saying, "It is easier to admit Nevada
than to raise another million of soldiers." At the same time
he went to the office of a former New York editor, who
had become Assistant Secretary of War, and said the
votes of three Congressmen were wanted for the required
three-quarters of votes in the House of Representatives,
advising, "There are three that you can deal with better
than anybody else. . . . Whatever promise you make to
those men, I will perform it." And in the same week, he
said to a Massachusetts politician that two votes were
lacking, and, "Those two votes must be procured. I leave
it to you to determine how it shall be done; but remember
that I am President of the United States and clothed with
immense power, and I expect you to procure those
votes." And while he was thus employing every last re-
source and device of practical politics to constitutionally
abolish slavery, the abolitionist Henry Ward Beecher
attacked him with javelins of scorn and detestation in a
series of editorials that brought from him the single comment, "Is thy servant a dog?"

.   .   .   .

He sent hundreds of telegrams, "Suspend death sentence," or "Suspend execution" of So-and-So, who was to
be shot at sunrise. The telegrams varied oddly at times, as
in one, "If Thomas Samplogh, of the First Delaware Regiment, has been sentenced to death, and is not yet exec-

cuted, suspend and report the case to me." And another, "Is it Lieut. Samuel B. Davis whose death sentence is commuted? If not done, let it be done."

While the war drums beat, he liked best of all the stories told of him, one of two Quakeresses heard talking in a railway car. "I think that Jefferson will succeed." "Why does thee think so?" "Because Jefferson is a praying man." "And so is Abraham a praying man." "Yes, but the Lord will think Abraham is joking."

An Indiana man at the White House heard him say, "Voorhees, don't it seem strange to you that I, who could never so much as cut off the head of a chicken, should be elected, or selected, into the midst of all this blood?"

A party of American citizens, standing in the ruins of the Forum in Rome, Italy, heard there the news of the first assassination of the first American dictator, and took it as a sign of the growing up and the aging of the civilization on the North American continent. Far out in Coles County, Illinois, a beautiful, gaunt old woman in a log cabin said, "I knowed he'd never come back."

An enemy general, Longstreet, after the war, declared him to have been "the one matchless man in forty millions of people," while one of his private secretaries, Hay, declared his life to have been the most perfect in its relationships and adjustments since that of Christ.

Between the days in which he crawled as a baby on the dirt floor of a Kentucky cabin, and the time when he gave his final breath in Washington, he packed a rich life with work, thought, laughter, tears, hate, love.

With vast reservoirs of the comic and the droll, and notwithstanding a mastery of mirth and nonsense, he delivered a volume of addresses and letters of terrible and serious appeal, with import beyond his own day, shot through here and there with far, thin ironics, with paragraphs having raillery of the quality of the Book of Job, and echoes as subtle as the whispers of wind in prairie grass.

Perhaps no human clay-pot has held more laughter and tears.

The facts and myths of his life are to be an American possession, shared widely over the world, for thousands of years, as the tradition of Knute or Alfred, Lao-tse or Diogenes, Pericles or Caesar, are kept. This because he was not only a genius in the science of neighborly human relationships and an artist in the personal handling of life from day to day, but a strange friend and a friendly stranger to all forms of life that he met.

He lived fifty-six years of which fifty-two were lived in the West—the prairie years.[14]

Thus we have an abstract of his own book, as it were, by Sandburg himself. And of course no one could write it as well or with as much understanding. It is an epitome of the life of Lincoln setting forth what the author considers to be a typical sampling of the voluminous work in which he far exceeded the limits which he at first placed for himself. It was, in a way, as if Sandburg were trying to rationalize himself out of the formidable job of finishing the Lincoln biography; but at the same time, one can detect his inner anticipation of the labor which was to come, the remarkable achievement which was to be.

Henry Steele Commager has stated that "it is fitting that from the pen of a poet should come the greatest of all Lincoln biographies." The six-volume work was great, Commager believes, in a way that Lincoln himself would have wished and would have understood: genuine, simple, broad, humane, dramatic, poetic, thoroughly American in its muscular, idiomatic words, in its humor, in its catholicity and democracy. "Here is the whole of the war President," adds Commager, "nothing of importance is omitted but there is much which before was thought unimportant but now is appreciated. Sandburg has realized that Lincoln belongs to the people, not to the historians, and he has given us a portrait from which a whole generation may draw understanding of the past inspiration for the future." [15]

Lloyd Lewis, after setting the stage for the remarkably dramatic Gettysburg Address, observed in regard to the event that Lincoln had not had time to get up much of a speech, even for the five minutes allotted for the Chief Executive of the United States. Most attention had been paid to the preparations for the main speaker, Edward Everett, president of Harvard University and the most renowned speaker in the country. Under the circumstances, Everett was the logical choice. There was also a question as to how many would listen to the somewhat discredited Lincoln at this time. Among his own party, the leaders said to each other that there was little need for them to be there because, in their estimation, Lincoln was not going to be elected the next year anyway.

Ironically, Lincoln's time at this crucial period was filled with appointments for days before the scheduled address and he did not get much done on the speech. In addition, Tad, the little son to whom he was closest, was sick and his wife was hysterical, she had already lost a son in the White House. But Lincoln with characteristic reliability had come through with some kind of a speech, and as he sat beside a friend he confided that he wished he had gotten up the thing with more care. How little did that friend realize with what memorable care the Gettysburg Address had been born.

But the London *Times*, in all its English stolidity, remarked that Lincoln's speech could not have been beaten for dullness. For that matter, *The New York Times* devoted very little space to the address and commented that it was an insignificant event indeed. Such appraisal may now seem ridiculous but it was apparently sincere at the time. Lincoln said in the address that the world would not long remember the remarks that he made on that day. Under the circumstances, he must have really felt that way; and Sandburg understood this when he wrote of the occurrence. It is in such simple but priceless moments in history that greatness is born, and so it was with Lincoln's Gettysburg Address. In two minutes he did what Everett could not do in two eloquent hours.

Sandburg's achievement in describing incomparably the address on the most important battlefield of the Civil War stands on its own merits. He discards the conventional technique of the historian—he does not include footnotes. Yet the very facts of his narrative are evidence of the great research that he has done, so that virtually no one questions the veracity of his account. Most historians, sensing at once from their own trying experiences that here was genuine primary research, received him into their midst without misgivings. At times he includes enough wordage in one chapter to suffice for a book of average length. Always the emphasis is on Lincoln, so that a battle or a campaign may be covered in whatever space necessary to show its effects upon the mighty subject of the text.

If the book were a Greek tragedy, two of the main characters, often adversely presented, would be Ulysses S. Grant and William Tecumseh Sherman. They loomed large upon the stage of their current history; less so in the retrospect of the more objective historian. No one could or does deny their effectiveness in their own time. They got the job done. But even modern accounts with Union leanings must question some of their actions on the basis of logic inherent in the national cause. As for McClellan, Sandburg takes up the conventional viewpoint and paints him with small strokes. "Little Mac" comes off not well at the hands of the author; yet time and new research have shown that he did have a substantial side which has often been overlooked in the light of Lincoln's judgment upon a seemingly static general who would not move until all was perfectly ready. In regard to Sandburg's conception of Benjamin Butler, the bitterness of the author seems more than justified by contemporary, as well as latter-day, judgment; if there were a worse example than Butler's of one-sidedness and crass opportunism in the Civil War and Reconstruction periods, it is still impossible to find.

Quite properly, Robert E. Sherwood compared the method of Sandburg in writing a biography with that of Homer. The modern poet started his *magnum opus* on Lincoln with a foreword that surveys his source material and is in itself a fine compendium of Lincolniana. Here Sandburg tells how he took his guitar and a program of songs and readings and went from coast to coast many times, performing before a large variety of audiences and at the same time meeting the sons and daughters of many of the leading players in that drama of the eighteen-sixties. From these individuals he obtained reminiscences and rumors that led to more such information. Others had sought out Lincoln sources but none had gone so far and wide to get it first hand. The singing of the songs themselves brought Sandburg into close communion with the very kind of people with whom Lincoln associated, and thus furnished a greater insight than could be gotten in hardly any other way.

Like Carlyle, Sandburg dealt more with the men who made the history than he did with events, and like Macaulay, when the generals advanced to the front, he retreated to the rear to write about the people who made it all happen. But Sandburg, unlike his English predecessors, preferred to concentrate on the private soldiers rather than the officers; he himself had been an enlisted man when he was in the Spanish-American War, and he had the viewpoint of the man in the ranks, who, after all, does the important job of fighting wars.

Almost like Greek tragedy is the period when Lincoln reached his lowest ebb, from the earlier part of 1863 to August of 1864, "the darkest month of the war," when Lincoln's party moved to replace him with another Presidential candidate. This Sandburg handles with immense taste and sympathy, feeling to some extent—from his own life—the depth of emotion which swept over the wartime President during his Golgotha. Appropriate too is the comparison here with the tragic-minded Nathaniel Hawthorne who at the time of his death seemed to despair of our nation and his own part in it and was ready to accept spiritual defeat as the price of having existed in such chaotic times. Then came Lincoln's temporary triumph, his re-election, and his brief moment again in the sun. And then the darkness.

Max Lerner observed that the surprising thing about Sandburg's work on Lincoln was that here was the writing of a democrat, a poet and storyteller, an earthy midwesterner and singer of the people, who has written about another democrat who was also something of a poet in his way, a storyteller and an earthy midwesterner and a product of the popular masses. He gave not only a biography of Lincoln but a history of the Civil War itself. It is itself a battlefield, a sprawling panorama of people and issues and conflicts held together only by Sandburg's absorption with the central figure. But Lerner felt that the work had one great flaw: the sense one gets of a curious one-dimensional plane, in which details get the same loving attention as the big event. Sandburg, it was felt, was a little like a painter in the primitive style. He is also the true democratic historian. In his universe, all the facts have been validated and are free and equal.

Henry Bertram Hill in reviewing the book sensed some of this spirit also. He observed that Lincoln's greatness did not come from the possession of astounding genius or flashing brilliance. It came in part from his humaneness and apparent humility as represented privately in his many pardons and letters and publicly in the almost Biblical measure of the Gettysburg Address and the last paragraph of the Second Inaugural. All of this is common pabulum for the usual biographer of Lincoln, but never before had that other part of the man, his closeness to the people, been so thoroughly and so well portrayed. Perhaps that was because no other biographer of Lincoln has himself been so close to the earth and its human inhabitants or possessed so much of Lincoln's animal warmth and simplicity.

Emanuel Hertz, who had written about Lincoln also, analyzed Sandburg's work by pointing out that John Hay and John G. Nicolay, private secretaries of Lincoln, made use of materials which had been used up to that time by no other persons. Seven and a half of their ten volumes were devoted to the war years and constituted about 920,000 words, while Sandburg covered the same period in four huge volumes containing almost twice as many words. Sandburg gathered material which disclosed every aspect of this complex human being. Not only the biographies of Lincoln, but every book, speech, sermon, or address on Lincoln which contained a pertinent idea or fact engaged his attention. The items of Lincolniana amounted to over 9,000 books, magazine articles, and pamphlets, besides the recorded lives of his contemporaries—Confederate leaders, Federal generals, Naval officers—and of soldiers or citizens who came in contact with Lincoln. Added to this were innumerable contemporary newspapers as well as the accumulated files of the *Congressional Globe.*

The long account records not so much the hatred expressed by so many against Lincoln as it does the charges brought against him by people in the North as well as the South. Quoted here are portions of the diaries of Hay, Welles, Chase, and others. Speeches made in Congress are quoted, and a large number of broadsides, messages, letters, and endorsements by Lincoln are reprinted. Hertz counted 170 anecdotes and an equal number of interviews and descriptions of the battles in both the North and South, as well as 150 photographs, besides the cartoons. Taken as a whole, *The War Years* forms a foundation as secure as the eternal hills of the Dakotas upon which rests Borglum's great stone face of Lincoln in its sublimity.

When the life of Lincoln was later condensed, there was omitted from it a story which proved catchy in *The Prairie Years.* It concerned an apocryphal letter Lincoln was supposed to have received from a New York firm inquiring about the financial standing of a Springfield, Illinois, man. His answer was brief: "Yours of the 10th received. First of all, he has a wife and a baby; together they ought to be worth $500,000 to any man. Secondly, he has an office in which there is a table worth $1.50 and three chairs worth, say $1.00. Last of all, there is in one corner a large rat-hole which will bear looking into. Respectfully, A. Lincoln."

The book runs from the ridiculous to the sublime. Lincoln could tell a joke and Sandburg would repeat it or recount what the President was said to have said, then go into poetic strains such as the following regarding the year 1863:

> The dew came on the White House lawn and the moonlight spread lace of white films in the night and the syringa and the bridal wreath blossomed and the birds fluttered in the bushes and nested in the sycamore and the veery thrush fluted with never a weariness. The war drums rolled and the telegraph clicked off mortality lists, now a thousand now ten thousand in a day. Yet there were moments when the processes of men seemed to be only an evil dream and justice lay in deeper transitions than those wrought by men dedicated to kill or be killed. Beyond the black smoke lay what salvations and jubilees? Death was in the air. So was birth. What was dying no man was knowing. What was being born no man could say.[16]

Such poetic beauty is also shown in Sandburg's classical description of the ending of the life of his subject. After the assassination, the biography concludes:

> The last breath was drawn at 21 minutes and 55 seconds past 7 A.M. and the last heart beat flickered at 22 minutes and 10 seconds past the hour on Saturday, April 15, 1865. Dr. Barnes's finger was over the carotid artery, Dr. Leale's finger was on the right wrist pulse, and Dr. Taft's hand was over the cardium when the great heart made its final contraction.
>
> The Pale Horse had come.
>
> To a deep river, to a far country, to a by-and-by whence no man returns, had gone the child of Nancy Hanks and Tom Lincoln, the wilderness boy who found far lights and tall rainbows to live by, whose name even before he died had become a legend inwoven with men's struggle for freedom the world over.

The voice of Phineas D. Gurley: "Let us pray." Kneeling at the bedside, his sonorous tones shook with submission to the Everlasting, to the Heavenly Father, with pleading that the dead man's country and family be comforted.[17]

Sandburg, toward the end of his book, summed up his own appraisal of Lincoln in words that live:

> Out of the smoke and stench, out of the music and violet dreams of the war, Lincoln stood perhaps taller than any other of the many great heroes. This was in the mind of many. None threw a longer shadow than he. And to him the great hero was The People. He could not say too often that he was merely their instrument . . .
> And the night came with great quiet.
> And there was rest.
> The prairie years, the war years, were over.[18]

They were over for Abraham Lincoln but not for Carl Sandburg. Never would he lose the aura of that great and grim experience through which he had lived in re-creating the career of America's most memorable martyr.

What did he derive from writing the biography?

Late in 1939, he told Janet Mabie of *The Christian Science Monitor:*

> Well, when I wrote the last chapters, which deal with the end of Lincoln's life, I observed certain things. The chief of them was that I could spend the next two years—or even ten—writing about Lincoln's life. It isn't just that, if I went on, I could make it a better job than what has gone before, though nobody knows better than I where and how my books on Lincoln could be bettered! But there's so much that hasn't been touched. Not that there is anything very new about that. Who has ever exhausted the subject of Washington? Or Napoleon? Of Lincoln? How little we really know of figures like these, compared with what we might know. . . . If I didn't learn anything else, I learned

humility and patience. I never foresaw what I would put into the subject in the way of study and exploration and thought—and it's a funny thing, but a good many of the really important materials drawn into the narrative were offered me when I least expected them—and I can't say now that I am really through with the subject. But I learned to be patient, dealing with it. Why, when I think of the patience Abraham Lincoln had with McClellan alone—it was simply superb! McClellan was a man who bore himself like a big executive yet who at heart was strangely naïve. There was a lot about McClellan that troubled Lincoln, but he made himself be patient with the man because there was a lot more that was worth conserving. Yes, I got a degree of patience, working with Lincoln.[19]

The Poetry

WHILE STILL AT THE *Chicago Daily News* Sandburg was rummaging through his desk one day and speculated out loud: "There may be letters in here that I shall be answering one of these days in the hope that the people haven't moved."

One letter that he did write—two in fact—elicited a reply. It was from Robert Frost, then at the University of Michigan, and was dated November, 1922:

> Dear Carl: I am glad you wrote me two letters at a time to recall me to my better self. Two should turn the trick; one wouldn't have done it. I must never be allowed to forget that though for the year I am the guest under God of

Robert Frost

this vast institution of various things, still a guest is not all I am. They may think they have outguessed me. Appearances may be against me. But all the time deep down in me in my dungeon keep I'm a poet ain't I? Thanks, thanks to thee my worthy friend for the lesson thou hast taught, as one of the poets we have superseded (I assume we have) has rather too beautifully said. All right then. I'm a poet and my name is R. Frost. You will bear me out in that. . . .[1]

Sandburg and Frost came to know each other better as both grew to be accepted and became more famous. They were to praise and criticize each other's poetry but always seemed to hold a strong mutual regard. Alfred Harcourt had written Sandburg who was at the American Embassy in Stockholm in October, 1918, and said, "Frost has read *Cornhuskers* and says: 'Sandburg is better and better. He was a great find for you. He's man, woman and child all rolled in one heart.'"

Thirty-five years later, Louise D. Gunn wrote in the *New York Herald Tribune*:

> Who is Carl Sandburg?
> You'd know him if you saw him,
> You'd know him if you heard him speak;
> He is a singer of songs,
> With a shock of white hair,
> And a singing guitar.
> I heard him once and I've never
> Stopped hearing him since.
>
> He said: "Go to it, O jazzmen."
> And I heard him in the jitterbug feet
> At a high school dance, in the pitter-pat
> Of a disc jockey's lingo, in the long
> Wild wail of our neighbor's boy,
> Practicing on his shiny new sax.

> He said: "The people, yes."
> And I could not say "the people, no,"
> After that; for I heard the heartbeat
> Of the crowds, the hammer-tick of time,
> The tide-wave of sorrow, the jump-up
> Of joy. Yes, I said, the people, yes.
>
> And so Carl Sandburg sang,
> And so we sing with him, now, today:
> "I have one remember, two
>   remembers, ten remembers:
>   I have a little handkerchief
> bundle of remembers—of Carl Sandburg." [2]

Probably most of the criticism of Sandburg has centered on his poetry. By some it is called "non-poetry." To him a poem was more than a succession of rhythmic sounds which are supposed to convey a thought. It was his purpose to let words express the subject matter even if he had to switch his meter from smooth to staccato and back again according to what he was thinking. Sandburg virtually dispensed with rhyme and shocked the romantic school of poets by selecting instead of love, dreams, or death such earthy subjects as stockyards and stevedores.

Robert Sherwood commented,

> . . . a poet is an inexplicable creature of unsound mind who rides on a flimmering floom with wild ducks. I hesitate to say whether Carl Sandburg qualifies as a poet under this definition. All I can say for sure is that he is a great Natural Force, comparable in heat, power and intensity to those which manifest themselves on the surface at such places as Vesuvius or Yellowstone National Park. . . . Viewed in its entirety, Sandburg's poetry, like the works of others (including Shakespeare's), appears wildly uneven in quality. Some of the pieces, including some of the most formless and seemingly incoherent ones, seem to have been fash-

ioned with the utmost care and precision and intellectual
sweat. Others seem to have been spewed out, which is not
to say that the spewed ones may not be good or even great.[3]

Pertinent comment also had come from Ezra Pound in London,
who wrote Sandburg, "The *Chicago Poems* have come at last.
Complimenti miei! The thing that strikes me most is that you have
kept the whole book down to brass tacks and that you have succeeded in this much better than Edgar Lee Masters, even in the
Spoon River Anthology."

Sherwood Anderson commented on the poem, "The Four Brothers": "A magnificent thing, Carl. It sings and it has time, sweep,
and bigness. Makes my heart jump to know we have a man like
you in our old town."

Perhaps the most eloquent tribute to Sandburg's poems came
from a fourteen-year-old girl who wrote: "I can scarcely say
whether or not his poetry will live . . . it shall live with me."

It seems that she may have had this poem in mind:

AT A WINDOW

Give me hunger,
O you gods that sit and give
The world its orders.
Give me hunger, pain and want,
Shut me out with shame and failure
From your doors of gold and fame,
Give me your shabbiest, weariest hunger!

But leave me a little love,
A voice to speak to me in the day end,
A hand to touch me in the dark room
Breaking the long loneliness.
In the dusk of day-shapes
Blurring the sunset,
One little wandering, western star
Thrust out from the changing shores of shadow.

> Let me go to the window,
> Watch there the day-shapes of dusk
> And wait and know the coming
> Of a little love.[4]

Here was a sentimental Sandburg, a poetic person who appreciated the nice nuances of love. Paul Rosenfeld had written in the
Bookman, "It is creation indeed that Sandburg has been about in
his earthiest, vivid pieces. He has been making us to be at home
here in the West. . . . He has been doing in his Chicago of the
new century what Whitman was doing in the Manhattan of Civil
War times: burning the mists off the befogged land, striving to
create out of the inanimate steel and the loveless dirt, the living
thing, America. . . . Sandburg has been feeling beauty in the
towns of the Middle Border, where beauty never before was felt.
This is a man filled with a warm, great love for men and women.
. . . He has the sense of the unity of mankind, the oneness of the
forgotten man of yesterday and the men of today. . . . His successful efforts are almost sparks of fire out of a chaos, sudden
tongues of flame that leap out of smoky matter and subside as
suddenly again." [5]

Yet by the time he was middle-aged, Carl Sandburg himself
said that there was puzzlement as to what he really was: poet,
biographer, singer, or newspaperman. One might conclude that he
indeed was all. Mark Van Doren in a eulogy at the Library of
Congress said that Sandburg was first of all a poet. He pointed this
out despite the fact that Sandburg's *Lincoln* contains more words
than the Bible or Shakespeare, he said. Even the biography of
Lincoln is compared with poetry or music and is saturated with
humor, despair, skepticism, and a sense of great things, especially
Lincoln and Sandburg themselves. Sandburg strongly brought out
that there is nothing more certain than death and nothing more
uncertain than the hour. The poet seemed to be deeply and often
concerned with death, yet unlike Hemingway, he was not fascinated by it and apparently had more religion than the late novelist. Van Doren felt that Sandburg's best poems are his short ones.

He could, for instance, find geese laughable and admirable at the same time. Sandburg pokes fun at pomp and could laugh loudly when he loved. Sometimes he is as happy as a child, in fact, he could speak in the child's language remarkably well. Yet he could be somberly philosophical, as in:

GRASS

Pile the bodies high at Austerlitz and Waterloo.
Shovel them under and let me work—
    I am the grass; I cover all.

And pile them high at Gettysburg
And pile them high at Ypres and Verdun.
Shovel them under and let me work.
Two years, ten years, and passengers ask the conductor:
        What place is this?
        Where are we now?

    I am the grass.
    Let me work.[6]

Another special quality is noted in the review which the *London Times Literary Supplement* gave to Sandburg's *Smoke and Steel* poems in 1920. "American poets may be divided into those who stay in America and those who emigrate," the sedate English publication pronounced. "Mr. Carl Sandburg is one of those who have accepted Americanism." Here the newspaper may well have touched upon the real reason why Sandburg never received the Nobel Prize: he was too American.

In describing *Smoke and Steel*, the *Times* commented,

> Now, the life which Mr. Carl Sandburg wishes to express is, generally speaking, the life of the Middle West, which is different from that of the aristocratic South, ruined in the Civil War, different again from the Puritan New England which found expression in Lowell, Emerson and Hawthorne, and yet again different from the life of the Coast.

> The distinguishing feature of the Middle West, to quote
> Mr. J. G. Fletcher is "its immense flatness and monotony";
> its population, after achieving a gigantic piece of pioneer-
> ing, is isolated on farms or concentrated in small provincial
> towns, in either case with an attitude towards life which
> renders it indifferent or hostile to the arts. Yet in this
> monotony of landscape there are great stretches of beauty;
> in this worship of material success there is a stirring of
> the ideal; and Mr. Sandburg is, as it were, a mouthpiece
> for this inarticulate idealism to make itself heard.[7]

The English appraisal stressed that mere material prosperity is
not enough, that to blaspheme wealth needs courage in any country, especially in the Anglo-Saxon ones. But the significance of the
criticism was that the poems came not from an exceptionally well
educated man in the United States, but from Sandburg who was
of the people. He used the materials which he found at hand, but
even though absorbing the natural beauty of his country, he had
a kind of predetermination to insist on the ugly and materialistic
side of his subjects. The tradition of Sandburg was held to be that
of Whitman, of journalism, and to a slighter extent that of the *vers
libre* poets. But in the writings of Sandburg was found vitality,
novelty, and Americanism at all costs. What does it matter, he
seemed to say, that the Parthenon is the extreme expression of a
supreme wisdom, that Shakespeare is the supreme poet of tragedy
and comedy, that anything supremely excellent and beautiful has
been created by the past?

Sandburg, according to this opinion, introduced themes which
had seldom been treated before, such as an impressive display of
energy in *Smoke and Steel*. His poems succeeded in doing what
they set out to do, whether this is art or not. Sandburg has chosen
to be down to earth "among the market carts" and the reader
would be remiss not to accept what he tries to convey, whether or
not he agrees with the poet's presentation. Technique may or may
not be present; realism presented in vivid local color is always
there.

Amy Lowell felt that Sandburg was a propagandist for the lowly with a prejudice against wealth that tended to blind him to the good qualities of men in higher stations of life, regardless of their merit.[8]

But Carl Sandburg was not merely defending the common people. He was giving vent to feelings deep within him which sprang up from the hardships of his youth and those around him in Galesburg and on the prairies. He felt he had a right to speak for these people and those whom he later met in Milwaukee and in Chicago. He defended this right by crying out against old houses, the ugly buildings which he passed going to and coming from work. They brought a lump to his throat and from this his poetic voice sang out a raucous protest. He felt the grief of the people there and he voiced their resentment. If this did not sound good to comfortable, wealthy people, it is not surprising.

Touching and typical of Sandburg's great compassion is the poem "And So Today" which was inspired by the burial of the unknown soldier in the cemetery at Arlington, Virginia. The following is a significant excerpt:

> And so today—they lay him away—
> the boy nobody knows the name of—
> the buck private—the unknown soldier—
> the doughboy who dug under and died
> when they told him to—that's him.[9]

Various philosophies have been read into this poem, principally that Sandburg was first of all a pacifist; this may be true, but probably his main intent was to show the madness of war itself, regardless of how those feel who take part in it. Some readers of the poem have felt pity, others anger, and others uncertain desperation. Uppermost is surely the lament for the unrealized causes for which the young soldier died. The aims are still unaccomplished; the goals are yet to be reached, whether by a League of Nations or a United Nations, united in formality only. In the poem is shown the spectacle of citizens paying tribute to the dead soldier by laying wreaths, placing roses, and indulging in oratory.

However, there is also shown the skeleton horses and the cynicism of those in the crowds who see the folly of war as well as its manifest glory. The corpse is laid away "under a sky of promises"; the powerful poem suggests that the symbolic acts are illusory because of a nation's tragic lack of understanding.

Here Sandburg is bewildered by the carnage of war and almost stunned by its catastrophic results. He is disgusted with the antics of the orators who are not expected to be so conscious of the folly of the conflict as a reflective poet. They seem to think that they know what the boy in the grave died for, but they do not make it clear—at least not convincing to the poet. They have, he believes, only a dense misconception of a respectable society. To him, war had "played hell with a community."

In his poem "Prairie," Sandburg expresses an exultant defense of his often-called drab native country. Here he says that "the past is a bucket of ashes" which indicates his position in regard to traditional values. But when he said, "there is nothing in the world only an ocean of tomorrows," one derives a different impression.[10] In this poem, Sandburg has been said to acknowledge that it is the prairie that fed him, that made him content. One critic even compared it with the Psalms of David or the Song of Solomon. Here the poet tells what he sees and is happy with the plain and simple values of the common life. He was born on the prairie and enjoyed "the milk of its wheat, the red of its clover, [and] the eyes of its women." It sings to him in the forenoon and at night he rests in its arms. Here are wagons, horses, plows, sod-houses, and towns—on the rivers and in Omaha, Kansas City, and Minneapolis and St. Paul. Here are described the flatboats, Indian homes, the grim smokestacks outlined against the skyline, the express trains speeding across the plains, and the bluffs of the Mississippi River.

Yet Henry van Dyke took a less poetic view of part of the description. He wrote, "Carl Sandburg says, 'The past is a bucket of ashes.' Now *ashes of the past* was once a poetic phrase, though it has now become a cliché. But when you lug in the bucket it makes one think of the janitor and the garbage can."

Sandburg was obviously contemptuous of old forms of poetry. He had a fairly good education in liberal arts in college but his interest was mainly in the English classics, with Keats and Browning as favorites. Never did he immerse himself in the Greek and Latin classics as did Longfellow, for instance, and his work shows this lack of form. Even when he obtained a book that he especially liked, his tendency was to tear out the pages that most interested him and throw the rest away. He expressed himself naturally, apparently using the dictionary and thesaurus frequently in search of just the right word; and he usually made an exquisite choice. He was convinced early in his writing career that Americans did not express their own life in the terms which should be used. The towns, the country, the people who lived in them were depicted vividly, he felt, but not accurately. Current language was alien to our poets.

His sense of rhythm and meter is admirable and frequently his lines can readily be set to music. Many of his poems are prose and much of his prose is poetry. He writes often in the Walt Whitman style but not enough so one can state positively that he imitates him. That Sandburg admired Whitman is evidenced by a letter that he wrote his sister Mary on June 2, 1904, in which he mentioned, "I was in Walt Whitman's old home last Sunday, and on Memorial Day threw a rose in his tomb at Camden."

There is no doubt that Sandburg has his own style and perhaps no poem brings this out more than his "Lost."

> Desolate and lone
> All night long on the lake
> Where fog trails and mist creeps,
> The whistle of the boat
> Calls and cries unendingly,
> Like some lost child
> In tears and trouble
> Hunting the harbor's breast
> And the harbor's eyes.[11]

Mostly, it seems, the poems of Carl Sandburg, like all of his other writings, are his own. They are examples of a man's expressing himself on paper, very consciously not following any rule, feeling deep down that he is bigger than most of the rules and in many cases, proving it. At first his audiences and his readers were against his verse form, but by the time he was through, reading and singing and writing, they were usually won over. He felt that men needed more courage in interpreting America, and he gave himself to this task with lifelong abandon. In his heyday, he was conscious of the revolt against existing standards in the arts and he made himself a vital part of this revolt. The scholar was at first opposed to him because here was a new form of earthy poetic expression unlike the classic forms which had been studied and revered so long.

Sandburg's own definitions of poetry seem fitting here:

> Poetry is a projection across silence of cadences arranged to break that silence with definite intentions of echos, syllables, wave lengths.
>
> Poetry is an art practiced with the terribly plastic material of human language.
>
> Poetry is a sliver of the moon lost in the belly of a golden frog.
>
> Poetry is a phantom script telling how rainbows are made and why they go away.
>
> Poetry is the achievement of the synthesis of hyacinths and biscuits.[12]

Of course, a vital element that distinguished the poems of Carl Sandburg was his own vocal delivery of them. In his sonorous voice which made even the commonplace seem dramatic, he sang out his rhythmic word pictures until his audiences were fascinated by the sounds alone—which is just what he meant for them to be. Some people who asserted that they found no beauty in the reading of Sandburg's poetry became entranced by his own rich intoning of the lines.

Among those who early recognized the power of Sandburg's verse on the printed page was Louis Untermeyer. He believed, after reading the first volumes, that the poet had the ability to make language live, to cause the printed page to dance and sing and even bleed. Whitman, Untermeyer felt, would have been overjoyed to have the opportunity and timely talent of Sandburg. It was pointed out that here was an angry opponent of Billy Sunday who responded to that ardent evangelist by charging that he was slangy and vilifying while pretending to be religious.

Untermeyer also appreciated Sandburg's gift for sharp and sympathetic etching of his firm, suggestive lines. Here was a passion for justice, a cry against the economic wrongdoings of America and the rage to kill beauty that appeared to be characteristic of the wealthy and predatory. Untermeyer felt that Sandburg evoked the background of his actors with the fewest possible strokes, and with a sympathy that few poets possess. His heat was a dynamic force which could distort and overbalance the effect of his work. Thus he regarded Sandburg as both soft- and hard-speaking, but beneath his brutality, possibly the tenderest of American poets. As an example he cites, as is so often done, the requiem note of "Cool Tombs": [13]

When Abraham Lincoln was shoveled into the tombs, he forgot
    the copperheads and the assassin . . . in the dust, in the
    cool tombs.
And Ulysses Grant lost all thought of con men and Wall Street,
    cash and collateral turned ashes . . . in the dust, in the cool
    tombs.
Pocahontas' body, lovely as a poplar, sweet as a red haw
    in November or a pawpaw in May, did she wonder?
    remember? . . . in the dust, in the cool tombs?
Take any streetful of people buying clothes and groceries, cheer-
    ing a hero or throwing confetti and blowing tin horns . . .
    tell me if the lovers are losers . . . tell me if any get more
    than the lovers . . . in the dust . . . in the cool tombs.[14]

Here beneath the slang one is conscious of the mystic quality of the poet. Here are blended sweetness and sonority and feminine grace. Here is a prime example of the new American spirit in poetry. This is not gained from dry tomes within the recesses of the library but from the real earth, the dirt as well as the sky. There are great gaps and boulders here, steaming ditches and the deep-chested laughter of workers quarreling, forgetting, building. Brutal, tender, full of anger and pity, his lines run light as a child's pleasure or stumble along with the heavy grace of a hunky, common as sunlight or tall on Third Avenue of a Saturday. Rough-hewn and solid; perhaps a bit too conscious of its biceps; too proud of the way its thumping feet trample down quiet places. But going on, on, gladly, doggedly—with a kind of large ecstasy. One thinks of a dark sea with its tides tossing and shouting. Or the streets of a crowd-filled city when a great wind runs through them.

The use of free verse by Sandburg brought upon him a strong attack by the traditional poets such as Amy Lowell and Ezra Pound—although they both admired him, for his work was in line with some of their main ideas, such as the use of the language of common speech, especially in employing the exact word, not just that which was nearly so, and the creation of new rhythms to express new moods, not the imitation of old rhythms. Sandburg agreed with them in their quest for a more effective use of language, derived from the experience of mankind. He believed that when men no longer possess a poetic feeling for life itself, then poetry may lose its means of exalting humanity.

Sandburg put a new stress on deriving his subjects as well as his language from everyday life and criticized severely the generally accepted process of what he termed subjugation of the intellect to well-matched syllables. He believed that the excessive use of verse forms tended to make the rhyme more important than the meaning and thus deceived the reader. Often, he believed, particular poets made a style of their own so that they could be recognized from this aspect alone. It is not easy to characterize Sandburg in this respect but certain things do stand out as typical

of him. His vignette technique is vivid and his brief character-
izations of personalities are unique. In describing motley humanity, his sketches form an artistic picture clearly recognizable as
his own. Sometimes one wonders what is poetry and what is
prose, but there is no mistaking that it is Sandburg and that in
short, bold strokes he has brought to life a myriad of human
prototypes. His dynamic portrayal of the city of Chicago is held
to be the most forceful description of it in poetry and was quoted
on television as recently as the 1968 Presidential election campaign.

This was a highly appropriate use of his verse, for he is ever,
when dealing with industrial subjects, the social historian who
elevates the commonplace to rhythmic heights. Here he shows
that this nation has grown more in material stature than in spiritual wealth and he may be said to have been in many ways our
first poetic muckraker.

As this poet progressed in personal experience and technical
prowess, he progressed markedly too in his artistic interpretation. It was increasingly clear that underneath his rough exterior,
his earthy manner and gruff demeanor, there was a highly sensitive approach to poetry. He became more restrained. This is shown
not only in his writing but in his choice of subjects. His caustic
criticism mellows into substance more kind and considerate. Not
so much does he cry out in *Cornhuskers* as he had done previously against the raw evils of society. Here is shown most clearly
the effect of his Scandinavian background, not only through his
mother's influence (she was still living), but also through some
knowledge of Swedish history which he had evidently spent more
time on than was known prior to this publication.

In this second volume of his poems, Sandburg emerges as more
mature in the field of poetry and with a new concept of the
beauties of the world. Time, increasing knowledge, and a greater
satisfaction with some phases of life show in his lines. His affection for the land shines through in his description of the prairie
grass, the flight of wild geese overhead, the antics of pet animals,
the songs of birds, and the music which ever exists around us if

we only hear it. He has come to accept more what is, rather than demanding what should be, and he shows a new ability to interpret this country in the light of world significance. His poetry has moved out from the din of the cities and their concomitant evils to the tranquil scene of the prairie in which he finds not only solace but even beauty. This of course brings to his work a more lyrical quality, better imagery, and more contrast than he had hitherto exhibited. Nature held for him affection as well as disaster. No doubt this was accentuated by the inspiration derived from a devoted wife and a happy family atmosphere. From his home grew not only poetry but music; and Carl Sandburg often put the two together in a beautiful way. He added a pastoral tone to his already rich treatment, and, though still downgraded by some critics, was well on his way toward significant literary heights.

In his war poems Sandburg shows that America had a strong determination to do its part in world events and help to achieve victorious results for what it mainly regarded as the right side. In a smoother style, he displays varying moods and subjects, emphasizing again the matchless value he places on human life. Being close to the heart of the United States, in more ways than one, Sandburg played out upon his poetic strings a concordant melody of strong protest against war.

Although Sandburg never had a son—a fourth child who died at birth was also a girl—he could write about a boy and his father with remarkable understanding. Here is shown as well a new tenderness in the poet and an emotional approach toward religion which he admitted mostly through the medium of verse. But not far from such sentimental expression is found also another element common to him; a denunciation of social conditions which he had so often found in the factories and slums of the Chicago area. Sandburg calls upon the compassion of mankind to rid itself of the scourge of exploitation of the poor. In scope, the poems range from powerful ones about the smoke and steel of the industrial scene to short and poignant ones depicting landscapes of the Middle West and South and colorful character studies of the denizens of the tenement sections. At times, Sandburg wonders what life is all about—as in:

HATS

HATS, where do you belong? what is under you?
  On the rim of a skyscraper's forehead
  I looked down and saw: hats: fifty thousand hats:
  Swarming with a noise of bees and sheep, cattle and
    waterfalls,
  Stopping with a silence of sea grass, a silence of
    prairie corn.
Hats: tell me your high hopes.[15]

Slabs of the Sunburnt West appeared in 1922 and covers a broader panorama than Sandburg had previously done. He appears to have come to view the past more in the light of a pageant of history than in the sharp stabs of its individual parts. From what was apparently a study of the westward movement as such, the poet turns to the shaping of the people's character by this movement and its significance to our whole civilization. Perhaps showing the effects of the theory propounded by Frederick Jackson Turner, Sandburg interprets broadly the experience which the western pioneers underwent in their struggle with the elements. They were tried in the crucible of the frontier and came out for the most part as conquerors of their environment. The people moved and with them went old customs and traditions which were soon caught up in new conditions and problems. Out of it all came a new type of American—and none was more typical of this new type than Carl Sandburg himself.

He even took a closer and longer look at his city of Chicago. Now he chose not simply to castigate it like a fond parent spanking a child, but to go back into the past and trace the growth of the windy city from its beginnings. Having understood this development better, he was able to express a deeper understanding of the forces at work in a new nation. Doubtless this study whetted his appetite for the large novel he was later to write and which is supposed to trace the story of America from its birth.

From this broadening there came more recognition among his fellows. Other American poets now held him in higher esteem. Even Amy Lowell who had so lamented his propagandistic work wrote a poem to him and admitted that for the first time she saw the Middle West clearly—through the eyes of Sandburg. In so doing, she paid high tribute to him for his vividness, his authenticity, and his musical contributions both in poems and on the guitar.

Other kinds of music came to him after publication of *The Prairie Years*, namely, critical praise and financial remuneration. By 1928, his reputation had so grown that he was invited to Harvard University to deliver the Phi Beta Kappa address. Ninety-one years before, Ralph Waldo Emerson had given on this occasion his famous speech entitled "The American Scholar." So it was obviously a high honor for this son of the prairies, who had not even finished undergraduate school, to be designated—as he was at that time—an honorary member of the fraternity.

At the meeting, Sandburg read a new poem, "Good Morning, America," which was soon published along with others in a new volume by that name. The title poem itself is a long and uneven work which is not rated as highly, in general, as most of the poet's output. It states that "America began young the same as a baby," with its swaddling clothes, its small shirt, and its long joints—then raises the question: who can tell the secrets of its moons now? In it there is great eloquence, but also much that is prosaic. It swings between the realistic and the nebulously ethereal, some of it apparently done for the occasion, always a risk in any such undertaking. There are many lines which leave the reader cold and make him wonder if at this point Sandburg may not have bogged down in preoccupation with some other thoughts or activity. He sings of the productive, early power of those who have built modern America and sounds the clarion for religious freedom. His passion for history growing, he goes back to the colonial days and shows the actions of our founders as they made their way against the new surroundings. The formative changes which took place in

the last century are pictured and then he brings us into the sweep
of the present one, with a flourish of poetic trumpets.

Yet he warns of trials to come, of a possible denouement like
that of Greece and Rome, and expresses the fervent hope that we
will not soon have to say, "goodnight, America." Despite the
poem's weaknesses, it also contains flashes of Sandburg at his best,
although they are somewhat obscured at times. One thing is clear:
the poem was and is a flat challenge. It seems to apply remarkably
to the present, with order and chaos existing side by side, with
despair and hope competing for our attention.

It was the element of despair existing so widely around him
that made Sandburg write his important poem *The People, Yes*
which appeared in 1936. America was in the depression, and although he now lived with his family on Lake Michigan in compar-
ative quiet and comfort, still, his acutely conscious being was
cognizant of the grievous conditions of the country as a whole.
Here in the melancholy of economic retreat, Sandburg rings out
a cheer for democracy:

> Man is a long time coming.
> Man will yet win.
>
>   .   .   .   .   .
>
> . . . one hears "Yes but the people what about the people?"
> Sometimes as though the people is a child to be pleased or fed
> Or again a hoodlum you have to be tough with
> And seldom as though the people is a caldron and a reservoir
> Of the human reserves that shape history . . .
>   "Man will never write,"
>   they said before the alphabet came
>   and man at last began to write.
>   "Man will never fly,"
>   they said before the planes and blimps
>   zoomed and purred in arcs
>   winding their circles around the globe.
>
>   .   .   .   .   .

        The people will live on.
The learning and blundering people will live on.
They will be tricked and sold and again sold
And go back to the nourishing earth for rootholds,
The people so peculiar in renewal and comeback,
You can't laugh off their capacity to take it.

            .   .   .   .   .

        Man is a long time coming.
        Man will yet win.[16]

This volume of poems is a mixture hard to describe. It has rhythmic verse which changes to irregular sounds and forms. Here is lingo as coarse as any that Sandburg writes, here are sayings from folklore, here are proverbs and superstitions and warmhearted passages expressing deep truths and wisdom so profound that one wonders whence the poet derived it all. Evidently this was the voice in which Sandburg wished to speak for people of all kinds. Why some of the prose sections are included in what is supposed to be poetry is difficult to fathom.

Some of his defense of democracy probably sprang from the attacks made on American society by Communist groups in the 1930s when our society was particularly vulnerable. Sandburg's answer is to point to the inexorable movement of nations with representative government toward their democratic goals, albeit at times through fire. In this march, humans of various types join in a common effort and objective, a combination of feelings and faiths, with all the ups and downs that go with any such great struggle. But from the mighty struggle emerges finally the brightness of success and the fruition of the common longing. In *The People, Yes* Sandburg successfully defends our democracy against its Communist opponents. He shows vividly that, although this country is made up of countless varied groups and interests, in the long run it acts as one when above it the great storms break.

From then on the time of Carl Sandburg was taken up mostly with his prose writings, on Lincoln, a novel, and various other forms. He did write more poetry but it was not regularly his major interest. In 1941, he penned a poem entitled "Mr. Longfellow and His Boy." It begins:

> Mr. Longfellow, Henry Wadsworth Longfellow,
>   the Harvard Professor,
>   the poet whose pieces you see in all the schoolbooks,
> "Tell me not in mournful numbers
>   life is but an empty dream . . ."
> Mr. Longfellow sits in his Boston library writing,
> Mr. Longfellow looks across the room
>   and sees his nineteen-year-old boy
> propped up in a chair at a window,
> home from the war,
> a rifle ball through right and left shoulders.[17]

Sandburg then quotes more of Longfellow, "Thou, too, sail on, O Ship of State! Sail on, O Union, strong and great!" and ends the poem with a comparison with President Franklin D. Roosevelt in the White House, struggling with the great problems of World War II which was then still confined to Europe. In conclusion, he again quotes the poem about the union. He copied it in his own hand and sent it to the President.

On April 7, 1941, exactly eight months before the disaster at Pearl Harbor, President Roosevelt wrote the following letter:

> The White House
> April 7, 1941
>
> Dear Carl Sandburg:
>   I have received through the kindness of Archie Mac-Leish that copy of your poem: "Mr. Longfellow and His Boy" so carefully written out by your own hand. Your treatment of this inspiring theme is masterly. It reflects deep poetic sentiment, expressed in lines of singular beauty and sinewy strength.
>   Naturally the poem makes a strong appeal to me and I need hardly assure you that this copy in your own hand-

writing will find a place among the personal mementos I cherish most. Please accept my heartfelt thanks.

Very sincerely yours,

Franklin D. Roosevelt [18]

On Carl Sandburg's eighty-fifth birthday, seventy-seven new poems of his were published under the title *Honey and Salt*. In these he dwells on his favorite themes—life, love, and death. Many who read the book were seeing Sandburg's writings for the first time and did not understand him. But to the older readers, here was the familiar poet—again speaking in much the same voice that sang of Chicago or of how the fog came on little cat feet. Here were found again the images of grim city streets as well as prettier scenes. The poet speaks of the prairies, the sun rising over them, the fogs and mists, the sun, moon, and stars. The formless handling is all his own and the tender vies with the tough. Sandburg is still wandering and wondering. But when he describes a boy and girl falling in love, there is a sureness that convinces one that he knows exactly what he is writing about, even at the age of eighty-five.

The praise for the new volume was not new. A decade earlier when Sandburg had received the gold medal of the American Academy of Arts and Letters, *The New York Times* commented editorially on his other achievements, then added,

> But it has been his poetry that expressed the man the most. Roughhewn and unconventional, its cadence has its roots in our midwest speech, and the idioms and slang that lie embedded in it are as American as Yosemite. Yet in spite of its regional dress, it speaks to the world in its compassion for the plight of man and in its attempt to feel the heart behind the world of the machine. He was among the first of our poets to accept our machine civilization for what it is and to try to see behind the dross and tinsel of metropolis the lineaments of beauty. His poetry has been sharply attacked and eloquently defended. But Sandburg has refused to enter the battle. 'Those who make poems,'

he once said, 'and hope that their poems are not bad may find readers and listeners—and again they may not.'[19]

He did. The next year, at Christmas, he penned a piece of poetry which appeared in the newspapers. It was called simply, "Names":

> There is only one horse on the earth
> and his name is All Horses.
> There is only one bird in the air
> and his name is All Wings.
> There is only one fish in the sea
> and his name is All Fins.
> There is only one man in the world
> and his name is All Men.
> There is only one woman in the world
> and her name is All Women.
> There is only one child in the world
> and the child's name is All Children.
> There is only one Maker in the world
> and his children cover the earth
> and they are named All God's Children.[20]

More expert appraisal of Sandburg's poetry appeared. A scholarly article by Professor Oscar Cargill, "Carl Sandburg: Crusader and Mystic," appeared in the publication, *College English*. This study was based on the concept that the early poems of Sandburg could be understood only if the reader was aware of the biographical and historical factors behind them. Cargill looked upon Sandburg as a mystical crusader who wrote so profusely that he sacrificed sensibility and inventiveness for the controversial. Writing in the *South Atlantic Quarterly* a few years later, Professor Gay Wilson Allen, a New York University colleague of Cargill's, interestingly observed that Sandburg had not only been ignored by serious critics since the peak of his reputation, but that reviewers of his latest poems had hardly read him since the 1920s or the 1930s. Allen called for a reevaluation of Sandburg and stated his own belief that the poet was not a thinker or philosopher so much as he was a seeker and wonderer.

On the other hand, Newton Arvin, writing in *The New Republic,* found that

> Carl Sandburg's continuous effort to find a poetic outlet for the fast, hard, noisy, smoky, machine-ridden experience of Middle Western city people and for the dry, unshaded experience of Middle Western villagers and farmers, has taken on the dimensions of a literary achievement, and one that no disparagement can minimize. In a generation in which most poets set themselves more manageable and more opportune tasks, he undertook to be the poet of a people among whom the sources of poetry, though by no means exhausted, were untapped, grown over and all but completely forgotten. . . . Sandburg's was the intention of a rhapsodist or (with important differences) of a modern "political" poet; and it led him to the attempt to get into verse the whole disorderly and humid life of the twentieth-century United States, with its violence, its grandiosity, its social tensions and its waste of human impulse and power. . . . His strength has lain in his closeness to the people, but they are a people whose impulses and affections have been nipped and stunted like trees in a city park or like wild flowers on a stock farm; and of so cramped an emotional existence this too cool, too inexpensive, too phlegmatic poetry—this poetry of half-lights and understatement and ironic anticlimaxes —is the inevitable expression. . . . Sandburg's words, it is true, have often come to him from the inexhaustible reservoirs of American slang; and, given his purpose, that was just where they should have come from: with no other language could he ever have rendered the surfaces or even the spirit of contemporary life as he has rendered them with his "galoots," his "necktie parties," his "fadeaways," and his "fake passes." [21]

In a more recent appraisal, T. K. Whipple takes a less lauda-
tory view of Sandburg as a poet. In his volume entitled *Spokes-
men,* he takes the poet to task for what is regarded as
uncontrolled power, and finds the poems uneven and uncertain.
According to this critic, the taste of Sandburg is lax and undisci-
plined and judgment is lacking. His poetry, it is felt, is seldom a
finished product but generally crude and raw. Much of the work
is not fully projected and it is unable to stand alone. But Sandburg is given credit for reflecting a fascinating world, even
though at times a strange and chaotic one. Its disorder is full of
inconstancy and contrast. No trait, the critic continues, is more
prominent in Sandburg's writing than his sensitiveness, even
though at times his expression is raucous. But he is conspicuous
among American poets for his great gusto and his zest for living
and his chief distinction in his power of realization. He appears
to be principally a psalmist.

Carl Sandburg has been compared with other poets of his
period with varying results. His poetry and that of Edward Arlington Robinson are both said to have substantial character
analysis and deep interpretation, with much of the verse of both
being that of protest. Both possess poetic imagery and both include many references, plain and subtle, to religion in their
poems. There is humor in the writings of the two poets but Sandburg's is of a lighter vein and more earthy, since he was more of
an optimist than Robinson, the brooding and Puritan-minded
New Englander who never quite came to accept life in its brighter
aspects. Then, Sandburg had more faith in people, and it was his
belief that no one could really be happy unless he did have faith.
Sandburg also dealt with more humorous phases of life. And
while he obviously had some doubts, he never lost faith in
humanity.

It would appear that there is also a common bond between
Sandburg and Vachel Lindsay who was likewise a middle west-
erner and a singer of folk ballads. But here it seems the similarity
stops. While Lindsay had a strong sense of idealism, he was
given more to fantasy than Sandburg and lived for only 50 years

compared to the 89 of our subject. Obviously both men were inspired by the same general subjects, especially by Abraham Lincoln, Lindsay having been born in Springfield, Illinois. But Sandburg possessed a deeper comprehension of these subjects than Lindsay, and he went on to delve profoundly into the Lincoln story, for example, whereas Lindsay—for a long time at least —appeared content to wander around the country singing and peddling his poems. Sandburg wandered too, but his main quest was visiting places which contained Lincoln material for his biography. Although Lindsay wrote some good poems, on the whole his work is less strong, courageous, and human than that of Sandburg. Judging from current concepts, the poetry of Sandburg will live longer than that of Vachel Lindsay.

Another midwesterner who for a while loomed strong as a contemporary of Sandburg's was Edgar Lee Masters. In fact they were close friends in their days in Chicago, and Masters wrote a tribute to Sandburg on the jacket of the first edition of *Chicago Poems*. But Masters was a lawyer at heart, a poet second. Both he and Sandburg became concerned with the social and moral side of American life, and at times Masters attacked it more sharply.

While there is continuing cynicism in the poetry of Masters, especially in his great *Spoon River Anthology,* such does not exist so strongly in Sandburg. Both write about the sham and unfairness of life, but Masters is more bitter while Sandburg always seems to retain his faith. Masters rightfully shows the smallness and meanness in village life, but instead of rising above it, he allows the darkness of the picture to dominate him more than it does Sandburg. Perhaps no one loved nature more than Carl Sandburg; but Edgar Lee Masters did not bring himself close enough to enjoy the full beauty of his natural environment as Sandburg did.

Often compared and with diverse results are Carl Sandburg and Robert Frost. The two have much in common; they corresponded and encouraged each other. But there are great differences. Frost was an important pastoral poet but he observed life more from the ivory tower of a professorship or from the quiet seclusion of his New England farm. Such a perspective naturally gave him a different viewpoint from that of a poor prairie boy thrust into a cruel city. This is reflected in the language of Frost who did not deign to use slang. While his poetry is pithy and some of it unforgettable, it is more provincial and abstract than Sandburg's, although it is often more graceful and balanced than that of the latter.

Both poets are realists, but Frost seems reluctant to recognize the grim aspects of industrial America, whereas Sandburg denounces them from the poetic housetops. Both poets do find deep significance in ordinary things—Frost in his mending wall and Sandburg in his skyscraper; and both find the hand of God at work where few would suspect Him to be. But where Sandburg is sad, Frost is serene; perhaps it is because of the latter's personal background, Frost having been born in California, moved to New England, traveled in Europe, and then settled down to a rather calm and successful existence here.

As a poet, Carl Sandburg has made his mark on the American scene, and it promises to be lasting. How it will rank in time to come, only the future can tell. There are some who think he was no poet at all; but they are vastly in the minority. He surely was a poetic voice, long to be heard. He set himself the mission of properly portraying America, and has done it.

In breadth of subject and in volume alone, his poems stand out. They have possibly been read by more people of more different kinds than the poems of any other major writer of this century. This is partly because of their popular nature and their wide diffusion through mass media; partly because Sandburg made himself even more famous through his prose writings. The millions who admire him have found stimulation and inspiration in his verse. There is a warmth to his approach found in few other messages. There is a humanity in his expression not to be lost upon anyone.

One does not have to turn to his poems to find the poetry of

Carl Sandburg. It is to be found abundantly in *The Prairie Years* and in *The War Years*. He simply cannot help being poetic, even in his speech. Wherever one finds Sandburg, there he finds poetry. He himself said, "Poetry is the opening and closing of a door, leaving those who look through to guess about what is seen during a moment."

Notable Associates

Sandburg worked with many, including the noted collector and student of Civil War photographs, Frederick Hill Meserve. The latter recalled how he and Sandburg sat together and talked about the pictures needed for the life of Lincoln. The biographer would read from his manuscript in a booming voice which varied at times from mouthing and rolling words on the tongue to a fast change of pace as the action increased. Or Sandburg would find in Meserve's collection some photographic negative from Mathew Brady, prominent photographer of the Civil War, and hold it up, exclaiming at its beauty and appropriateness. He would linger over the pictures of Lincoln as if they were of some member of his own family—which in a way they were.

Sandburg told Meserve that ignorant people had been talking about Lincoln in a way that made him tired. He felt that it would take one a week to read *The War Years* and that some would feel insulted, regarding the big book as "a bale of hay" when what they wanted was "a ham sandwich." According to Meserve, bedtime would come for him but not for Sandburg, who expressed his thoughts out loud as his mind raced on and on. Some of these were on Lincoln's fine sense of justice, and Sandburg admired it almost with adoration. He felt the President's personality had more shadings and colors than any other in American history. He dwelt also on Lincoln's sense of human tragedy and feeling for the lives of others who toiled without reward.

In the early 1940s, Sandburg became acquainted with the late historian James G. Randall, of the University of Illinois, and his wife, Ruth. Randall was writing his four-volume *Lincoln the President* and of course the two men had much in common. One cold day in Urbana, the Randalls heard on the phone the sonorous voice of Sandburg saying he was in town for a day and would like to come over. He did and Mrs. Randall found that he had a headache and cold feet, so after she had given him two aspirin tablets and a pair of wool socks, they were warm friends. The conversation that followed included Professor Bruce Weirick of the English Department; they discussed such topics as poetry, William Saroyan, goats, Shakespeare, Whitman, and of course the inevitable Lincoln.

So cordial became the friendship that Sandburg invited Randall to visit him at his home in Michigan. The invitation was accepted and Randall later related that he was given a course on the subject of goats. He apparently slept in a room near them, drank his first goat's milk, and was given a firsthand opportunity to observe these interesting animals. But of more interest to the professor was his chance to go through Sandburg's Lincoln collection. One night on a walk along the shores of the lake, the two discussed the hard work required in writing a biography of Lincoln. Sandburg remarked that he felt his energy for the task was

derived from his Swedish ancestors and only wished that he had
the zest for work that he had had when driving a milk wagon in
Galesburg. When Randall's work appeared and received high
praise, Sandburg told him to enjoy it while he could and to have
a thick skin about adverse criticism, a quality which he himself
did not always enjoy.

Robert Sherwood recalled that after he had reviewed Sandburg's *The War Years* in *The New York Times,* he received a telephone call one day from the author, who was in New York at the
time, asking that the two get together and take a walk. They did,
starting from East 45th Street northward on a cold day in December. By the time they had reached Central Park, Sherwood
was winded. Mainly they had walked in silence; then Sandburg
began talking about life after death and apparently assumed
that such a life existed. He wondered out loud what the spirit of
Abraham Lincoln hovering above them thought of these two
writers. Finally Sherwood answered he did not know but wondered what Lincoln would say to the idea of these two stopping
and having a drink. Several minutes later, Sandburg replied that
he thought Lincoln would approve. So they did.

Sandburg liked the 21 Club in New York. Once when he went
there with friends, he was asked where he would prefer to sit. He
replied that he just wanted to sit where he could see the celebrities. It happened that at that time he was the only celebrity in
the restaurant.

Later on, he called on the late Tallulah Bankhead, the actress,
and, according to her, drank two bottles of Jack Daniel's whiskey,
after which he walked steadily down her long stairs out into the
night, singing loudly, "I'll Be Seeing You."

Sandburg observed after World War II that we forget or have
never learned that George Washington had the support of only
a patriotic minority in the building of this nation, and pointed
out that there were at times more native-born Americans in arms
and fighting on the side of the British than Washington could
ever muster for his own troops.

As for fighting, the family came to feel they had been in conflict with the Lake Michigan weather for all too many years. So in 1945, they decided to look elsewhere. Mrs. Sandburg made a study of weather conditions throughout the United States and eventually came to the conclusion that the area around Hendersonville, North Carolina, in the western part of that picturesque state and in the edge of the magnificent Great Smoky Mountains, was the best place. Specifically, they decided to locate in the little wooded and quietly residential town of Flat Rock, and purchased the former home of Christopher G. Memminger which was built in 1833. He was at one time Secretary of the Treasury of the Confederacy under Jefferson Davis. Here was irony indeed. The biographer of Abraham Lincoln, the opponent if not the enemy of Davis, moving into a Southern domestic stronghold. But such irony appealed to the grim Sandburg humor. Carl felt it was just the place he had long sought; here was the poet's end of the rainbow, to be his last domicile, a huge house and estate which caused his friend Harry Golden to remark, "Your old Socialist colleagues up in Wisconsin must be turning over in their graves."

Perhaps Memminger was turning over also. This Confederate cabinet officer had been born in Germany, the son of an army officer in the duchy of Württemberg. After the father was killed, the mother came to Charleston, South Carolina. When she died, the son, at the age of four, was placed in an orphanage, but showed promise as he grew and eventually graduated from South Carolina College. Memminger became a commissioner of schools for Charleston and held this position for thirty years. As a lawyer, he opposed nullification and even wrote a booklet on his beliefs. But he did believe in slavery and after the John Brown raid, he addressed the Virginia Legislature in 1860 on the need for joint defensive measures. He became chairman of the committee which drafted the provisional constitution of the Confederate States. As Secretary of the Treasury under Jefferson Davis, he faced a difficult if not hopeless task because of inadequate tax laws and military reverses. When the credit of the Southern government collapsed, Memminger was generally held responsible for the disaster. In 1864, he retired to his country home in Flat Rock where he stayed until after the war was over. In 1867, he received a Presidential pardon from Andrew Johnson and returned to Charleston where he practiced law. His later years were distinguished by his efforts toward good schools for both whites and Negroes.

Another example of Sandburg's sympathetic interest in those on the southern side is shown in a letter he had written on July 3, 1941, to John C. Pemberton, III, prominent New York attorney who had sent the biographer of Lincoln a copy of his own biography of his grandfather, *General John C. Pemberton, Defender of Vicksburg.* "Thank you for sending me a book so strictly in my field," wrote Sandburg, "that I have read it carefully in toto. Of course I am among those who believe events had moved to the point where reconciliation by any devices of negotiation was beyond possibility. . . . I came to respect General Pemberton for his tenacity and his superb use of meager resources, and other qualities."

The Memminger home, regardless of background, had a beautiful view, Carl Sandburg thought. According to his daughter Margaret, he held the same kind of compassionate attitude toward southerners as did Lincoln, and got along with them well. She feels that he never was regarded as a "real Yankee" in North Carolina, a state which welcomes progress. In the midst of discussing the new home, somehow the subject of Sandburg's long white hair came into the conversation. Margaret recalled the story about her father's being at the home of Robert Frost, who was asked where the other poet was.

"Oh, he's upstairs fixing his hair," was the reply.

"You mean, combing it back from his eyes?"

"No, combing it into his eyes. He likes it that way."

Another reason for the move south was not simply a change of scenery. Sandburg needed more warmth. Often now he would wear a scarf around his neck and an afghan over his knees, as perhaps befitted a 68-year-old man who had lived a strenuous life and whose long night hours of work were already beginning to tell on him. But he did not wear a shawl, as some have believed. He at times wore a sweater with the sleeves tied behind, as this gave his arms more freedom of movement to write.

Although the house was impressively large and set in a picturesquely beautiful landscape, it needed changing. For the Sandburgs, the ceilings were too high. So they had these lowered. There were only two bathrooms and these were increased to four. There were virtually no closets, the old-fashioned families having used separate wardrobes. So the Sandburgs had built in some, as they were "a family that just simply can't do without closets." The bookshelves in Michigan were taken down and moved to Flat Rock, for this was a time of shortage of lumber and furniture because of the recent war. Some 12,000 books were also brought along to adorn the new house; they were not only on the subject of American history, but as Margaret pointed out, included American literature, Swedish, Japanese, Russian, and Chinese literature, and many books by French writers. The huge Lincoln library had been given to the University of Illinois.

On approaching the Sandburg home at Flat Rock, one makes a turn in the tree-lined road through a cool leafy recess and suddenly the house appears—high on a hill, very white, and framed by white pine trees towering up to 125 feet tall. From the dormer windows a view for forty miles can be seen across the majestic Smoky Mountains. The squarish house itself sits on an elevation of about 2,500 feet, at the center of a 245-acre plot of woods and pasture. It had been named "Connemara" by previous occupants who were Irish. Inside on a clear day, the sun poured brightly through uncurtained windows, and in one room was a white mantel beneath which the hearth was filled with various kinds of walking sticks, for there was lots of walking in the Sandburg family. The high bookcases—some of them with eleven shelves—held every type of subject from the *U.S. Camera Annual* to southern volumes on the Civil War.

In each room there was a fire extinguisher and a guitar case. On the first floor stood stacks of Sears, Roebuck catalogs, in reverent memory of the outbuildings of yesteryear, which were used as footrests when Carl felt the urge to hold forth on his guitar. In an upper room, as in Michigan, was the realm of the author himself, a place of orange crates and other such boxes but now these were close to a chrome-and-leather chair and his type-writer. There he maintained his reputation for making changes on the proofs of books, and for keeping poems in his desk drawers for as long as twenty years. There again he slept through the early part of the day, usually, and worked in the evening hours. Upon arising, he did his calisthenics, walking in the airy outside, and raising a heavy cedar chair above his head to keep his body in shape. Perhaps he would visit the goat pasture in the after-noon or show up at the big rock with moss on its top where he often worked for awhile. For a time he and his family were in-vited out socially by the prosperous neighbors; but soon they learned that Carl was likely to show up in an old red shirt—that is, when he did not entirely forget the invitation. Finally, the neighbors decided that the Sandburgs were living in "another world."

But the man of Connemara was not entirely aloof to his sur-roundings. On January 17, 1946, he appeared by request at the local Moore General Hospital and spoke, read, and sang for the patients and personnel. He was introduced as the "greatest living authority on Abraham Lincoln." Sandburg prefaced his recital by saying that "but for certain circumstances, the late war might still be running and have years to run." He referred to the atomic bomb as a weapon that had brought new problems to this coun-try, but he felt that the problems were an acceptable price since the bomb had shortened the war. At one time in his performance, he quoted the proverb, "Nothing is more certain than death, nothing more uncertain than the hour." He added that it applied well to the recent passing of General George S. Patton; and as he lingered upon the saying, there was a feeling that he was also thinking of himself.

However, it was to be years before Sandburg entered that "un-discover'd country from whose bourn no traveller returns . . ."

As the family gathered—Mrs. Sandburg and two daughters arrived there in late 1946, Carl and his daughter Margaret in
early 1947—the place began to hum with activity. Besides the
immediate family, Helga's young son and daughter, Joseph Carl
and Paula, arrived to enliven the proceedings. Jackson, a shaggy
cocker spaniel also appeared as did Chula, a fine-looking Siamese
cat. Of special importance was the arrival of the goats. Although
Carl spent some time with them, they were really the personal
concern of Mrs. Sandburg who continued her expert interest in
them, one which turned to a pretty profit as well.

The father now found that climate was not the only necessity
for a satisfactory life for him. He found at long last that six hours
a day was the limit for his writing at this stage, four being better.
But he also discovered that even if this were his planned schedule, he often became so enwrapped in his research that his companions, "the night stars," soon slipped away and over the deep
blue Smoky Mountains came the sun "and rosy-fingered dawn
appeared." With the very boxwood and bamboo which Christopher Memminger himself planted, this quiet vista must have
seemed a throwback to those days of which Sandburg had so
eloquently written.

But the Sandburg women were not to live like ladies of the
Old South. They had been too accustomed to hard housework.
The few servants they tried turned out to be too town-loving and
hour-conscious, so they were soon allowed to spend all their time
away from Connemara. The wife and daughters got down to
their old routine, and liked it. And one reason they did was because the lord and master of the household was nearly always
close at hand, coming into the kitchen or laundry from time to
time to pass along a bit of poetry or homely philosophy, often
accompanied on his "gui-tar."

It was a happy home, probably because it was busy in a nice,
leisurely way. At times, it seemed that Carl was now almost in
the background—especially when the goats were attended to.
Mrs. Sandburg would go to feed and pet them and sometimes he

would go with her. One day as one of the goats nuzzled up against her, she explained that the goat would not eat her clothing but added that they were fond of nylon. At a recent stock show she recalled that a visitor had been standing and talking and not paying any attention to the Sandburg goats. She was wearing a nylon skirt and one of the goats came up behind her and started nibbling. The moisture from the goat's mouth made the fabric soften, and before the woman knew it, the goat had eaten out the back of her skirt.

Mrs. Sandburg could quote production figures, butterfat percentages, and breeding methods related to her animals. Milk from the goats was sold to a Hendersonville dairy, and many letters regarding the herd were received from different parts of the country. A Cuban wrote that he wanted "to buy some of the goats from the farm of that wonderful biographer of Lincoln."

Asked if she was lonely when her husband was away, Mrs. Sandburg told Karl Fleming of the *Asheville Citizen-Times*, "Dear, no. I look forward to it in a way because it gives me a chance to catch up on my own work. I think it is good for couples to separate occasionally. And Mr. Sandburg always has such interesting things to tell me when he gets home. I have never felt left out. And I have never felt that I had a right to interfere with Mr. Sandburg. When we were first married, I felt that what he was trying to do was wonderful and gave him credit for his wonderful vitality and energy. He was working sixteen hours a day, part of the time at the paper and then at home on the first Lincoln biography. But I think a woman should create interests of her own. It would be a lonely life if a woman didn't get interested in things for herself."

She told how she had come down from Michigan and selected the place—how Asheville did not have the kind of house they were looking for.

"The decision came when Mr. Sandburg came down and saw the view from the front porch," she said. As to the house, she added that she did not like rooms that look like a window in a furniture store, because these windows look so cold and unlived in.

Referring to the Sears catalogs and books piled around, she commented, "And if he wants to leave that stack of books there for a month, that is all right with me."

She admitted proofreading the Sandburg copy, saying that she herself usually remained at the farm all the year around except when she visited her brother, Edward Steichen, the renowned photographer. She felt that the two most understanding men she had ever known were her husband and brother, both of whom she felt had attained some degree of greatness. She felt that understanding and greatness go together. "Mr. Sandburg," she said, "is interested in everything and has been interested in every person he ever met. He likes people. I believe this leads to understanding. He is very easygoing. I can put a dish on the table about which I have some doubts and he'll say, 'My dear, I couldn't have gotten a better dish at the finest hotel in New York.'"

Now and then, Carl Sandburg did visit New York. He also went to New Salem once for a televised visit through the prairie; later he went to Moscow with Steichen to show the Russians a photographic exhibit entitled, "The Family Of Man." On one occasion he went to Washington and delivered a speech to Congress.

Where did the money come from, to buy and live at Connemara and to make such trips? Obviously from the sales of his books which were now soaring, the one-and-a-half million words he had written on Lincoln, the one-volume condensation, etc., were now before the eyes of millions of people, selling tens of thousands in hardcover and paperback, in literary club editions and in foreign language translations. Asked how much of an estate he left when he died, Margaret replied with a look of satisfaction, "Father did all right by his family."

Much mail was received at the Flat Rock home. Much of it went unanswered. This writer recalls being with Sandburg once when he received an inquiry. He explained that if he answered all the letters he received, the would not have time to write his books. When people wrote to ask the meaning of some Sandburg poem, Mrs. Sandburg would often reply for him in the words of Browning, "When I wrote that poem, God knew what it meant and I knew what it meant. Now only God knows."

But more goats than poems kept popping up at Connemara. Bill Sharpe, a writer for the state news bureau at Raleigh, noticed that

> Nubians, Toggenburgs, and Saanems are fine goats but not literary goats and show little interest in Sandburg and his work. . . . One of them, a fine creature known as Alison, is the American champion, so far as giving milk is concerned. There are some 80 others on the farm, but Alison is exceptional because weighing only 135 pounds, she produced 136 pounds of butter fat, but it never was clear whether she produced this in a day, a month,or a year. No difference; whatever it was, it is the record, and Alison's kids are sold for $100 each just as fast as she can produce them. . . . The goats are clean, aristocratic looking, and quite docile. They do not, alas, eat tin cans but do get a fine diet from the Connemara pastures and from scientifically determined feeds. "Just like cows," Helga says. . . . They have only two teats and a man with two hands and a willing heart can milk one in a jiffy. A good goat will yield three and one-half gallons a day. The milk is wholesaled to a downtown dairy and is in demand by people all around, especially by hospitals.[1]

One goat was named "Felicia Agawam" and she also produced her weight in milk. Sometimes when he was not working or mixing with the goats, Sandburg sat at a cozy window by the radiator in winter and watched the birds fly by, among which were rosy-breasted purple finches which took full advantage of the bird feeder behind the house. When Carl passed across his front porch, he usually took his daily exercises by stretching and turning his body, trying to keep in what he liked to call "baseball trim." Helga recalled how he would open his pocket knife and throw it up in the air, then catch it by the handle with the blade still open, to the consternation of his family.

"Can't you stop him?" she once asked her mother.

"I never tell Carl what to do," was the significant answer.

Then she asked him what he wanted for supper and he responded that he didn't care, that he had "been a bum all his life."

When they brought him his guitar, he strummed the chords and asked if they wanted to hear "Red Iron Ore." Then he admitted he might have forgotten the words. Instead he asked, "How about 'When the curtains of night are pinned back by the stars, and the beautiful moon swept the sky?'"

Meantime, the Michigan neighbors were lamenting his leaving. The Associated Press story stated that Lake Michigan was losing one of the best stone-skippers ever to hurl a piece of shale across its rolling waters. There it was felt he was leaving a veritable writer's paradise on a site "reminiscent of the Bay of Naples where in 1929 he began the almost unbelievable task of putting into a million and a half words the story of Lincoln's role in the War Between the States."

Sandburg was quoted as saying about the South, "If anything, I've found the colleges and universities and teaching there even more liberal than in the North. Tolerance is there in great measure today." He added that he never let a day go by without doing some writing. "You know, you've got to let the hook down and float a sinker to see what's going on in the old bean. . . . For many centuries, it has been taught that mankind is of one blood and the family of man is a unity. And now the airplane, radar, and above all, the atomic bomb, tell us we must change our habits and think in terms of global humanity. Otherwise, the two world wars we have seen will each look like a pleasant picnic compared to what can and may come."

In 1947, Sandburg and the J. G. Randalls, among others, went to Washington for the opening of the papers which had been deposited in the Library of Congress by Lincoln's son, Robert Todd Lincoln, who had specified in his will that these documents were not to be opened until twenty-one years after his death. James Randall prepared an article on the event for *The New York Times*, Sandburg for the *Washington Post*. The date was to be July 26th, so those concerned gathered in the Library at midnight of the preceding night. As the clock struck, Dr. C. Percy Powell of the Library staff twirled the knob of a big safe and its door swung open. There, where they had been lying for eighty-two years, were the manuscripts. Sandburg and the Randalls took over, and, amidst lights and the click of press cameras, worked away at the papers until four o'clock in the morning.

At first glance, the collection did not seem to the two Lincoln experts to be anything exciting. Sandburg soon left Washington, the Randalls stayed on for months, but the former returned in a matter of weeks and spent half a month going over the documents more carefully. He and Dr. and Mrs. Randall worked at one of the big tables in the Manuscript Division, and when either of the men found what he considered to be a choice item, he would signal the other. At noon they went out to one of the few restaurants around the place and there carried on shop talk about the research. Then after lunch, they would walk until Sandburg gave the word that they would have to return: "Back to the salt mines!"

Sandburg and Randall commented that working in these "new" Lincoln papers made them feel like preachers attending a theological convention: they returned home refreshed in spirit. Although the contents of the papers of Robert Todd Lincoln were not sensational, they did contain many letters to President Lincoln from ordinary citizens involved in the Civil War, telling him their vivid impressons of the conflict. This of course Sandburg liked. After dinner, the researchers would often walk past the majestic Capitol building, lighted at its dome with a brilliance that always inspired Sandburg. It made him feel poetic and reminded him of Lincoln and he spoke of this to his friends and they well understood.

All too soon September came and the friends parted. James Randall saw Carl Sandburg off at Union Station and that night wrote in his diary, "Gosh, how we will miss him." A few years later, it was Sandburg's turn. Randall had developed leukemia and Sandburg went to see him in Urbana, Illinois. The pale, thin face of the popular professor lighted up when he saw his old friend for the last time. On this occasion, Sandburg spoke movingly of Randall's last volume of *Lincoln the President,* describing it as a lovable book. For his part, Randall said,

> We need our poets. They are our eyes, our ears, our voices and a good deal more. In Carl we have a great American poet. Sometimes he is whimsical, sometimes in dead earnest when aroused by social injustice, but always he is Sandburg and that is enough. He has given us our own America. He has given us Lincoln. There are three great words that belong together: America, Lincoln and Sandburg.

Meantime, the nation was beginning to prepare a lasting tribute to the poet who had sung of its many moods. In Galesburg, a restoration of his birthplace had been undertaken. First there was a search for the house and it was finally found near the railroad yards, in a dilapidated condition and owned by an Italian woman. Over her protest, a plaque about Sandburg was hung by the front door and a large rock was placed on the terrace. Sometimes the indifferent woman would hide the plaque and try to remove the stone.

When she died, her son sold the house to the Carl Sandburg Association which was formed to receive donations and the restoration project was incorporated as a nonprofit educational institution. A fund-raising campaign to purchase the house was launched and the price was raised within sixty days. Work on the birthplace was begun, appropriately, in the early spring of 1945, as sums small and large came in from all sections of the country, including the pennies and nickels of small school children.

It was found that the siding, plaster, and laths underneath were in a deteriorated condition, and these were duly restored. A fence of split hickory pickets was erected around the yard, an old wooden pump of the 1870s was installed, and shrubs were set in proper places around the yard. The original walls had consisted of wide interior boards standing upright and papered repeatedly, but lath, plaster, and siding were used in the restoration.

From the Sandburg family came the Bible which had been used when Carl was a boy, some old wooden chairs, dishes and cooking utensils. On view also is the stereopticon used by Sandburg when he sold similar instruments during his summer vacations when he was a student at Lombard, now Knox College. Old families around Galesburg contributed rope and trundle beds with hand-woven coverlets harking back to bygone days. On the walls hang pictures of the parents, of their children and grandchildren, and some photographs by Edward Steichen. Conspicuous in the collection are three of the earliest works of Sandburg, written while he was in college, and entitled *Incidentals, The Plaint of a Rose,* and *In Reckless Ecstasy.*

Adding a touch of realism in the little bedroom is a radio-phonograph with recordings by Sandburg, including selections from his songs and his poem *The People, Yes.* Here, too, is a venerable typewriter on which he wrote some of his Lincoln biography and his children's stories. Other items on view include deeds to a home the family owned later on which the father had made his "mark" in 1894, not being able to write his name.

Perhaps the outstanding room in the Sandburg birthplace in Galesburg is fittingly called the Lincoln Room and is the result of donations of friends. Its walls are of knotty pine and the bricks in the chimney came from an old Galesburg house that had been a stopping place for the "underground railroad," secreting slaves on their way out of the country in Civil War times. On the mantel is a picture of Lincoln, given by the widow of the artist, N. C. Wyeth. Beside the fireplace are a pitcher and platter which Lincoln presented to his friends Elizabeth Burner and Isaac Gulliher on the day of their wedding in New Salem in 1831, donated by local descendants of that couple. Beside a wall is a pine desk taken from the Bishop Hill Swedish community, and on this is a model of a covered wagon by Earnest Elmo Calkins. A rifle of pioneer times reposes over the collection. An iron grease lamp which hangs beside the fireplace is said to have been presented by the Lincolns to their neighbors when the former left Indiana for Illinois. Just before he died, the collector Oliver R. Barrett sent an original copy of an 1863 call for additional troops from Massachusetts, which was signed by Lincoln.

The Carl Sandburg birthplace was dedicated on October 7, 1946, the anniversary of the Lincoln-Douglas debate in Galesburg. Speakers paid tribute to the man who had made the town famous. The main address was by Marshall Field, the noted Chicago merchant. From the *Chicago Tribune* had come Fanny Butcher to talk on the appearance of Sandburg's *Chicago Poems* and his subsequent rewards. Quincy Wright, Harry Hansen, the Reverend Alan Jenkins, and Ralph G. Newman paid warm tributes to Sandburg. Inside the cottage may be found these words by Stephen Vincent Benét: "He came to us from the people whom Lincoln loved because there were so many of them, and through all of his life, in verse and prose, he has spoken of and for the people. A great American, we have just reason to be proud that he has lived and written in our time." [2]

So this three-room birthplace, though restored, breathes warmly of the earliest days of the poet-biographer. Here Carl Sandburg lived until he was three years of age, while his father worked as a blacksmith in the nearby C. B. & Q. railroad shops for $9 a week. Those in charge of the home do not pretend that it is all authentic. In fact, only three chairs in the living room, the washstand, and two wall whatnots in the bedroom are from the original birthplace. The rest of the picturesque furniture was selected as representative of that used in small homes of people with small means in the days when Sandburg was born.

At the rear of the tiny house is a large stone called "Remembrance Rock" after Sandburg's novel of that name. Dedicated on June 4, 1966, it was used the next year to shelter the ashes of Sandburg himself, which were placed there by his widow during memorial services for him on October 1, 1967. Surrounding the sturdy stone and its buried treasure is a small park which has been planted with dogwood, white pine, and red maple trees—brought here, along with soil, from Connemara.

Credit for the restoration goes to the late Mrs. Adda George, a former English teacher and widow of a professor at Northwestern University, who had retired to Galesburg and became interested in bringing to public view the Sandburg birthplace. When Mrs. George was unable to carry on the restoration work, her place was taken by Mrs. Juanita Bednar who served actively as head of the project until her death in early 1968.

Lauren W. Goff, a retired transportation official, and his wife, Mary, now act as hosts and show a dedicated interest in Sandburg as well as in his birthplace. Goff likes to reminisce about the days of the poet and is impressed by the belief that Sandburg was strongly influenced by the writer of "Little Drops of Water", Julia Carney, about whom he wrote, "She has a tiny, quaint niche in the history of American literature."

Goff recalls animatedly the occasion when Sandburg came to the restored home in 1958 for the observance of the centennial of the local Lincoln-Douglas debates at Knox College. When he visited the cottage, Sandburg seemed at first embarrassed, Goff recalled, but soon got over it. Someone asked him if he had actually slept in the bed in the bedroom. Sandburg paused a moment, then lay down on the bed and closed his eyes. Rising he said, "Now you can say that I slept in it."

Remembrance
at Connemara

In North Carolina, it was inevitable that Sandburg should make friends with newspapermen. Prominent among these was Don Shoemaker, editor of the *Asheville Citizen*, who wrote an editorial about the decision of the poet and his family to move from Michigan to the southern state, a decision of which Shoemaker definitely approved. So it was not long before Sandburg turned up at the newspaper office to accost Shoemaker good-naturedly and fraternize as one veteran scribe with another. When he first met the editor, Sandburg presented him with half a cigar, he himself smoking the other half. But it was not long before the doctor ordered Sandburg to stop smoking and he gave Shoemaker his humidor and pipes as well as a box of half-used stogies. With the tobacco was a small card from Sandburg which stated, "Dear Don, Kicking the bitch lady Nicotine. (Scooze, she no bitch.)"

"He had a way with children," recalls Shoemaker, "the way some people have with animals: he could talk to them. Elizabeth [Shoemaker's small daughter] became 'Hunkahoova Princess.' He was simply 'Carl' [which he preferred to the pompous 'uncle' business] and they understood one another thoroughly."

On one of Sandburg's visits to the Shoemakers, he inscribed a copy of *The People, Yes* as follows: "For the Shoes, who already know most of the answers and are asking merely a little music with our modicum of ascertained truth—whereto subscribeth their friend and sober visitor, Carl Sandburg."

Shoemaker also recalled that "Carl ate sparingly but consistently. He liked a little soft whiskey. His clothing was simple and often included a rough wool scarf and an eyeshade. When he sat of an evening in the cool shadows of a Carolina sundown, he tucked a sweater around his knees. Once he gave me a leather vest; he had worn it nearly to shreds.

"No man of course was ever larger in these parts," Shoemaker reminisced, "although Asheville claimed the young Tom Wolfe who fell at thirty-seven. Carl was interested in Wolfe and in the surviving members of his family, who in a manner endearing rather than crude, lived off Tom's memory."

The Asheville editor, later editor of the *Miami Herald*, told how much demand there was on Sandburg's time and how he helped the poet to fend off those who would take advantage of him. There was no time for bores and gushers. Sandburg seemed, according to the editor, to like listeners best of all, and was a great soliloquist.

> The conventions that came to town, the celebrity-sightseeing politicians that drifted in, the jackleg literateurs, all tried to put a hand on Carl. He was a quick man on the withdraw. No politician could capture him intact. He was a loner who could say "No" with tenderness and grace or

with brutal finality . . . but publicly he would never acknowledge any idols. . . . But he had his heroes. The
living ones.[1]

In June of 1944, *The New York Times* had announced that
Sandburg had signed a contract with Metro-Goldwyn-Mayer for
"a biographical novel of American life, manners and morals". A
quarter of a century before, Sandburg had planned such a book
but his time had been taken up with the Lincoln biography.
Now that *The War Years* was finished, he could devote his time
and talent elsewhere. So he went to work on the book and spent
four years completing it, hoping it would be the great American
novel.

He felt that to do the American scene justice, a novel twice as
long was called for. But as it was, a thousand pages resulted. He
at first thought of naming it *The Angel of the Backward Look*,
an expression he had found in the journals of William Bradford,
a leader of the Plymouth Colony. But to his publishers, this title
sounded too much like another, *Look Homeward, Angel,* by
Thomas Wolfe. So they decided on *Remembrance Rock.*

In the book, which received mixed reception, there is a prologue, a series of three parts, and an epilogue. The prologue is laid
in Washington, where a former justice of the Supreme Court is
spending the period of World War II with his daughter-in-law
and grandson. In his front yard is a large stone called "Remembrance Rock" under which is buried earth from Plymouth, Valley
Forge, Gettysburg, and the Argonne Forest. This judge resembles
the author himself, generous, well-versed in American history,
and often sentimental.

The first story in the book is set in 1608 at Scrooby, England,
whence the Pilgrims embarked for America. Here a woodcarver
fashions a little plaque of bronze on which he inscribes the four
stumbling blocks to truth, as set forth by Roger Bacon. He pre-
sents this plaque, hung on a silver cord, to a young woman of the
Separatists with whom he is in love, and it becomes a symbol of
the theme of the novel. The second story occurs during the Ameri-

can Revolution and concerns the hero who is on his way from New York to Boston to see his sons. He runs athwart the feeling between the Whigs and Tories and realizes that there will be two sides to the coming conflict. Military operations and many adventures follow. The third story takes place sixty years later and is about a man who, like earlier characters in the book, has a face half warlike and half peaceful. He marries a promiscuous woman and is caught up in the turmoil and suffering which such a union usually brings, especially in her tendency to continue in the same loose way. The epilogue of the book returns it to Washington in 1945. It is recognized that now is a time of crisis for the country but the characters know that the country has gone through fire in search of fulfillment of the American dream. So they bury beneath Remembrance Rock gravel from Anzio Beach, sand from Utah Beach in Normandy, and some volcanic ash from Okinawa.

In these pages is undoubtedly shown the affection which Sandburg had for his country. He seemed to be trying to show that the present is based upon the past and that without realization of mistakes which have gone before, there is little hope for the future. The novel is 1,067 pages in length and abounds, as does his life of Lincoln, in songs, proverbs, anecdotes, and folklore. Much of the criticism of the book held that it was unrealistic and that the characters were wooden. Yet Sandburg had gone back into history, beyond Lincoln, and in fact beyond the Founding Fathers, presumably to give the book a rich background of realistic detail. He was one of the few who, from his research on the novel, was familiar with the subject of a biography by this writer, Henry Knox, the noted artillery leader and first Secretary of War, and he helped on it with material from his own wide collection and that of Oliver Barrett.

The Scripps-Howard newspapers, catching the spirit of *Remembrance Rock*, quoted excerpts from it, pointing out that in 1777, for example, the cause of American independence seemed hopeless. Philadelphia swarmed with Tories who had boasted that the Continental Army was nothing but a phantom and that leaders of the Revolution soon would be swinging from the gallows. Many

Americans thought the Tories were right. General George Washington, in a gesture designed to show both sides that the American dream rested on something more substantial than words and paper, marched his army through Philadelphia. Sandburg told how the citizens of Philadelphia, gathered on doorsteps and streetcorners,

> . . . stood waiting, stood two hours watching the army march by, the wheeling columns of an army the world was wondering about, an army that came and went to return after it vanished, an army that lost in afternoon fog had hammered its attack at sunrise, an apparition army in tatters and makeshifts, an army lacking nearly every essential but visible flesh and invisible faith and vision, a paradoxical army of tatterdemalions who could take defeat after defeat and come on for more, an army more barefoot than well-shod, an army with slim rations and great expectations in its knapsacks, an army that lived on hope and that hope kept alive by one dreamer in ten who saw a continent and a world republic of free men to be won by fighting, by the will to resist till the enemy gave in—an array of nationalities, breeds and crossbreeds where the native-born shared with English, Scotch, Welsh, Yorkshiremen, Irish, Germans, Dutch, Swedes, Jews, Poles, Bohemians, Negroes, Protestants, Catholics, Lutherans—an array of farmers, mechanics, hunters and trappers, fishermen, day laborers, indentured servants, vagabonds, looters and criminal plunderers who had been punished and warned by the headquarters command, pious descendants of Puritans who fought under Cromwell against King Charles I, drifters and rollicking men who wanted to taste fighting and blood, landless men who wanted the hundred-acre farm promised them by the Continental Congress, men holding title to wide fabulous tracts of land—dreamers and desperadoes with dawn in their eyes—chimney-corner heroes who wished they were home and wondered whatever got them

into the army—they marched—they wheeled in the column that turned the corner of Front and Market Streets that day.

Marching they came with drums beating and the fifers shrilling "Yankee Doodle" and "The White Cockade"—Marching four abreast and spaced out with dignity, sprigs of green on many a hat and twigs of pine that gave out like little songs—Ragged men marching with here and there a British or Hessian uniform stripped from prisoners or battlefield dead and wounded—Marching farm boys in homemade jackets without sleeves and black-and-white checked shirts torn and splotched and over the shoulder the squirrel rifle from home—Marching lean and worn men, middle-aged and old, hard and battered, slouching at a gait that wasted no muscle or breath—Marching rough men with nameless gleams in their eyes, men of drink and carousal who had nevertheless proven they could fight, kill, and stand hunger, rain, snow and sleep on the cold ground—Marching barefoot men and men with shoes tied and bandaged to their feet, men with shoes patched and repatched and bound and rebound with thongs and strings till the wonder was they didn't drop off the feet—Marching raw recruits who couldn't keep step, their fresh clothes from home standing out against the rags of veterans—Marching they came with drums beating and the fifers shrilling "Yankee Doodle" and "The White Cockade"—Horsemen there were with sabers and pistols, teamsters and the commissary wagons, brass and iron cannon with the huge figure of General Henry Knox heading his artillerymen—Marching, they were more than two hours marching around that corner of Front and Market Streets—At their head with other horsemen rode the Commander-in-Chief, the responsible head, General George Washington—a man, a legend, a hope, a bulwark, a threat and a promise—a born rider, he and his horse one piece, a unit—Washington in his faded buff-and-blue giving the people of Philadelphia and the delegates to the Continental Congress a good long look at the Continental Army of the United States of America—

Soon were to come his words: "The time is now near at hand which must probably determine, whether Americans are to be Freemen, or Slaves, whether they are to have any property they call their own. . . . The fate of unknown millions will now depend, under God, on the Courage and Conduct of this Army. . . . We have therefore to resolve to conquer or die." [2]

Perry Miller, writing in *The New York Times Book Review* said of the novel,

Thousands will read the book and find in it solace and reassurance; of the innumerable recent efforts, this is the supreme and lengthiest celebration of the mystique of America, the most uninhibited, and the most naïve. "They ought not to be forgotten," it croons, "the dead who held in their clenched hands that which became the heritage of us, the living." *Remembrance Rock* is not really a novel; it is the chant of an antique bard who fills out the beat with stereotypes and repetitions. . . . Page after page of *Remembrance Rock* is patently an uninhibited paraphrase of history, wrapped in a turgid rhetoric, that descends to such small tricks as working whole segments of Bradford and Winthrop verbatim into the dialogue of unconvincing characters or to printing a letter of Roger Williams and the Declaration of Independence as though they were free-verse lyrics by Carl Sandburg. The reiteration of his triangular drama is tedious. The effect is to show, unmistakably, some of the things a bard falls short of when he tries to construct a novel out of no more intelligible or dramatic a comprehension of the past than his blind assurance that "Life goes on." [3]

But Charles K. Robinson, writing in the *Asheville Citizen-Times*, stated

that with this background of knowledge and experience, in his first novel he has written both novel and history of the dimensions which Americans have long waited for in the

ultimate American novel. If *Remembrance Rock* is not that
novel, it must anyway be the greatest historical novel so far
conceived and written on the scale of this book . . . in
what is truly the grand style.[4]

O. D. Hormel in the *Christian Science Monitor* perceived sev-
eral similarities between the book and Tolstoi's *War and Peace*.
"Here for the first time is a novel comparable with the greatest—
one which should certainly take its place beside *War and Peace*.
Remembrance Rock is a rich and perceptive embodiment of the
American Dream."

The volume was also hailed as a great aid to young students in
their American history classes, and as "a lamplighter along the
highroads and back lanes of American history."

Sandburg himself said of it, "Some day this book will be discovered. It's my favorite—next to the Lincoln books."

Don Shoemaker commented:

> in the ten years I knew him best, Sandburg wrote and com-
> pleted *Remembrance Rock,* a sprawling novel which never
> caught fire with the critics but which, I humbly predict,
> will be revived in years hence as Americana distinctive of
> the twentieth century. The cool reception of this novel hurt
> him. If it was, as I think it was, a prose expression of his
> poet's being—earthy, lyrical, haunted by his love of Lin-
> coln, a singular example of primitive Americanism—it was
> not a base of recognized excellence from which he could
> move forward.[5]

The Asheville editor also took note of what happened at a reception when a little old lady asked Sandburg for his autograph,
and he demanded to know if she had read his current book. "No?"
he asked. "If you didn't take the time to read my book, why
should I take the time to write my name in it?"

"Unfortunately," added Shoemaker, "she did not see the twin-
kle in his eye. The great thing about Carl was his intense interest
in individuals and his unflagging loyalty to them. I think he is the

only authentic genius I have ever known." Apparently Sandburg complained frequently about television, calling it "a thief of time." Yet he watched it when he achieved triumphs on it. At about this time, the Asheville Public Library put on an exhibition of Sandburg works, and testimony concerning them was requested from many prominent Americans. One of these came from a public official in Texas who assumed that this was a postmortem affair and wrote, "All America mourns the passing of this great poet." Nobody laughed harder than Sandburg himself.

Such humor was in line with that of Mark Twain. Herbert Mitgang said that Carl Sandburg was in direct line from Twain and Walt Whitman, and he became more and more convinced of his unique American quality after editing a recent volume of Sandburg's letters.

Ralph Newman, proprietor of the Abraham Lincoln Book Shop in Chicago, was a friend of the poet-biographer and remarked that

> He was a giant who belonged to the world. He was a friend and neighbor whom we claim as our own in Chicago and the State of Illinois. . . . He was many things to many people—a Swedish leprechaun, a folk singer, a poet and punster; a friend of the mighty and a playmate of children; a socialist and a rugged individualist who believed in the capitalistic system; a writer of social tracts and a long historical novel; a historian and a part-time Bohemian. Like his great hero, he too could be both velvet and steel.

Perhaps it was in both such capacities that Sandburg visited Governor Adlai Stevenson of Illinois in October of 1948. The new governor, who was to become a two-time presidential candidate in years to come, welcomed the native of Galesburg with enthusiastic praise. Stevenson recalled that, long before, Sandburg had visited his father, Lewis Green Stevenson, and asked to meet an ex-Governor of the state, "Private Joe" Fifer who had fought in the Civil War.

Adlai Stevenson related:

Joe Fifer loved good whiskey, and, having arranged a meeting with him, my father went to the cellar and brought up a pint of rare Bourbon, which he had kept under lock and key for many years. Armed with the whiskey, Carl and my father set forth for Governor Fifer's, confident that it would stir his recollections, and assured that he would share it with them. Sight of the whiskey added to the warmth of Fifer's greeting, but when Father presented him with the bottle, he placed it, uncorked, on his desk, where father and Sandburg cast frustrated glances at it throughout the interview.

Doors open hospitably to Carl Sandburg, wherever he may be, but he also brings trouble with locks. The day after the Fifer interview, my father took him to a popular local restaurant, the Village Inn, to meet other Bloomington men. Soon after they arrived, Sandburg disappeared into the men's room, where his stay seemed unduly long. As the guests began to look concernedly at one another, loud poundings came from the direction of Sandburg's exit, with calls to be let out. Several minutes elapsed before local strength and ingenuity overcame a faulty lock, and the famous author emerged.[6]

At Indiana State Teachers College, a full house was gathered one morning at ten o'clock to hear Sandburg. He failed to appear and the audience finally filed out. At two-thirty in the afternoon, the students were summoned to a special meeting. Sandburg had arrived. Questioned in regard to his belated appearance, he explained that the weather had been so inviting he had decided to hitchhike to the college.

In 1949, Sandburg brought out another book, this a sort of run-of-the mill comment on the great Lincoln collection of Oliver Barrett of Chicago. In 1950 Sandburg brought together and published all of his volumes of poetry under the title, *Complete Poems.* This big volume, containing over eight hundred poems, won for him his second Pulitzer Prize, the first having been for history in 1940. That he was not overawed by such awards was brought out in a letter he wrote to a Mrs. Marie Bullock who had asked him to sponsor an organization. "You may know," he told her, "that on the two occasions when I received Pulitzer Prize Awards, the jury was so divided that I was given half and some one else was given the other half. I am not even sure whether I could be designated as a Pulitzer Prize winner through having twice received half an award. Arithmetically it works out. In spirit it doesn't."

In the same year there appeared his one-volume biography of *Abraham Lincoln,* intended for those who do not have time to read the six volumes. This handy book has 430,000 words and is condensed from the 1,800,000 words in the original work. It also has some new material based on the Robert Todd Lincoln papers.

On a January day in 1953, the Superintendent of Schools visited the Douglas Elementary School in Galesburg. Having in mind the fifth Lincoln-Douglas debate held in Galesburg, October of 1858, the superintendent asked a class in the fourth grade, "Did Abraham Lincoln ever come to this town?" A hand was raised. "Yes," the young student answered, "He came to see Carl Sandburg."

It was also in 1953 that Sandburg published a small book entitled *Always the Young Strangers* which was autobiographical. It depicted not only his life up until 1898, but also the life of an immigrant Swede in Galesburg. The previous year, he had been awarded the coveted gold medal for history and biography by the American Academy of Arts and Letters.

Coincident with his publication of an autobiography occurred Carl Sandburg's seventy-fifth birthday. The country sat up and took notice of this three-quarters-of-a-century milestone reached so vigorously by the poet and biographer. *The New York Times* in an editorial said:

> He is more than a poet, biographer, historian, more than a man of infinitely entertaining and moving words. Child of Swedish parents, son of the Middle West, epic interpreter of Abraham Lincoln, poet laureate of Chicago, he has

been a kind of literary Liberty Bell ringing across the prairies and the decades. His poetry often breaks into prose, his prose often heightens into poetry, but the rich imagery, the sensitiveness, the pity and the humor are never lacking . . . unlike Whitman, he has never been a poseur, never self-conscious, never pretentious. He has been honestly a seeker, never sure that what he sought he has found or ever will find.[7]

Harvey Breit in the same newspaper described Sandburg as "a bony, fine-looking fellow, with flattened-down, white, symmetrical hair (that can get quite disheveled), enigmatic eyes, a bold nose and mouth." Asked about his recent gold medal, Sandburg replied that he would wear it under his coat "and when a railroad dick stops me and flashes his badge, I'll flash my gold badge right back at him." Lewis Nichols saw him "with a laugh so booming as to threaten chandeliers, and an informal manner that would be the envy of a schoolboy. In a warm room, he peels off his coat; in a truly hot room, he probably would peel off his shirt. He does not sit, but slouches."

The *New York Herald-Tribune* rhapsodized:

> That Carl Sandburg's seventy-fifth birthday should have turned into a kind of informal tribute in a national celebration is altogether fitting to a literary man who, perhaps more than any other living figure, is a voice of American democracy. . . . He is a kind of poet laureate of the people, collecting their ballads, commemorating their heroes, asserting their hopes, affirming their worth. Out in Chicago, they gave a big dinner for him, at which he jubilantly appeared replete with Lilian and his guitar. Asked if he had attained all his ambitions, Sandburg said, "I'm only amazed that I'm ambulant and in my right mind."[8]

Whether the Nobel Prize Committee was in its right mind the next year when it gave Ernest Hemingway the award was questioned by the recipient himself when he stated that if he had been on the board, he would have "voted for Carl Sandburg. He is a very dedicated writer." Hemingway added that Sandburg's six-volume work on Lincoln would have influenced him. Years later when asked why he had not won the Nobel Prize, Sandburg replied that he had; that Hemingway had given it to him in 1954.

Ed Murrow, the late television personality, once asked Sandburg on a national program what he answered when people asked him how he wrote. He replied:

> Much depends on who is asking the question, "How do you write?" I say, "Simple. It's easy. You just sit up to the typewriter and you put down one word after another. If you try to put down two or three words, you're sunk." And they take that as very valuable advice.
>
> And then there are some nice, earnest, serious college boys and I try to reduce it to the formula, of say, Ty Cobb. There were some baseball writers got around him at the end of one season and they asked him, "You have eleven different ways of sliding to second base. Now we'd like to know at what point between first and second do you decide on which one of those eleven ways you are going to use?" And Ty said, "I don't think about it. I just slide."

As to what was the most detestable word in the English language, Sandburg said that it was the word "exclusive." When you are exclusive, he added, "you shut out a more or less large range of humanity from your mind and heart—from your understanding of them."

Edward R. Murrow was also a North Carolina man, being a native of the state, and he was a purveyor of news in the colorful manner of Sandburg's earlier days. Murrow observed that Sandburg had been a newspaper man for some fifty years and, like very few writers in the United States, knew what the country was like from extensive traveling over it.

On a trip to New York in the spring of 1956, Sandburg was asked to comment on the state of things in this country and his reply was that one of its troubles was a "fat-dripping prosperity."

He was in the metropolis to receive an Albert Einstein Commemorative Award. "To make a goal of comfort or happiness has never appealed to me," he added, giving credit for the thought to Einstein himself. There is a danger, Sandburg said, in the deep desire and main goal of Americans to obtain the articles of comfort and happiness when this goal overrides others.

Whether such an occurrence was a goal of his or not, a kind of windfall came to Sandburg in June when the University of Illinois paid him $50,000 for four tons of his books, manuscripts, pictures, and other materials. The collection filled 150 cases and contained not only original documents but typescripts and proofs with the author's personal corrections. Of course there was much Lincoln material and it has since grown into one of the important such repositories in the country.

Collected in another form was a selection of Sandburg's works which appeared in 1957 and was titled *The Sandburg Range*. In the foreword to this impressive and handy volume are found the words:

> Carl Sandburg is a symbol of the abiding virility of an America whose continuity from the past binds it to the present. His words bite and sting with independence of judgment. They also erupt into beauty and surge with power. . . . He is of the high tradition of creative letters, a figure which, in times of timidity, cautious speculation, and poetic obscurantism, is rare enough but which will find its successors. . . . Even as he has sought the hearts and minds of the anonymous multitudes, exploring their dreams and scourging their mediocrity with the lash of a prophet, so he has lashed with caustic phrase those who would crib and cabin men's minds.[9]

An example of this lashing was Sandburg's advocacy of a pardon for the convicted and imprisoned Nathan Leopold who was serving an eighty-five year sentence for his and Richard Loeb's murder of young Bobby Franks in Chicago in 1924. Sandburg had previously written in behalf of Leopold to the Illinois State Parole and Pardon Board:

> For a long time it has been known in the circles in which Richard Loeb and Nathan Leopold moved at the time their offense was committed that the initiative was in the hands of Loeb—that after the offense the one who was hardened and light-minded about it was Loeb, while those who interviewed Nathan Leopold saw him in tears and contrition. . . . If I were a member of the board I would vote for immediate and unconditional pardon for Leopold. I would add that if he were a neighbor of mine I would want to see him often if only for benefits from association with a great and rare intellect. I would have him on the basis of numerous reports I consider unquestionable as a guest in my house whose companionship would be valued.

Sandburg stated that Leopold's pardon "would have a good many people saying that we live in a sane world where sometimes at the right moment may come mercy and justice. The people, yes, they respond to acts of authority having grace and meaning." This appeal, along with others, apparently helped, for Leopold was eventually freed.

Later, at a memorial dinner for Clarence Darrow, the famous lawyer who defended Loeb and Leopold, Sandburg paid his tribute to the late attorney who had also been counsel for another favorite person of the poet-biographer, Eugene V. Debs. Said Sandburg about Darrow: "He was audacity and he was loneliness and he was genuine. His speech was bare and simple, understandable by plain folks. He knew gobbledegook but didn't talk it. Once in a debate on the question, 'Is the Human Race Getting Anywhere?' he said it WASN'T."

But Carl Sandburg was getting somewhere. United States Steel, an organization about as unsympathetic to the ideas of Debs and Darrow as can be imagined, engaged him to read a poem at a banquet in Chicago in salute to Chicago's construction industry as well as the steel business. The *New York Herald-Tribune* observed that perhaps this odd combination of poet and "big steel" came about because of the Sandburg poem, "Prayers of Steel," which opens with the lines:

> Lay me on an anvil, O God.
> Beat me and hammer me into a crowbar.

"It's rare for the literary world and the steel industry both to wait expectantly for the same event," the newspaper continued. "Still spry at seventy-nine, Mr. Sandburg is a great talker and speaks with a deep, resonant voice, once described as making 'hello' sound like the opening words of the Gettysburg Address."

Mervin Block recalls that he was attending a dinner in 1958 for the Adult Education Council in Chicago, which was held in memory of Justice Oliver Wendell Holmes. Sandburg was a guest of honor and sat next to Mayor Richard J. Daley of Chicago. A newspaper reporter approached Sandburg and asked him how often he got his hair cut.

"That's an impertinent question!" snorted Daley. "He doesn't have to answer that. He's the poet lariat!"

Such occasions were more festive than the birthday observances which Sandburg found were coming all too often and were all too remindful of the relentless march of time—even for a man as sturdy and lasting as himself. Usually he would work quietly at home, perhaps having a few friends at Connemara for whom Lilian would prepare a special dinner. As he neared eighty, his eyesight, as expected, grew dimmer and he found that he had to limit his reading. Always, it seemed, he had worked to meet deadlines on a tough, rigid schedule. Now when asked about an unfinished book or article, he began to reply, "It's past the time for deadlines. When it's finished and ready, it will be ready."

As the late afternoon of his life wore on, sometimes he would just sit and look out at the Great Smokies and work once in a while. To the end of his life, he received a large amount of mail, some of which he complained were "deluded letters from people attempting to establish the bastardy of Lincoln." About his own life, he said that four things were required to keep him happy: 1. To be out of jail. 2. To eat and sleep regular. 3. To get what I write printed in a free country for free people. 4. To have a little love in the home and a little affection and esteem outside the home.

In regard to the home, Sandburg spoke before the General Federation of Women's Clubs meeting in Asheville, and lashed out at television's "inanity, asininity, silliness and cheap trickery. When we reach the stage where all of the people are entertained all of the time," he said, "we will be very close to having the opiate of the people." He also stated that the contemporary poets "ain't doing so good," adding that Shakespeare, Leonardo da Vinci, Benjamin Franklin, and Abraham Lincoln never saw a movie, heard a radio, or looked at television. "They had conversation and creative solitude. They had loneliness and knew what to do with it. They were not afraid of being lonely because they knew that was when the creative mood in them would work if they could capture it."

Early in 1958, Henry Belk, blind and astute editor of the Goldsboro, North Carolina, *News-Argus*, suggested to Sam Ragan of the Raleigh *News and Observer* that the state should pay a tribute to the famous writer who had come from Michigan to make his home in the "Tar Heel State." The idea was well received; Ragan took it up with Governor Luther Hodges and plans were made for a luncheon, with Sandburg as honor guest. Jonathan Daniels, editor of the Raleigh newspaper, telephoned Sandburg and received a hearty acceptance of the invitation to be present at the affair on March 27th in Raleigh.

Governor Hodges then issued a proclamation designating "Carl Sandburg Day," in what appears to have been an unprecedented official recognition of an individual by the state. After some 250 persons including writers, businessmen, politicians and educators had accepted the invitation to be present, it was thought wise for Daniels to contact Sandburg again to remind him of the forthcoming day. Mrs. Sandburg answered the telephone, said she knew nothing of such plans and revealed that Carl was then in Spring-

field, Illinois. So Mr. Daniels called there and was told that Sandburg had gone on to Chicago. Again the editor telephoned Mrs.
Sandburg and asked whom Carl might be seeing in Chicago. She
replied that the only one she could think of was his dentist. A call
to this individual brought forth the information that Sandburg had
left Chicago for New York. By this time, the luncheon was only a
day and a half away, and it appeared that its guest of honor had
forgotten all about it. Again Jonathan Daniels telephoned Mrs.
Sandburg at Flat Rock and inquired whom Carl might be visiting
in New York. She pondered a minute, then mentioned that sometimes he stayed there with a friend who played the guitar. Daniels
forthwith telephoned Harcourt, Brace and was told that this
friend must be Segovia. A call there—and Eureka!

Carl Sandburg answered the phone.

Arrangements were made for him to catch a plane for Raleigh
the night before the luncheon. He missed two planes but finally
arrived at 11 P.M., "feeling fine," according to Sam Ragan, "and
ready for a night-long session of drinking and talking." At 4 o'clock
the following morning, Sandburg was still at the Jonathan Daniels'
where he was a guest. But he appeared at the luncheon next noon,
spry and full of good spirit.

Edwin Gill, state treasurer, had been asked to speak and he up-
held his reputation as an expert at such moments. "Our guest of
honor, Carl Sandburg, is an *original*—something that has never
happened before," he intoned.

> Something new under the sun. And how does this come
> about? Those schooled in science might call it a *mutation*!
> Those steeped in religion will call it a *miracle*! Of course,
> after making a bow, both to heredity and Divine inter-
> vention, Mr. Sandburg might add that *he* had something
> to do with result in terms of the sweat of hard work and
> the toil of patient effort! I do not mean to suggest that men
> like Sandburg do not owe a debt to the past—all men do.
> I simply mean that they absorb all the influences of the past

and with that alchemy that is the essence of genius put words or other components of a masterpiece together in a way that is quite new and without precedent. And may I say that Mr. Sandburg, both in his method and in his outlook, is as modern as the latest invention of the space age and as timely as the morning paper. . . . Surely free-swinging Walt Whitman was his great-uncle and shy, sensitive Emily Dickinson was his great-aunt. Among his distant relatives I find Bret Harte and Mark Twain, while his first cousins could be Vachel Lindsay, Edgar Lee Masters, and Robert Frost, and I would think that among his nephews we might even find our own Thomas Wolfe. But when I come to name his *literary* father, I hesitate and then go on to say that he could have been that tall, angular man with the stovepipe hat who went to Gettysburg one day and made there a brief, immortal address. And if I were to be so bold as to attempt to name his spiritual ancestor, I would suggest that patriarch whose gifted hand wrote the book of Job! [10]

In this year when he reached the age of four score, Carl Sandburg received the tribute often given the renowned when they have come to a venerable milestone. He was asked what it was like to be famous. Standing on the bare front porch of his mountain home, he looked out across the hilly horizon and a faraway gaze crept over the pale blue eyes. Then he grinned and wagged his white-thatched head.

"It's like a communicable disease," he replied with relish. "Nothing can be done about it."

After a pause, he continued. "But it's kind of nice. When I walk down a street, people smile toward me as though they know me and like me. I've got accustomed to nodding every so often to a complete stranger as though we were old schoolmates. Plain folks who wouldn't think of bothering you—but they feel they know you and they smile."

It was at this juncture that Frankie Sharp, writing for the Associated Press, described Sandburg as follows:

> Now, he's slowing down. His public appearances are rarer, his writing comes more slowly. But there's plenty of pepper in him yet. He says he's living the life of Riley on his farm. Here he pets his goats, strums his guitar, and sings folk-songs in the twilight and scribbles notes. He sits on top of his steep hill, joking with friends and newsmen who journey to see him, tossing barbs at modern poetry. . . . He looks like a proud-backed Indian with hooded eyes and straight, long white hair that falls across his forehead. He walks a bit unsteadily and there are brown age spots on his big hands, but there is nothing old in the shrewd, merry eyes under his green eyeshade.[11]

In regard to the younger generation, Sandburg philosophized that "never was a generation told by a more elaborate system of the printed word, billboards, newspapers, magazines, radio, television—to eat more, play more, have more fun." Then he quoted General Robert E. Lee as telling a mother with a child in her arms, "Teach him to deny himself." And Sandburg added that whatever Lee meant by that, it is a teaching almost never heard nowadays. The young do not hear it, he felt.

Carl Sandburg was given the biggest tribute by Congress to a private citizen in nearly a hundred years when he was invited to address a joint session on the 150th anniversary of the birth of Abraham Lincoln, February 12, 1959. Not since George Bancroft, the historian, spoke to Congress following the assassination of Lincoln, had an American private citizen been so honored.

Sandburg came up from Flat Rock for the occasion and seemed perfectly at home in the capital as he was escorted to the rostrum where Vice President Richard Nixon and Speaker of the House Sam Rayburn were waiting for him. Sandburg was introduced by Rayburn as the man who probably knew more about Lincoln than any other human being. But before he spoke, the House chamber had filled until there was only standing room in the galleries. Northerner and Southerner, Republican and Democrat sat side by side in a friendly atmosphere. Outside there was winter sunlight which filtered down on the marble structure and on the statue of General U. S. Grant. A Coast Guard Academy chorus had sung "Dixie" and "The Battle Hymn of the Republic" and Frederic March, the actor, gave a superb reading of Lincoln's Gettysburg Address. Appreciation was expressed by members of the Supreme Court who were present as well as the diplomatic corps and other luminaries. It was a day of solemn observance.

Peering out from under the thatch of white hair which still fell lank over his temples, Carl Sandburg became for a time the personification of his subject. His face was crisscrossed with the lines of a man at eighty-one, his voice was resonant but becoming softly hoarse at times. His audience was hushed as he began:

> Not often in the story of mankind does a man arrive on earth who is both steel and velvet, who is as hard as rock and soft as drifting fog, who holds in his heart and mind the paradox of terrible storm and peace unspeakable and perfect. Here and there across centuries come reports of men alleged to have these contrasts. And the incomparable Abraham Lincoln, born one hundred and fifty years ago this day, is an approach if not a perfect realization of this character.

> . . .

> During the four years he was President, he at times, especially in the first three months, took to himself the powers of a dictator; he commanded the most powerful armies till then assembled in modern warfare; he enforced conscription of soldiers for the first time in American history; under imperative necessity he abolished the right of habeas corpus; he directed politically and spiritually the wild, massive, turbulent forces let loose in civil war.

> . . .

Millions there are who take him as a personal treasure. He had something they would like to see spread everywhere over the world.[12]

Sandburg spoke for eighteen minutes. He evoked in his own repeated words the image of a tall, somber man looking at the world with sad eyes, a man who had confined his greatest speech to two minutes.

When Carl Sandburg finished, he stood looking out over the House. His noted audience sat as if under a spell—which it was. Not once did the distinguished personages there interrupt him with applause, for it was not that kind of a speech. Then as they suddenly realized that the Lincoln tribute was over, the emotion created by his biographer broke into a great thunder of applause. Moving with great dignity, the erstwhile boy from Galesburg who had been diligent in his ways and now stood before the mighty, stepped down from the Congressional dais and strode across the well of the House and out the door. Said Congressman Carl Albert of Oklahoma, his voice choking with emotion, "Never in my life have I ever heard anything like it."

In late spring of the same year, Gene Kelly and Sandburg gave what was termed "a unique television performance," in which the Hollywood star danced to one of the poet's compositions while the latter strummed his guitar. Then in late summer, Sandburg and Steichen went to the Soviet Union as cultural ambassadors, to open the "Family of Man" exhibit. Some five hundred pictures had been chosen from millions taken in many countries and the exhibition portrayed the common brotherhood of humanity in scenes of everyday life, such as loving, praying, weeping, dancing, laughing, and fighting. It had previously been shown at the Museum of Modern Art in New York City, where Steichen was Director of Photography. Although no event of note occurred during the visit of the two Americans to Moscow, the Russians received the pictorial exhibit well. Sandburg thought "Russians in the streets of Moscow hurry more than Americans in New York and Chicago."

En route home, they stopped in Sweden where Sandburg visited a cousin named Erik Carlsson, as well as some other relatives. Sandburg remembered enough Swedish to be able to chat a bit with his kinfolks and he also sang a few old Swedish songs. While in this country, he received from King Gustav VI a special medal for his achievements. The prime minister gave a special dinner for the visitor and at the same time, Upsala College of New Jersey announced the award of an honorary degree to him. He had already received such degrees from Lombard, Northwestern, Lafayette, Wesleyan, Yale, Harvard, Syracuse, Dartmouth, Rollins, Augustana, Upsala in Sweden, the Universities of Illinois, North Carolina, Louisville, and New York University.

Asked by a reporter how he preserved his silvery mane, he replied, "Every morning, for a wake-up, I give myself a dry shampoo for two to three minutes. Not a massage, a shampoo." Queried as to whether he used any hair lotions, he quipped, "I have no notions about lotions." He revealed that three or four times a year, he gave himself a real shampoo.

Asked if he thought the marriage of Abraham Lincoln to Mary Todd had been successful, Sandburg responded, "When you have four fine boys in ten years, that marriage ain't a failure."

Successful, too, was the program of dramatic readings which was launched at this time by Bette Davis and her husband, Gary Merrill. She had known the poet-biographer only through "his Lincoln and his 'little cat feet' poem," she said. But she became interested in the script by Norman Corwin, an arrangement of extracts from Sandburg's works, which the radio-television writer had acquired from years of adapting them for broadcasting. Speaking of Sandburg, Miss Davis said, "This man is more vital than anyone I have ever met in my life. He is *au courant.*"

After studying the script and rehearsing for the show, which was named "The World of Carl Sandburg," she said, "I have never known three weeks of so much intensive education and illumination. When people see this show they will say, 'I had no idea of the facets of this man. He wrote about rockets to the moon years

ago. He has written of the 'unknown war'—a third world war—
and of the nuclear age." Commenting on the language of Sandburg, Miss Davis added, "It is an experience in this day to work
with great words. We don't often have great words any more. It
is an age of economics in the theater—everything said in the quick-
est and most commercial way. The play demands about twenty-
five parts in two hours—it is like playing the full range of every
part you have ever done, in fragments, during one evening."

Apparently the Davis-Merrill team were pleased with the results of their performances for she later commented that the reviews were "among the best of my career."

"The World of Carl Sandburg" toured the United States for a
year with Bette Davis and Gary Merrill and then had a run on
Broadway with Miss Davis and Leif Erikson. Then it "came home"
to North Carolina and played to some 200,000 high school students around the state before arriving at the Vagabond Touring
Theatre at Flat Rock where it enjoyed a successful engagement
right in the front yard, so to speak, of its original author.

Interviewed in Hollywood, Norman Corwin recalled how he
cherished his long friendship with Sandburg, stating that the
latter arrived at one time on the West Coast with only one shirt,
two pairs of sox and two handkerchiefs.

> He had backwoods simplicity," Corwin said, "but he was
> unspoiled. He was not even a heavy drinker but was first
> of all a poet. He told me that *The People, Yes* was his best
> work. Once he met Charles Laughton in the studio and
> demanded that the actor recite Lincoln's Gettysburg Ad-
> dress on the spot. Laughton did. Sandburg had a scorn for
> phoneys as Lincoln did. Carl had a distrust of people who
> liked him only because he was a celebrity.

A master showman himself, it was inevitable that Sandburg
would land in Hollywood. The event did not concern Lincoln, or
any of his books, for that matter. He had seen the movie about
Texas entitled *Giant* three times and had sent the director, George
Stevens, a copy of his novel, *Remembrance Rock*, autographed

with a complimentary note for Mr. Steven's work on the film. Whether this was pure tribute or also a hint that the novel might be considered as subject for a picture is not known; probably both elements were involved.

At any rate, Stevens was duly impressed, especially as he already had a warm admiration for Carl Sandburg. Correspondence and negotiation ensued and soon a press release from Twentieth-Century-Fox announced that Sandburg was to be a "creative consultant" on the forthcoming movie production of *The Greatest Story Ever Told,* a life of Jesus Christ, based on the book of that name by the late Fulton Oursler.

The announcement was made in Hollywood style from the picturesque Sandburg home in Flat Rock, North Carolina. Stevens was on hand and was greeted by Sandburg with: "Hello, Boss." Whereupon the producer replied, "Hello, God."

Bantering with reporters who were numerous, as well as photographers and Twentieth-Century-Fox publicity men, Sandburg quipped, "Why ain't I got a right to write for the movies? That's a header; that's a high dive I haven't made. Why ain't I got a right to take a dive in the Twentieth-Century-Fox lot?"

On posing for the publicity pictures, Sandburg remarked, "It is the grief of those who live for pleasure only."

He took occasion to remark about the lake near his home, "The lake belongs to God but He leased it to us."

And of motion pictures, he added, "We have to live with it."

He recalled that forty years before, when he was motion picture critic of the *Chicago Daily News,* he had visited Hollywood and apparently did not like all he saw. From the set of an early Cecil B. De Mille Biblical film, *The King of Kings,* he wrote: "Today I picked a pink paper carnation from a papier-mâché tomb of Jesus."

Sandburg, then eighty-two, duly arrived in Hollywood on July 18, 1960. In an endeavor to forestall cynical comments from people who might think that he was taking advantage of Sandburg's prestige, Stevens issued a statement noting, "There's one thing I wish to make clear. Mr. Sandburg's association will not be merely nominal. He will make complete contribution in all creative areas of the production and will devote his full time working with us from the start to the finish of this dramatic undertaking."

Soon after he had arrived, Sandburg was interviewed for four hours by reporters from newspapers, magazines, radio, and television. He seemed to ignore the rules of the usual Hollywood interviews by saying what he pleased and taunting reporters. He sat back easily in an armchair, his sturdy hands crossed in his lap, with his white mane dropping over his right eye. He took the reporters by surprise by first singing a little song about the apostles of Christ, in order, he explained, to give the meeting the proper spiritual atmosphere. Then he impishly added that he was ready for any cross-examination they might throw at him. Asked to give the major character traits of Jesus, Sandburg quipped, "Go hang out your lawyer shingle!"

To another questioner he answered, "get my book of poems. Eight hundred and sixteen poems. $7.50. Less than one cent a poem. Cheaper than tomatoes or onions."

When asked what he was doing on the picture, Sandburg passed this one along to Stevens who explained that while Ivan Moffat was writing the screen play, Sandburg was engaged in basic development and would work on the lineal poetry and visual poetry.

The poet himself then commented on movies on religious subjects, saying that as a rule they were less interesting than Sunday School classes.

"Oh, I have had my periods," he went on, "when I have had my cinema drunks. And then very often for months I don't see a movie. I may go to see *Ben Hur* just to see if the chariots are like they were in the hippodrome when I was a boy."

Sandburg revealed that this was not his first experience with Hollywood. In his newspaper days, he added, he had for awhile done interviews with stars of the silent films; and once D. W. Griffith wanted to produce a movie about Lincoln based on the Sandburg works.

"I told Griffith that I wanted $30,000," Sandburg stated, "and he offered me $10,000. He got Stevie Benét [Stephen Vincent Benét] for the job. Stevie was good. I forget the name of the picture."

In a later interview, he recalled, "In 1944, I was attending a dinner here for Harold Ickes. This was during the Presidential campaign. There was a pretty girl sitting on the other side of Ickes, and after the dinner I was introduced to her. I didn't catch her name and I had to ask her for it." Then he laughed loudly. "That was quite a scandal, to think that I didn't know who Joan Crawford was."

Sandburg admitted that this was his first adventure into dramatic writing, but he quickly added that he had written everything else. Not exactly with modesty but with accuracy, he said, "After all, I have a wider range of writing than any other American author, living or dead." He reeled off a list of his activities including newspaper reporter and motion picture critic; Lincoln biographer ("a million and a half words, longest biography in this hemisphere"); poet ("eight hundred in print and two hundred more I am still playing with"); songster (*The American Songbag* had one hundred songs that had never been printed"); writer of children's books; novelist (*Remembrance Rock*). The last named, he said, belonged to Metro-Goldwyn-Mayer but had never been produced.

In his Hollywood interviews, Sandburg supplied incidentally some illuminating facts:

> When I wrote *The War Years,* I used to work sixteen, eighteen hours a day, and there were times when pains used to crash through my head and I used to say, "Jesus, could that be the preamble to a brain hemorrhage? Pain like that?" And I said an oath like some old-timer in the Old Testament: "Oh Lord, if thou wilt permit me to finish this task thou canst ha-a-a-ve me." I was willing to bargain with God: "Strike me dead when I have read the last page proof of this book!"

But for all the well-laid plans for the film on Jesus, Twentieth-Century-Fox in early September of 1961 decided to postpone its production. An obvious reason was that in the preceding year the company had lost $13,000,000. The sum of $3,000,00 already had been spent on the biblical film, including $170,000 for Carl Sandburg's services. Of course the poet-consultant was disappointed but did not seem discouraged and neither did George Stevens. Before he left for his Flat Rock home, Sandburg gave an explanation of what happened: "They went on what you might call an economy binge." He blamed the decision to stop production on "Wall Streeters who have been buying heavily in Twentieth-Century-Fox. This picture will be made," he predicted, "and it will be a great all-time picture."

He was at least partially right. *The Greatest Story Ever Told* was later made by United Artists, directed and produced by George Stevens in Technicolor and Cinerama, in association with Carl Sandburg. It appeared in 1965 and starred, among others, Max von Sydow as Christ, Charlton Heston, Pat Boone, Richard Conte, Jose Ferrer, Van Heflin, Angela Lansbury, Sidney Poitier, Claude Rains, John Wayne and Ed Wynn. The film ran three hours, forty-one minutes. Critical reaction was mixed.

On March 4, 1961, the centennial of the first inauguration of Abraham Lincoln was re-enacted on the east front of the Capitol in Washington before a crowd of 20,000 people. This was twice as many people as witnessed the original event. Referring to its occurrence when the nation was on the brink of the Civil War, Carl Sandburg said:

> It was a great day in American history of which we might say it was sunset and dawn, moonrise and noon sun, dry leaves in an autumn wind, and springtime blossoms, dying time and birthing time. Lincoln would have wanted us of the latest generation to remember how he stood amid the terrific toils and turmoils he was under compulsion to face.[13]

Television appearance by Sandburg on a Columbia Broadcasting System program on April 13, 1961, was entitled "Carl Sandburg at Gettysburg" and attracted wide attention. Howard K. Smith was the reporter and the two met on the memorable battlefield in Pennsylvania. Asked by Smith why people wish to celebrate so bloody an event, Sandburg replied that it was "a little artificial . . . it's overdone. . . . War is terrible to look at. Those who are enjoying this Centennial don't have the imaginations to see the war that was. . . . Lee rode his horse along roads winding through bright summer landscapes to find himself looking at the smoke of a battle he had not ordered or planned."

Sandburg further declared in answer to a question that if Lee had commanded the Union forces—as he had the opportunity to do—the war might well have been shorter, but he might also, as a Southerner, have had some difficulty in handling the Northern troops. As to why Lee continued to fight after his defeat at Gettysburg, Sandburg was of the opinion that it was a matter of honor. "The South was known for its chivalry, and Mark Twain used to say that *Ivanhoe* caused the war, the ideas which it gave the South about chivalry, and a Northern editor said that 'the war was between the shovelry and the chivalry.'"

In regard to what might have happened had Lee not lost his "right arm," Stonewall Jackson, before Gettysburg took place, Sandburg stated that the outcome of that battle could have been different if Jackson had been in command of "Pickett's Charge" instead of its own commander. Sandburg surprised some by saying the battle of Vicksburg was more important than that of Gettysburg which took place at the same time and received more attention then and since. Unlike Winston Churchill, Sandburg felt it was the American Revolution, not the Civil War, that "was the noblest and least avoidable of wars till that time." Grant was a better general than Lee, Sandburg believed.

In late 1961, Sandburg kicked up a kind of controversy when he was visiting Washington and saw President John F. Kennedy, whom he admired, for a brief visit in the White House. A reporter asked him a question and he took the occasion to blast former President Dwight Eisenhower, whom he did not admire, about a speech the latter had made the day before criticizing the newly created Peace Corps. "Eisenhower has yet to know the people of the United States," said Sandburg.

> With him the words 'socialist' and 'socialism' are dirty words—very nearly as dirty as 'welfare state.' But ever since he left the creamery at Abilene, Kansas, he never bought a suit of clothes or a meal. He never was out of work for a day. All the anxieties that go with the free enterprise system, he hasn't known them. He's lived in a welfare state ever since he left Abilene and went to West Point.

The statement brought forth protest and none was more marked than that of David Lawrence, the journalist. He wrote that "Mr. Sandburg has a strange misconception—shared by many other people—that each of the armed services provides all the needs of its men and officers. The fact is that the commissioned officer himself buys all of his clothes—his uniforms as well as the civilian clothes he wears when off duty." Lawrence went on to point out that the military living allowance only partially covers the cost of providing a home for the officers and their families, that many of them cannot afford college educations for their children.

By this time, Sandburg himself had done well enough financially not to have to worry about his family expenses. Not far away lived a genial Jew, Harry Golden by name, who had also succeeded in life and who saw in Sandburg a kindred spirit. So he became acquainted with the sage of Flat Rock and in time wrote a light-hearted and entertaining book about him. Golden described his subject as

> a white-haired man who lives in Flat Rock, N.C., and plays the guitar very well. . . . Despite the race riots Carl witnessed and the vicious labor wars he reported and the oc-

casional futility of the democratic process he has seen and despite the poverty he lived through and the cruelty and prejudice he knows others had suffered, the message of his books was that Americans are really nice guys. . . . One of the reasons Carl Sandburg was able to affirm his faith in *people* was that he did not look back to another time and wish vainly for it. He made the best of the time he lived in.[14]

John K. Hutchens, America's eminent reviewer of books, agreed with this observation, writing on an occasion which took note of the more than four-score years of Sandburg's sojourn upon this earth,

He is the prairie-haunted bard, the biographer of Lincoln, the teller of stories for children, the guitar-strumming troubadour and song-collector, the novelist invoking the American dream from Plymouth Rock down the years to our time, the memoirist looking back on his youth. . . . His robust, delicate, throbbing songs of city streets and distant prairies and mighty rivers are still as stirring as they originally had been. . . . He is today's America.[15]

But the song was dying down. Life at Connemara during the octogenarian years seemed to be mainly a succession of birthdays with more or less celebration, and in between some literary achievement of a modest nature as befitted the evening of the writer's career. He would be asked leading questions such as what would Lincoln have done about dropping the atomic bomb on Japan. "Let us permit our imagination to conceive of Lincoln free of his Springfield tomb and resident in the White House," Sandburg answered, "as Chief Executive in the year 1945, and before him the reports from the War Department on the estimated casualties of 500,000 to be expected in an invasion of Japan. For myself, I believe Lincoln would probably have made the same decision as President Harry Truman."

His eighty-fifth birthday was celebrated in New York City at a literary dinner in the Waldorf-Astoria during what Sandburg himself termed "a beautifully tumultuous evening." The occasion also marked the publication of his new book of seventy-seven poems entitled *Honey and Salt* and the publisher, Harcourt, Brace & World, had scores of other celebrities in attendance. When the guest of honor dropped his short cigar and arose to read the title poem of the new book, he remarked that the occasion was so "rare"—a favorite adjective of his—and unforgettable that he could not express his feelings even in a poem. But he declared the evening's fine remembrances "will help me live a little longer—perhaps a year or so." These words were prophetic. After a session of autographing books, he admitted that he felt toward the end "like something the cat drug in." John Steinbeck was there and commented: "Carl, all of us could have learned from you—and a lot of us did." Mark Van Doren read a poem he had composed "To Carl Sandburg, lover of the long view." A telegram from President Kennedy was read which stated that Sandburg "as poet, story teller, minstrel and biographer, has expressed the many-sided American genius." So Sandburg stood "before kings."

"How does one live to be eighty-five and still be producing poems which are wise and profound, merry and sad, prophetic of phrase and beautiful with imagery?" asked his friend the late Ralph McGill in his syndicated newspaper column. Then he answered it himself. "Why one lives, of course. This is what Carl Sandburg has done—and still does—he lives."

At his eighty-sixth milestone, the sage of Connemara remained quietly there on January 6, 1964, and now and then he and his devoted wife would look out across the snow-covered fields and woods and reminisce. Of his reliable colleague, he remarked, "We've been married fifty-five years—and we ain't never had one real storm." She was now eighty. He went on to muse, "Life is a series of relinquishments"; to remind people that at forty, he gave up baseball; at sixty, he stopped bounding up stairs; in his seventies he cut out most of his cherished cigars; and in his eighties he reduced his taking of whiskey to very small amounts.

"I don't like the phrase 'old age,'" said Sandburg. "Frank Lloyd Wright and I agreed that we did some of our best work in the seventies."

"I'm going to make a little address to God," he declared, "thanking Him for the eighty-six years."

And in regard to the race question, he remarked, "The most important thing is that the Negro Slaves were freed in the Emancipation Proclamation, which can never be revoked. It is up to the Negroes to perform now."

His eighty-seventh birthday he celebrated by lifting the same heavy oak armchair over his head that he had been lifting to keep himself in condition over the years. He also did considerable reading and continued to work on a sequel to his autobiography, *Always the Young Strangers.* By now, he was avoiding the telephone, and his wife and the two daughters at home, Margaret and Janet, protected him from intruders. "He's a great family man," Harry Golden observed. "They hold hands all the time. And they don't do it for effect. Fantastic."

But by the time the eighty-eighth year of his life had ended, Sandburg had been slowed down by illness. The year before, he had been bothered by an inflammation of the intestines. Since then, he had suffered a fall and his physical discomfort was increased by gall bladder trouble. At long last, the marvelous physical machine was forced into low gear. He spent much of the time in bed—reading, eating a steak, and worrying about a transit strike in New York. But seclusion in his picturesque home could not prevent greetings from the low and the mighty pouring in. He received "well-wishes" from Mark Van Doren, Archibald MacLeish, Harry Golden, and the late Ralph McGill.

A telegram from President Lyndon Johnson stated:

> You once wrote that "The People Will Live On"! Thanks to you, the people live on with a deeper insight into their nation, their fellow citizens, and their own inherent dignity. You spoke to them in verse, you sang to them of their traditions. You wrote to them of Lincoln's greatness and

of the greatness of the land that produced them. And now
in return we say "Happy Eighty-eighth Birthday" to you.
It does not ring with poetry, but it comes from deep within
a nation's heart.

By the time another year had passed, Carl Sandburg was more
his old, ebullient self again, though weakened. By now he had
given up writing in favor of reading history and poetry. Rarely
was he seen tending to his goats, strumming the guitar, or roam-
ing through the hilly countryside. He even stopped granting interviews, but his Lilian did give one over the telephone. She
said her husband usually spent mornings in bed but got up in
the afternoons. "He sometimes walks around the house," she
said. "And he likes to watch television, especially news programs."
As to his attitude, she added, "He has a wonderful disposition.
Some people fight aging, but he doesn't. And he loves everybody. Mr. Sandburg doesn't like sweets and won't eat cake, so
there's no sense in baking one."

When spring came again to Connemara, there was a new quiet-
ness about it. The dimming eyes of Carl Sandburg looked out on
what Professor W. C. Burton called

> a vision of verdure soothing to his aging but ever-keen, blue
> eyes. . . . He loved it better and was more lavishly con-
> tented in it than any place he had ever lived. . . . The
> barnyard where his goats gathered and where they nuz-
> zled any member of the family, and all visitors in the bar-
> gain, to be petted, was so overlaid with a rustic peace that
> it seemed to exist in another, earlier century. Sandburg's
> real tower and fortress, however, could not be truly said
> to have been a place but a person, his devoted wife, Paula,
> the former Lilian Paula Steichen. She fended him from the
> world when he wanted fending and let him rove when he
> wanted to rove. She kept the home fires banked or burning
> as need be. She sheltered him, encouraged him when
> courage and faith and admiration were his needs, and

walked by his side when he might otherwise have walked alone.[16]

But even such sustaining inspiration has its limits. As the spring wore on, Sandburg became weaker and weaker. In June he suffered what was described as a "heart stroke" and lapsed into semiconsciousness. It was becoming clear that the evening was nigh. As the July days passed, he talked to hardly anyone and it became difficult for him to recognize anyone—anyone, that is, except his beloved wife. She remained in his consciousness endlessly and now and then he would arouse his failing faculties and softly speak her name. Then she would stand beside him until he recognized her. "But his great strength was failing," she noted; and she would be the last to give up.

On Saturday morning, July 22nd, as the sun broke brightly over the Great Smoky Mountains, Sandburg awoke but was in a barely conscious condition. By eight o'clock, his breathing came with difficulty. The two nurses who were with him applied artificial respiration. Dr. D. I. Campbell King, his attending physician, was quickly summoned. But it was to no avail.

The pale horse had come.

At nine o'clock, Lilian Sandburg close beside him noted that her husband "slowly breathed away." She added, "I thought it was a wonderful way of going. He had a beautiful passing."

Across the nation, obituaries flashed across newspaper pages in vivid prominence. *The New York Times* brought out its full-page tribute, long set in type as is customary with this great newspaper, and gave it a front-page position as the start of the glowing article.

"What does a man care about his obituary?" Sandburg had once asked a reporter who had come to see him to freshen up his paper's own obituary file. People evidently did care about that of Sandburg. It was news of the first order for days.

Mrs. Sandburg immediately announced that the body would be cremated and the ashes placed at "Remembrance Rock" in Galesburg. Known to be one of Sandburg's favorite spots around

Flat Rock was a beautiful little early nineteenth-century church known as St. John in the Wilderness. It is an Episcopal church and stands on a knoll, wooded by tall white pines, long-leaf pines, firs, and cedars interspersed with ancient boxwoods and rhododendron, a lovely sylvan setting. Here the funeral services were to be held.

The Sandburg family asked the Thomas Shepherd & Son Funeral Directors of Hendersonville to select a Unitarian minister. They recommended a young man, Reverend George C. B. Tolleson of Charleston, South Carolina, and he and the family quickly agreed on the arrangements. He was also a musician and played drums with the Charleston Symphony Orchestra. "My first awareness of Carl Sandburg began when I was eight years old and my mother sang to us from *The American Songbag*," he revealed. In a conversation with the family, the Reverened Mr. Tolleson learned that there was no need for any sort of ritualistic funeral. "Sandburg's own belief was not in a God of ritual but in a God of reality," he concluded.

It was decided that most of the words to be used in the service were to be Carl Sandburg's own. So on Monday afternoon, a small procession wound down from Connemara to the little church of St. John in the Wilderness. There was Mrs. Sandburg, brave and unassisted, their three daughters, Margaret, Janet, and Helga, and Edward and Mrs. Steichen. The family had wanted private services but said that the church door would not be closed. So two of Sandburg's friends, the late Ralph McGill, publisher of the *Atlanta Constitution,* and Harry Golden were among the small gathering.

The funeral service lasted only fifteen minutes. During the organ prelude, Mr. Tolleson's six-year-old daughter broke into tears. When her mother took her outside and asked her why she was crying, the little girl replied: "Because he was such a nice man and he wrote such good stories for children and I didn't get to meet him until he died."

The organ prelude was "John Brown's Body," a favorite of the deceased. Then from one of the Sandburg poems, "Finish," the young minister quoted, "Death comes once, let it be easy."

"We are gathered here on this July afternoon to take note of a landmark," the minister said, "to celebrate a great life and to acknowledge its ending. Death is a gate through which all must pass. Each of us has died a little with the death of Carl Sandburg. This is how it has to be when a man whose voice was our voice has left us."

Edward Steichen entered the church and walked to the coffin carrying a single green pine bough from Connemara. He quietly placed it on the white pall and then took his seat.

When the minister had ended his words to the small, hushed group, the organ again pealed forth. This time it was "All of God's Children." The funeral service was over.

From all parts of the country, tributes poured in. *The New York Times* in an editorial recalled that Sandburg had said in 1950:

> It could be, in the grace of God, I shall live to be eighty-nine, as did Hokusai, and speaking my farewell to earthly scenes, I might paraphrase: "If God had let me live five years longer, I should have been a writer." Carl Sandburg lived to be eighty-nine. One of the nation's truly significant writers, he celebrated America's people. . . . Now midnight has come for the poet, but his millions of words will continue to say, as did the title of one of his books, "Good Morning, America." [17]

From President Lyndon Johnson came the message:

> Carl Sandburg was more than the voice of America, more than the poet of its strength and genius. He was America. We knew and cherished him as the bard of democracy, the echo of the people, our conscience and chronicler of truth and beauty and purpose. Carl Sandburg needs no epitaph. It is written for all time in the fields, the cities, the

face and heart of the land he loved and the people he
celebrated and inspired. With the world, we mourn his
passing. It is our special pride and fortune as Americans
that we will always hear Carl Sandburg's voice within our-
selves. For he gave us the truest and most enduring vision
of our own greatness.

These Presidential words seemed to echo some of Carl Sandburg's own, which were usually the most fitting and meaningful
of all:

I have spent as strenuous a life as any man surviving three
wars and two major depressions, but never, not for a moment, did I lose faith in America's future. Time and time
again, I saw the faces of her men and women torn and
shaken in turmoil, chaos and storm. In each major crisis, I
have seen despair on the faces of some of the foremost
strugglers, but their ideas always won. Their visions always came through.

I see America, not in the setting sun of a black night of
despair ahead of us. I see America in the crimson light of a
rising sun fresh from the burning, creative hand of God. I
I see great days ahead, great days possible to men and
women of will and vision.[18]

CHAPTER 1.

The Young Idea Takes Shape

1. *Prairie Town Boy* (Harcourt, Brace & World, 1953), 22.
2. *Prairie Town Boy*, 30.
3. *Prairie Town Boy*, 42.
4. *Prairie Town Boy*, 113.
5. *Prairie Town Boy*, 135–36.

CHAPTER 2.

Into the Main Stream

1. Letter from Marshall Goodsill, Office of President, Knox College, September 4, 1968.
2. *The Letters Of Carl Sandburg* (Harcourt, Brace & World, 1968), 61.
3. Interview with Margaret Sandburg, November 22, 1967.
4. *Ibid.*
5. *Chicago Poems* (Henry Holt and Co., 1916), 3.
6. *Chicago Poems*, 6.
7. *Chicago Poems*, 8.
8. *Chicago Poems*, 9.
9. *Chicago Poems*, 15.
10. *Chicago Poems*, 17.
11. *Chicago Poems*, 20.
12. *Chicago Poems*, 71.
13. Conversation of Hansen with author.
14. *Ibid.*
15. *Ibid.*
16. *Ibid.*
17. Letter from Stephens to author, April 10, 1968.
18. Conversation of Hansen with author.
19. Weirick, Bruce, *From Whitman To Sandburg* (The Macmillan Company, 1924), 212.
20. *Chicago Poems*, 24.
21. *Journal of the Illinois State Historical Society* (winter, 1952).
22. *The Chicago Race Riots*, July 1919 (Harcourt, Brace & World, 1919), 27.

23. *Ibid.*, 35.
24. *Ibid.*, 42–43.
25. *Bookman* (January 1921), 290.
26. *Smoke and Steel* (Harcourt, Brace & World, 1920), 3–4.
27. Interview by author with Margaret Sandburg, October 12, 1967.
28. Weirick, 215.

CHAPTER 3.

Enter Father Abraham

1. Letter loaned to author by Sandburg family. Also in *Lincoln Herald*, Sandburg edition.
2. *Cornhuskers* (Henry Holt and Co., 1918), 46.
3. Letter loaned to author by Sandburg family.
4. *Ibid.*
5. Anderson, Sherwood, "Carl Sandburg", *Bookman*, LIV (December 1921), 360–61.
6. Letter loaned to author by Sandburg family.
7. *The New York Times*, February 14, 1926.
8. *Abraham Lincoln: The Prairie Years* and *The War Years* (Harcourt, Brace & World, 1954), Vol. I, 45.
9. *Ibid.*, 140.
10. *Lincoln Herald* (Lincoln Memorial University, Harrogate, Tenn., Spring, 1968), 8.
11. *The Sandburg Range* (Harcourt, Brace & World, 1953), 377.

CHAPTER 4.

To An Advanced Retreat

1. Letter loaned by Sandburg family to author.
2. Associated Press Dispatch, May 28, 1952.
3. *American Songbag* (Harcourt, Brace & World, 1927), 93.
4. *Journal of IHS*, pp. 386–87.
5. *American Songbag*, viii.
6. *Ibid.*, 168.
7. Letter loaned by Sandburg family to author.
8. *New York Sun*, March 24, 1936.
9. Hansen, Harry, *Midwest Portraits* (Harcourt, Brace & World, 1923), 24.

10. *Ibid.*, 25.
11. Letter loaned to author by Sandburg family.
12. *Saturday Review,* June 15, 1963.
13. Letter from Warner to author, March 3, 1968.

CHAPTER 5.

The War Years

1. *Complete Poems* (Harcourt, Brace & World, 1950), 521.
2. *Journal of IHS,* 329.
3. *The New York Times Book Review,* December 5, 1939.
4. *New York Herald Tribune Books,* Devember 3, 1939.
5. *Journal of IHS,* 361.
6. *Ibid.*, 363.
7. *Ibid.*, 366.
8. Speech by Levine before Overseas Press Club, New York City, Sept. 6, 1967.
9. *New York Herald Tribune,* December 5, 1939.
10. *Atlantic Bookshelf,* Stephen Vincent Benét, *Abraham Lincoln: The War Years,* CLXIV (December 1939), 22.
11. Beard, Charles A., "The Sandburg Lincoln," *Virginia Quarterly Review* (winter 1940).
12. Nevins, Allan, "Sandburg As Historian" in *A Tribute To Carl Sandburg* (Harcourt, Brace & World, 1958), 63.
13. Comment of Sandburg to author.
14. *A Lincoln Preface* (Harcourt, Brace & World, 1953).
15. Commager, Henry S. "Lincoln Belongs To the People," *The Yale Review* (winter 1940).
16. *The War Years,* (Harcourt, Brace & World, 1926), Vol. IV, 488.
17. *The War Years* (Harcourt, Brace & World), Vol. IV, 296–97.
18. *Ibid.*, 298.
19. *Christian Science Monitor,* 1939, Janet Mabie, October 7, 1939.

CHAPTER 6.

The Poetry

1. Letter loaned to author by Sandburg family.
2. *New York Herald Tribune,* October 10, 1953.

3. *The New York Times Book Review,* December 3, 1939.
4. *Chicago Poems,* 115.
5. *Bookman,* LIII (July 1921), 390.
6. *Cornhuskers* (Harcourt, Brace & World, 1918), 126.
7. *London Times Literary Supplement,* February 2, 1920. Review by J.G. Fletcher.
8. Lowell, Amy, *Tendencies In Modern American Poetry* (Houghton-Mifflin, 1917).
9. *Slabs of the Sunburnt West* (Harcourt, Brace & World, 1922), 20.
10. *Cornhuskers,* 3, 11.
11. *Chicago Poems,* 7.
12. *Good Morning America,* VII, VIII, X (Harcourt, Brace & World, 1928).
13. Untermeyer, Louis, Carl Sandburg, *Modern American Poetry* (Harcourt, Brace & World, 1936), 240.
14. *Complete Poems* (Harcourt, Brace & World, 1950), 134.
15. *Smoke and Steel,* 23.
16. *The People, Yes,* Complete Poems, Carl Sandburg (Harcourt, Brace & World, 1950), 160.
17. *Home Front Memo* (Harcourt, Brace & World, 1943), 21.
18. Letter loaned by Sandburg family to author.
19. *The New York Times,* August 10, 1963.
20. Associated Press Dispatch, December 25, 1964.
21. Arvin, Newton, *New Republic,* "Carl Sandburg," LXXXX, VIII (September 9, 1936), 120.

CHAPTER 7.

Notable Associates

1. Press Release, N.C. State News Bureau, July 1948.
2. *Journal of IHS,* 1945.

CHAPTER 8.

Remembrance At Connemara

1. Letter of Shoemaker to author, March 15, 1968.
2. *Remembrance Rock* (Harcourt, Brace & World, 1948), 614–16.
3. *The New York Times Book Review,* October 10, 1948.

4. *Asheville Citizen Times,* August 10, 1959.
5. Letter from Shoemaker to author.
6. *Journal of IHS,* 297.
7. *The New York Times,* January 6, 1953.
8. *New York Herald Tribune,* January 6, 1953.
9. *The Sandburg Range* (Harcourt, Brace & World, 1957), foreword.
10. Letter of Gill to author, March 27, 1968.
11. Associated Press Dispatch, June 1, 1958.
12. United Press International Dispatch, February 12, 1959.
13. Associated Press Dispatch, March 4, 1961.
14. Harry Golden, column "Only In America," *New York World Telegram and Sun,* January 6, 1960.
15. *New York Herald Tribune,* April 7, 1963.
16. *Greensboro N.C. Daily News,* July 30, 1967.
17. *The New York Times,* July 23, 1967.
18. *Asheville Citizen Times,* January 5, 1953.

Index

247